Future Nostalgia

Future Nostalgia

Performing David Bowie

Shelton Waldrep

Bloomsbury Academic
An imprint of Bloomsbury Publishing Inc

B L O O M S B U R Y
NEW YORK · LONDON · OXFORD · NEW DELHI · SYDNEY

Bloomsbury Academic

An imprint of Bloomsbury Publishing Inc

1385 Broadway	50 Bedford Square
New York	London
NY 10018	WC1B 3DP
USA	UK

www.bloomsbury.com

BLOOMSBURY and the Diana logo are trademarks of Bloomsbury Publishing Plc

First published 2015

Paperback edition first published 2016

© Shelton Waldrep, 2015, 2016

Library of Congress Cataloging-in-Publication Data

A catalog record for this book is available from the Library of Congress.

ISBN: HB: 978-1-6235-6692-0
PB: 978-1-5013-2522-9
ePUB: 978-1-6235-6993-8
ePDF: 978-1-6235-6679-1

Cover image @ John Adie Brundidge

Typeset by Deanta Global Publishing Services, Chennai, India
Printed and bound in the United States of America

For Jane, Chloe, and, Lily, again.

Contents

Acknowledgments

To the people who have written about David Bowie over the years—fans, critics, scholars, reviewers—I owe a genuine debt of gratitude, and I hope that some of my own enthusiasm for what Bowie has accomplished comes through here. I am especially excited by the work of Ian Chapman, Alex Carpenter, and others who have been working on Bowie in recent years and have helped to shine a new scholarly light on him. Closer to home, I would like to thank Bob Ludwig of Gateway Mastering for answering some of my questions about the technical aspects of Bowie's records; Nathan Kolosko for generously helping me to parse and understand some of Bowie's musical structure and evolution as a musician; and especially, John Brundridge for taking excellent photographs of Bowie in the 1970s and allowing me to reprint them for the first time here. I would also like to thank Ally-Jane Grossan at Bloomsbury for her efficient and seamless editing and the whole staff at Bloomsbury for helping me to bring this project to fruition. I was inspired by Bloomsbury's 33 1/3 series and their pop music list in general, and I am thrilled to be a part of it.

I would also like to thank students and friends who have provided insights and enthusiasm for my work over the years, such as Benjamin Rybeck, Csaba Toth, John Evelev, Philip Shelley, Caren Irr, and Phil Wegner. Martin Conte put together an excellent index.

Portions of this book were presented in early form at conferences and invited presentations, and I am thankful to the coordinators and audiences at those venues for the opportunity to share my ideas. Shorter versions of some of the chapters were published as "David Bowie and the Art of Performance" in *Global Glam: Style and Spectacle in Popular Music from the 1970s to the 2000s*, eds. Ian Chapman and Henry Johnson; "The 'China Girl' Problem: Reconsidering David Bowie in the 1980s" in *David Bowie: Critical Perspectives*, eds. Eoin Devereux, Aileen Dillane, and Martin Power; and "The Persistence of the Dandy in Contemporary Culture: On David Bowie, Subcultures, and Resistance" in *Sur le dandysme aujourd'hui: Del maniquí en el escaparate a la estrella mediática*, eds. Rocío Gracia Ipiña, Sergio Rubira, and Marta de la Torriente. Grateful acknowledgment is given to the editors and publishers.

Support for this project came from the University of Maine System in the form of a Trustee Professorship, for which I am profoundly grateful. The largest debt I owe is to my family, Jane Kuenz, Chloe, and Lily, who daily perform the acts of kindness and love that made this project possible.

Preface to the Paperback Edition

At the time that this book was completed, just before the summer of 2015, there was no way to know that David Bowie, that is, David Jones, was entering the last months of his life. Indeed, it is not certain that Bowie himself knew how little time he had left. He died, unexpectedly to the general public, on Sunday, January 10, 2016, just two days after his 69th birthday. Always a private man, Bowie seemed to have engineered his farewell in a peaceful, orderly way by keeping his disease a secret, even hiding his physical deterioration, and then dying peacefully with his family, who cremated him shortly thereafter. He protected them, and the life he had with them, until the end. Whatever we may think about Bowie and his extremely flamboyant public personae, it is also important to remember that he was also someone who needed to inhabit a character on stage in order to feel comfortable before an audience and that music, however adroit he became at it, was never something that he claimed to do well—or to even be his primary identity as an artist. There was always something private and hidden about Bowie, the autodidact and intellectual, that was not shared and that gives his music the cerebral edge that it has. As a listener, you are either drawn to this aspect of his work or repelled by it. As Bowie notes on "Ashes to Ashes," "I never did anything out of the blue." That fact seems especially evident in his preparation for his death—not only in terms of how he died but in his final artistic legacy as well. In the last eighteen months of his life, when he must have been at his weakest and during which he endured bouts of chemical therapy to combat liver cancer, he completed a live musical, *Lazarus* (2015) with cowriter Enda Walsh and director Ivo van Hove; recorded his last album, *Blackstar* (2016); and starred in two music videos for the songs "Blackstar" and "Lazarus," respectively. While the play sold out immediately despite meeting with somewhat bewildered reviews, the album was extremely well-received critically even before it dropped on his birthday. While his death sent his album sales into the stratosphere, earning Bowie his first number one United States sales position, besting Adele's *25* (2015) for the top spot, it is likely the album would have been an artistic success anyway, and probably some kind of commercial one as well. The superhuman effort that Bowie displayed in these final months was matched, at least on the album, with a strong set of compositions. Bowie recorded the album with a new band, primarily Maria Schneider and Donny McCaslin, utilizing their skills as jazz players to meld with his own aural experiments to create a unique sound on the album—unlike anything Bowie had ever done before, but certainly echoing his most self-consciously avant-garde treatment of rock on *Low* (1978) and *Outside* (1995). Bowie always claimed that his music was at its core an African American rhythm section onto which avant-garde European stylings had been layered. Bowie had come to America in search of black music, to celebrate it, and wondered why everyone else didn't. Bowie's explicit homages to black music—*Young Americans* (1975) and *Black Tie, White Noise* (1993)—are taken further here not only in the experimentation with jazz but the explicit references to Kendrick Lamar. Lamar's free use of saxophone and theatrical rapping can be heard on the title song and on "Girl Loves Me." While two earlier songs released in 2014 are here updated for the album, "Sue (Or in a Season of Crime)" sounds like it would have felt best on *Baal* (1981), the jazz accompaniment and production fit the music together into a startlingly new sound.

The asymmetrical opening track, the title song "Blackstar," like almost every song on the album now sounds like a farewell by Bowie. Perhaps it is no longer possible to parse what the tracks are supposed to be about outside of his death. Certainly, lines throughout the album and images in the music videos, especially the last, "Lazarus," seem to be a summing up of his life on Earth and a final message or two that he wanted to leave us with. While it is possible that each song may have its own elaborate meaning and the album as a whole has a mythology signaled by the song "Blackstar," it is also possible that the main subject of the song and of the album is Bowie's own autobiography. Despite his penchant for character creation, Bowie was, arguably, always writing about himself and some of his best songs are self-consciously about his creation of his own mythos. The video for "Blackstar" opens with a shot of an astronaut in a spacesuit on a lonely planet. He is long dead, his head now a calcified skull that looks like some sort of sacred object—a sort of Day of the Dead totem as designed by Damien Hirst. His suit has a 1970s "smiley face" patch sewn onto it. It is clear that Bowie is referencing Major Tom from "Space Oddity" (1969) and the subsequent decade of the seventies that Bowie was so mightily to influence. The black sun that dominates the planet's atmosphere, the blind seer prophet that Bowie plays, the young men and women whom he seems to control with his words—all touch on Bowie's career and his construction of a final persona. I'm not a "gangster" or a "pornstar" or a comic book "marvelstar," he sings, "I'm a blackstar." He is something at the edge of the known—someone in the darkness serving to offer a different approach. He is also dying. His black star has come and whether it is a metaphor for his cancer (a black star tumor) or for the lack of an event horizon (the black hole) or even a symbol of ISIS (one explanation), it is clear that the death of his mortal body is also a part of the album. The "skull designs on his shoes" on the album's closing song, "I Can't Give Everything Away," link to the death of Major Tom. For once, the characters and the man behind them are clearly put in the same frame. And though Bowie continues to play characters throughout the album— the blind seer and the showman with his book are two different characters in the video and the character of "Lazarus" is clearly a version of Thomas Jerome Newton from the book, film, and stage play—Bowie is also singing about himself and wondering how he will be remembered. Line after line in song after song seem related to Bowie's imminent farewell. In "Lazarus" he prods, "Look at me, I'm in heaven" and "I've got scars that can't be seen." In "Sue (Or in a Season of Crime)" he notes, "The X-ray's fine." In "Dollar Days" he intones, "If I never see the English evergreens I'm running to" that "it's nothing to me." While this song may be about being artistically or politically "against the grain," its lyrics also sound like another ambiguous self-reference in which Bowie is headed back to England and to death itself, which perhaps is nothing to him.

"I'm falling down," he says, and "I'm trying to / I'm dying to." The album's last song begins with Bowie singing, "I know that something's very wrong." And indeed, by the time most of us heard this album, we knew that there was, that there had been. This song takes us back to the album's beginning, to the title song, where Bowie says that "something happened on the day he died / spirit rose a meter then stepped aside," but, perhaps importantly, "Somebody else took his place and bravely cried: / I'm a blackstar." Bowie seems to suggest that we should all take up his mantle and try to do as he did now that he is gone.

Whatever balm we might take from Bowie's passing perhaps it is that a life well lived is worth living. Despite Bowie's extreme fame and wealth, it is his sober time at the end that he wants to be remembered for—as the family man, artist, and quiet citizen of an adopted country that he had become, or had always been. He died as he had lived, self-consciously, elegantly, and with thoughts for his family and his fans. He did not go out as a rock star, young, violently, or inadvertently at his own hand. He died as he had lived, not as he had written about. While it will always be difficult for those of us lucky enough to have lived during his time to imagine the future without the man of the future to guide us to it, it was also deeply inspiring to witness the world's reaction to his death. The tributes, encomiums, and memorials came in rapidly and the raw emotion was overwhelming. Who knew that he had touched so many? Who knew that his worldwide fame ran so deep and so broadly? Even people who did not know or like his music, or who did not think that it was particularly significant, paid notice and realized that, yes, this was the passing not of a musician but an artist, not an artist, but someone who had altered the fabric of culture itself. Here, finally, was our Leonardo, or Beethoven, or Picasso—a great, towering figure whose work could not be dismissed because it flowed through everything and everyone. As one student responded on social media, "So now we know where what we listen to comes from."[1]

It is still difficult even now to talk about Bowie in the past tense, to write or say "was" rather than "is" in reference to him. His musical influence will live on as will his outsider identity. Many commentators after his death had to explain to younger people how important Bowie had been in terms of sexuality and gender, and how he had presciently foreseen the replacement of the former with the latter. There is little in contemporary culture that he did not touch and it is satisfying to see many of his approaches to the art of rock music become accepted canon. The popularity of his last album proves that the public liked him best when he was most himself—difficult, "indulgent," and eccentric. Perhaps our best current definition of art is that an artist can best please the public by pleasing himself. And by this definition, Bowie ended on a high note having created an album that is the type of music that ultimately served him well artistically by being difficult, obscure, and wholly original. The public was ultimately to embrace him at his least commercially viable, his strangest and most difficult. They finally caught up with him, so he left. The album, and the ending, could not have been more poignant, or more perfect.

What is unique or interesting about Bowie is that he tried to stay honest with himself over a very long period of time. He summed up in his long career a great number of approaches to art, life, and songwriting. He took it all in. Bowie's career, unlike, say, the Rolling Stones', was a cultural dialogue—one that showed what people went through, how culture changed and evolved as it dealt with various issues. His work was not just about longevity, but also about constantly changing and evolving. Some musicians might last through or represent a period or two, but not as many different ones as Bowie did. His career also showed that even though he created a superhuman persona and body of work, that ultimately his work was subject to human limitations and represents being human—sex, drugs, and rock and roll, but also starting a family, having a heart attack, and aging. His work was a public laboratory for experimentation, but he ultimately couldn't get away from who he was as a human being.

Popular music will never be significant again because the economic and technological system has changed so dramatically. For better or worse, there is no vetting process for albums anymore and albums that are released by major labels are now provisionary and can be subject to constant change, tweaking, and revision by the artist. An album collection used to be an identity—the choice of a record became part of who you were in an intimate, physical way. We could never have a Bowie again. All we can do now is look back. Occasionally someone comes along who really does make a difference or captures a moment, but culture moves on so quickly now that someone with Bowie's stature seems unlikely to come again. For the future, for which we now live nostalgically, there will always be a past.

This book can now stand as one of the many memorials to him and to what he did and could do to make us all better versions of ourselves.

Note

1   Jeff Nunokawa, "4655. What David Bowie Said.," *Facebook*, January 11, 2016. https://www.facebook.com/jeff.nunokawa.

List of Figures

Figures 1.1, 1.3, 1.4, and the cover used by permission of John Brundidge.

Introduction: The Pastiche of Gender

Over the course of a long career, lasting from the 1960s until the first decade of the twenty-first century, then after a ten-year hiatus to recover from a heart attack, until now, David Bowie (David Jones) has been not only a major force in popular music but a major artist as well. We are only now coming to terms with some of the influences he has had on the arts in general, as interdisciplinary studies allow us to appreciate someone who has not only come from the "low" art form of rock and roll but who has also affected so many forms of art simultaneously—not just music, but acting, directing, costume design, and dance choreography as well. Bowie has been as much a visual artist as an auditory one, and his unique position as a ubiquitous influence on contemporary popular music comes out of his ability to affect so many different media at once. Bowie's career sums up and amplifies the work of pioneering sixties artists who focused on transforming rock music into its own art form—from the Beatles to the Who—and bringing an art school sensibility to blues-based fifties rock. Bowie carried this direction further into the realms of pop art, fusing a commercial sensibility with high-art pretension.

David Bowie is the name given to the performance of self by the real person David Jones. As Bowie, Jones has long performed himself performing an alter ego who himself frequently performs as someone else—Ziggy Stardust, Halloween Jack, the Thin White Duke, et al. At the core of Bowie's performance is always a persona, though spinning out from this core, like so many concentric circles, are various other performances. While the musical text is always the primary one, there are the secondary visual texts of the album cover, the costumes (on stage and off), the music videos, and the concert sets, staging, and choreography. Allied to these visual performances are other aural ones as well, as the original songs are frequently reworked for the concert stage and, after the 1980s, remixed and reimagined by other artists as extras to be included on CDs and later releases of albums. While many of these examples of performance are givens in the commercial world of popular music, in Bowie's hands they often become something more than mere rote advertisement for the musical product. They instead become their own works of art or interpretations of his songs and personae that refract the album that is being promoted in new and interesting ways.

While Bowie's sudden end to his Reality tour in 2004 created a hiatus in his career that was luckily broken by his reemergence with *The Next Day* in 2013, the album came with a rethinking of Bowie's long career. His new album, the first in ten years, debuted at number two in the United States and at the number-one spot in twelve countries. Several new books on Bowie were published at around the same time, such as Paul Trynka's *David Bowie: Starman* (2011) and *The Man Who Sold the World: David Bowie in the 1970s* (2012) by Peter Doggett, and, most significantly, the Victoria and Albert Museum in London held a major retrospective exhibit of artifacts from Bowie's personal archive that emphasized not only his music but his contributions to fashion, set design, and music videos as well.[1] Now is the time, in other words, to reassess Bowie's contributions, especially as he has made it clear that his new album does not signal a return to touring. He has stated that he wants only to create new records and is not interested in interviews or promotion of any kind. Still, Bowie's new music has been accompanied by new music videos and at least some miscellaneous journalism on Bowie's part, and while he is hardly presenting us with the full-scale media attention that some of his albums have had before, he is producing new material while at the same time encouraging (or allowing) a more thorough reassessment of his past than ever before.

While Bowie has long been a subject of journalistic scrutiny and certainly one of the most photogenic rock stars of all time, the amount of serious work on him as a musician and an artist has actually been limited. In their pioneering *David Bowie: The Illustrated Record* (1981), Charles S. Murray and Roy Carr created a prescient roadmap for future Bowie scholarship, all the more astonishing for being written at a time when it would be difficult to have much distance on Bowie's dense and complicated seventies career. Work on Bowie since then has taken the form mostly of biographies, all unauthorized, themselves based upon articles and interviews of Bowie and his cohorts over the years. Unfortunately, many of these books have tended to repeat the same errors and, arguably, failed to shed a great deal of critical light on Bowie's actual artistic production. The trend in these books has gone from those that might be considered little more than fanzines whipped together at key points of commercial success (mainly, the early eighties) to books that at least provide some new material for better understanding Bowie in the form of interviews with people who worked with Bowie such as Trynka's book and, to a lesser extent, Marc Spitz's *Bowie: A Biography* (2009). This genre has occasionally been supplemented by books that concentrate on a particular era within Bowie's career. Two of the most helpful are *The Pitt Report* (1985) by Bowie's first influential manager, Ken Pitt, and Hugo Wilcken's *Low* (2005), which says much about Bowie's Berlin trilogy in a short space. The latter book itself formed the basis of Thomas Jerome Seabrook's *Bowie in Berlin* (2008), which represents a renewed interest in Bowie's late-seventies period in particular. Unfortunately, that book, like many others, repeats much of what has come before, and does so without referencing the work of others so that one cannot even trace the references. Of much more help are Elizabeth Thomson and David Gutman's *The Bowie Companion* (1996), which collects many of the more interesting reviews of Bowie's albums, and Nicholas Pegg's *The Complete David Bowie* (2011), which not only traces every Bowie song, album, video, concert, and film role, but comments, however briefly, on it with at least some insight. The biographies provide the linear (temporal) story of Bowie's life and career while the annotated discographies spatialize Bowie's work and organize it as something to be dipped into as one prefers. This buffet-like structure is perhaps good for both the novice fan and the completist, but it works against creating a sustained analysis of any of Bowie's work. Actual work on Bowie as an artist, while now, finally, beginning to be generally acknowledged, is more assumption than reality.

I believe that the time has come to begin a major reassessment of his career in the form of a book-length study devoted to him as a performer. *Future Nostalgia* is an overdue intervention into our understanding of Bowie and his multifaceted influence on a number of media and art forms. This book looks at key moments in his career (1972, 1977–79, 1980–83, and 1995–97) through several lenses—theories of subculture (Dick Hebdige and others); gender/sexuality studies; theories of sound (Roland Barthes, Simon Frith); postcolonial theory; and performance studies (in the art-historical sense). I try to make sense, not only of Bowie's auditory output, but also his many reinterpretations of it via music videos, concert tours, television appearances, and occasional movie roles. In terms of the book's methodology, I would like to emphasize that while musicological analysis is a part of the book, this is not primarily a musicological study, since that is not my training. Instead, I discuss Bowie's music as the foundation for a larger set of performances, the totality of which one must understand in order to make sense of Bowie at any particular moment in time. Much as Raymond Williams described the notion of culture as "structures of feeling," I try to tease out some of the ways in which Bowie's career is made up of interacting aural and visual tropes and influences that reflect and refract both high and low culture at a given moment.

All of the work in the following chapters builds upon and expands observations that I first made in the last chapter of *Aesthetics of Self-Invention: Oscar Wilde to David Bowie*, entitled "The Phenomenology of Performance: David Bowie." The argument of that chapter emphasizes Bowie's performativity, his merging of art with life. I trace some of Bowie's queer tutelage under Lindsay Kemp and the Asian influences on Bowie's creation of his Ziggy Stardust persona. The chapter moves on to discuss the separate media in which Bowie has distinguished himself—performance in songs, films, music videos, and on the Internet. In the section on sound, I emphasize the inherent virtual nature of the creation of rock music as a genre and the development of Bowie's use of personae as a way to feel comfortable on stage. This approach to rock also broke with the notion of rock and authenticity—that the singer-songwriter is presenting a coherent self. His use of personae in his concert, film, and video work is a natural extension of his approach to writing and performing music.

In many ways *Future Nostalgia* unpacks, updates, and extends those discussions while staying close to my original thesis—that Bowie gives us a way to understand the vicissitudes of performance, aestheticizing the link between rock music and everyday life by calling attention to the artificiality of both.

The chapters that follow focus on Bowie's influence on mass culture as he has developed his own uniquely personal approach to music and the visual aspects of music culture. The introduction includes an overview of Bowie's career and a discussion of why the notion of performance is key to understanding Bowie's oeuvre. I situate

Bowie in terms of avant-garde performance in the twentieth century and then move on to discuss the importance of his performance of gender specifically. Beginning with an overview of Bowie's historical antecedents in the nineteenth-century cult of the dandy, the discussion in the second chapter broadens to include his influence on twentieth-century subcultures and, more recently, visual artists. I deal specifically with Bowie's appeal to the middle class in Britain and the United States and how this appeal was connected especially to the medium of television. Chapter 3 focuses on the musicological analysis of individual songs from different moments in his career, but especially from *Hunky Dory* (1971) through *Scary Monsters (and Super Creeps)* (1980), and changes in how he approached the construction of his music in terms of harmony, melody, and rhythm. The chapter also looks critically at the idea of the concept album, especially in terms of his most famous LPs, *The Rise and Fall of Ziggy Stardust and the Spiders from Mars* (1972) and *Scary Monsters*. Chapter 4 continues to look at his songwriting with a discussion of his songs as autobiographical texts, especially during the latter half of the 1970s, when his work was seen as experimental and seemingly at its least personal. This chapter includes an analysis of Bowie's voice and, specifically, his aural output using theories from Roland Barthes' seminal *Image-Music-Text* such as "the grain of the voice," but also his theory of "*musica practica*" as it applies to how we listen to music and what actually constitutes the "text" of music—especially important concerns for Bowie and his work. Chapter 5 takes up his work after the long seventies, when his bouts with commercial fame in the 1980s seemed to produce a striated body of work with which we are only now able to come to terms. In this chapter I talk about Bowie's attempt to fuse what he had learned in the seventies about avant-garde art and theater with the dictates of a more popular style that he experienced on the album *Let's Dance* (1983). My discussion here is informed by postcolonial theory and how it plays into his interest at the time in the Orientalizing of his own work on "China Girl" and elsewhere. Chapter 5 also analyzes Bowie's interest in Asian culture generally by reading that interest through the concept of "Orientalization" put forth by Edward Said. The book concludes with an in-depth look into Bowie's interest in and relationship to science fiction and fantasy. Chapter 6 focuses on a discussion of the representation of queer disability in Lady Gaga's recent video for her song "Paparazzi" from her debut album, *The Fame* (2008). I discuss the video as it references other examples of queer disability in popular music. Drawing parallels between Bowie and Gaga's fusion of the mechanical and the human, I also discuss the work of William S. Burroughs and J. G. Ballard, whose science fiction often deals with the biomechanical erosion of the inside with the outside, the beautiful with the horrific, which I believe correlates with Bowie's central aesthetic. This chapter also places Gaga's and Bowie's work in relation to Rob McRuer's "crip theory" on queerness and disability. Taken as a whole, the chapters attempt to intertwine notions of performance as it relates across the spectrum of Bowie's work, especially as it provides an architecture for understanding the personal nature of his experimentation.

The title of this book refers to a phrase promulgated by Bowie at the time of the release of *Scary Monsters*. Bowie said that his album represented "future nostalgia . . . a past look at something that hasn't happened yet."[2] While this description is an apt one to describe the specific setting for the album's title song, it is applicable to Bowie's aesthetic generally as well. As Bowie seemed to begin to acknowledge in the mid-nineties, around the time he made the albums *Buddha of Suburbia* (1993) and *Outside* (1995), he has always been postmodern avant la lettre.[3] The distinctive way in which Bowie seems always presciently to forecast the future is often tinged with a sense of futures that never were, or alternative timelines that are just as likely to result in a dystopia—"we have five years left to die in"—as a utopian dream of a "better future." The future from which Bowie looks back is always nostalgic for our present, which is where his futures emanate from.[4] By taking us into the future, he burrows more deeply into the present. The future he presents can be excitingly strange and fascinating, but it is never simply celebratory. Indeed, his glimpses into the imagined future are poignant and effective precisely because they are rooted in the present and have, therefore, sympathy for the now-ness of time, the very inability to ever imagine the future as anything other than desire. The present is future's nostalgia, but the future is the desire on the part of those living now to know what will become of them, to strive for something else. Wilcken, the author of a book on Bowie's *Low*, locates within Bowie "a sadness" that Bowie picks up on from Kraftwerk: "They look back to the golden age of the radio, or the futurist visions of a 1920s movie like *Metropolis*."[5] While Wilcken characterizes this feeling as ultimately a form of Romanticism, he also notes that "both blended postmodernist pastiche with a retro-modernist aesthetic."[6] This mixture of the past with the future, or the future by way of the past, is central to the music that Bowie creates especially during the important years from 1977 until 1980, when he secures his reputation as a musical innovator who is unafraid to take his music into uncharted territory and to transcend the cultural avant-garde of the Ziggy period with work that will place him completely outside of the pop musical mainstream and in a new orbit completely.

Career overview

The general story that people tell about Bowie focuses on his upbringing after the Second World War in London in a middle-class family that was cued in to modern entertainment—whether it was the television or the cinema. His father worked as an entertainment booker and his mother as an usher in a movie theater. They owned a television before other families on their block and lived a fairly comfortable life given the drab grayness of much British postwar existence, which was markedly spartan and contained.[7] Britain had barely survived the aerial bombardment of Hitler and suffered the scars—literally and psychologically—for years to come. As Davy Jones, Bowie was brought up in a somewhat unusual family atmosphere that included parents with several overlapping relationships and children from them, one of which included an older half-brother, Terry Burns, who lived in the home. Burns, a schizophrenic, was a major influence on Bowie's intellectual development, exposing him to jazz, the Beats, and other cultural influences that were to play a major role in developing Bowie's psyche. Bowie's earliest desire for a career, he often claims, came from seeing

Little Richard on television and wanting to be a saxophone player in his band. The first instrument that Bowie owned was a plastic (tenor) sax and Bowie would, in the future, privilege this instrument on several recordings, often played by him.

The mixture of glamour and sexuality that are the hallmarks of Little Richard fit almost too well into the Bowie mythos. Bowie's lifelong interest in otherness is well summed up by Richard's open bisexuality and racial marginalization. He was certainly a key figure in rock historiography, and one could certainly understand Bowie's particular attraction to him. Bowie began to become involved in music in a serious way in his early teens, when he was already involved in several bands. During most of the 1960s, Bowie moved from one band to another seemingly searching for a musical style to call his own. He was involved in jazz, cover bands, doo-wop, and various other styles (the Kon-Rads, King Bees, Mannish Boys, the Lower Third). Slowly he began to master the rudiments of pop-song craft. The work from this early era of Bowie's long career shows quite a variety of approaches to music and what would be for most musicians, solid pop hits. Bowie's work then sounds mostly like the work of others—from the Anthony Newley-ish vocals to the often generic family-film music sound of the orchestration—as Bowie had clearly yet to create his own unique sound or approach to songwriting. It is important, however, to also note the creativity on display here—especially the inherent drama in many of the songs, the role-playing and use of character voices that are already a hallmark of Bowie's writing and performing. In terms of content, many of the songs already suggest directions that Bowie will follow. Darker subject matter permeates many of the tunes—whether the postapocalyptic themes of "Please Mr. Gravedigger" or "We Are Hungry Men," which also adds a messiah figure that prefigures Ziggy Stardust and the set of Hunger City for *Diamond Dogs* (1974). "She's Got Medals" is his first gender-bending song, about a girl who passes as a boy in the army, and most of the love songs suggest some sort of psychological complexity that undercuts the underpinnings of the genre. Most significantly, perhaps, is "Maid of Bond Street," which already contains references to the notion of a self-made star, which is associated both with the "maid," who pictures "clothes, eyes of stars," and with her boyfriend, who "doesn't have a limousine/really wants to be a star himself." Bowie clearly attempts to give these songs more attention than they received at the time by rerecording some of them for the album *Toy*, which was rejected by Bowie's label in the early 2000s but eventually made its way to the Internet. In this context, the songs were paired with cuts that eventually appeared on *Heathen* (2002). Some of the songs, such as "In the Heat of the Morning," indeed suggest the harder rock direction that Bowie was to go in after "Space Oddity," when his backing band of Mick Ronson and Woody Woodmansey would meld with Bowie's voice to create a complex syncopated rock sound. Most of the 1960s sounds are more reminiscent of the direction that Bowie took on *Hunky Dory*, his first genuinely great album, and one that makes clear that the 1960s experimentation with pop music was taken by Bowie perhaps as far as he would before he branched out into the sounds of *Ziggy Stardust*. The rest is history.

Beginning with *The Man Who Sold the World* in 1970 and ending with *Scary Monsters (and Super Creeps)* in 1980, Bowie's long seventies resulted in an astonishing string of albums, one released every year, that had an unprecedented effect on music from the seventies onward. Although each of Bowie's albums is different from every other—and they and him are both unusual for their time in their constant reinvention—the decade as a whole can be divided roughly into three major phases. *The Man Who Sold the World* and *Scary Monsters* bookend the period. *Hunky Dory* is transitional, but like *Man*, shows Bowie's dawning interest in sexual personae, though also like *Man*, it is arguably a musical cul-de-sac. *Scary Monsters*, rather than being a proper 1980s album, is really a looking back and summing up of all of the work that Bowie had done since 1969's breakout hit, "Space Oddity," which signals the moment when Bowie discovered his own voice, style, and subject matter. The first major phase constitutes the Ziggy or glam/glitter era—from *The Rise and Fall of Ziggy Stardust and the Spiders from Mars* to its sequel, *Aladdin Sane* (1973), to *Diamond Dogs*. The album of cover tunes, *Pin-Ups* (1973), and the first live album, *David Live* (1974), also fall in this phase. Some musical critics then and now would say that this sub-era of Bowie's long career is the only one that really counts, that his work on *Ziggy Stardust*, especially, was his one significant moment—the time when his own interests and that of the cultural zeitgeist synched up. While this viewpoint is certainly churlish, it highlights how much the early seventies were the high-water mark for Bowie—the one time that even critics and detractors would have to give him. And, indeed, it is difficult to underestimate Bowie's achievements with Ziggy, giving voice not only to a new decade, one having to contend with the long shadow of the 1960s influence on culture in general and rock music in particular, but that established sexuality as a fit topic for rock music—arguably an inherently conservative medium. Bowie managed to meld classic rock music sound—short, muscular songs with hooks and rifts galore—with British music hall theatricality, playing with artifice and gender in ways that stretched the tradition of rock music in new artistic directions, not the least of which was the melding of the music with the various visual media through which Bowie refracted it.

While *Ziggy* tends deservedly to get most of the praise for this period, *Aladdin Sane* fits a pattern typical for Bowie and other musicians: a studio album followed by an album composed (and maybe even recorded) mostly on the road during the subsequent tour, with the band that was assembled for the tour (and road-tested on it). A collection of great songs that nevertheless work better separately rather than together, *Aladdin* is both a continuation of the style of *Ziggy* and a further intensification of its theatricality—"Time," with its wonderfully surreal lyrics, and the cover of "Let's Spend the Night Together" both representing the extremes of Bowie's camp aesthetics (the former successful, the latter not). "The Jean Genie," perhaps the album's most famous cut, is set to a blues rhythm and follows in a line of great rock anthems by Bowie: "Suffragette City" and "Rebel, Rebel." The lyric "He's outrageous/he screams and he bawls" originally read, "He screams and he balls."[8] *Sane* was followed by one of the most underrated of Bowie's albums, the wonderfully dark proto-punk *Diamond Dogs*. It is in this album that Bowie takes the artifice of *Ziggy* to its logical extreme, creating an entire dystopian world that, like the set for the concert tour, was rendered three-dimensionally. Begun as a version of George Orwell's *1984* (1949) that was blocked by his widow, the album is perhaps all the better for being based on

Bowie's own invention and is a pastiche of J. G. Ballard, Orwell, the Stones, funk, and Bowie's usual partners in crime—William S. Burroughs, Stanley Kubrick, and Nietzsche. One could make a successful case for all of the songs on the album, but perhaps for the first time in his career, the songs really do have an existence mainly together, in their relationship to each other. Though *Ziggy Stardust* announces itself as a modern remake of a Brecht/Weill opera (*The Rise and Fall of the City of Mahagonny* [1930]), it is not really a concept album, but *Diamond Dogs* is. "Rebel, Rebel," for instance, arises out of a juke box that in this barren city landscape has been made to play again, the song seeming to start up like an old 45-rpm single that is slowly chugging to life. The song, about sexual confusion, both echoes earlier Bowie songs and extends them into this distaff future.

Bowie follows this phase of his career with something that we might call an interim between two great periods: the Ziggy era and the Berlin "trilogy." In the middle of the decade, Bowie ensconced himself in Los Angeles, feeding an alarming addiction to illegal drugs. He produced *Young Americans* (1975), an ode to Philly Soul, and the eponymous *Station to Station* (1976). He also starred in *The Man Who Fell to Earth* (1976), securing a new crossover status in film. While *Young Americans* has been dismissed as packed with "plastic" or "blue-eyed" soul, it contains two of Bowie's most enduring songs: the title track, whose raw, one-take vocal anticipates rap music and finds Bowie creating, sui generis, an effective political song that manages to be both sympathetic and damning of the American cultural scene simultaneously, and the brilliant single "Fame," which was Bowie's first number-one song in the United States. That song, a sort of sideways James Brown rift, is brilliant and perfect in its syncopation of guitar, bass, and percussion. While other songs on the album might be considered lesser songs—"Win," "Right," etc.—and definitely have a similarity in feel, they are all (with the exception of the atrocious cover of "Across the Universe") more interesting than they might seem to be at first, with "Fascination," introducing Luther Vandross, still a remarkable rhythm and blues number. It is *Station to Station*, however, that most people consider the highlight of Bowie's mid-decade period. Many people would now place it near the top of Bowie's albums, if not at the very top. At the time, it was an album about the transition from Los Angeles back to Europe—not to the United Kingdom, but to Switzerland (where Bowie would live off and on in tax exile through the 1980s), and, more famously, Berlin. Its strange mixture of American soul and European experimentation was the template for the upcoming Berlin period. Bowie seemed to wed the hard-edged with the human, the "sure white stains" of the title song with bizarre whimsy ("TVC 15"), nostalgia ("Golden Years"), religion ("Word on a Wing"), and pure funk ("Stay"). The cover version of "Wild Is the Wind" is an example of what makes the album work: Bowie manages to give a blistering technical performance, in which his voice slides up and down octaves, and to make an essentially melodramatic, rote song pulsate with genuine feeling and warmth, while also making us self-conscious about what he is doing as he does it. The desperate nature of Bowie's fragile physical and psychological condition comes through on the album in a controlled way: help me help myself. The album is a perfect fusion of the United States and Europe—saying good-bye to the United States, Bowie, in a way, makes his most direct statement in decades, one that contains the most feeling while also being an album that constantly surprises in its unusual construction, its odd mélange of styles.

While perhaps not constituting a phase as such, this important middle period shows Bowie finally conquering the American market yet moving on to the rest of the world via a return to Europe. Increasingly in recent years, critics and fans have lavished praise on the Berlin period, which has perhaps begun to eclipse the Ziggy one. In some ways, Bowie surprised even himself from 1976 to 1979, creating music that was equally as experimental as the Ziggy period, but as music not as content. What the Ziggy period did with performance and what was permissible as subject matter, the albums *Low* (1977), *"Heroes"* (1978), and *Lodger* (1979) did for rock music itself, pushing into the range of the avant-garde, creating soundscapes, ambient music, and chants to rewrite the rules of rock music from the standpoint of composition. With his partners, Tony Visconti and Brian Eno, Bowie used the studio in wholly new ways to create albums that were just as electrifying and terrifying as the Ziggy albums of the first part of the decade. *Low* finds Bowie almost unable to articulate, wordless and numb. *"Heroes"* is a bleak look at a divided consciousness. *Lodger* is a portrait of a peripatetic world traveler beginning to return, for better or for worse, to pop-rock consciousness. Taken together, the three albums represent a major contribution to rock music that extends it into performance art and twentieth-century classical music (especially serial music) and shows Bowie abandoning any and all musical conventions he has used before, pushing innovation almost (on *Lodger*) for the sake of innovation, restlessly trying to top his former self. In this sense, *Scary Monsters* is a necessary break from the avant-garde pose of the European phase of his career. Returning to America, but to the East Coast, not the West, Bowie ends his great decade where he began it—with the song of Major Tom. "Ashes to Ashes" is arguably Bowie's greatest song, reflecting back across the years, settling some important debts with himself and his fans, and clearing the deck for a reemergence in the 1980s with a new sound, image, and approach to making music.

The identification of Bowie with the 1970s was inevitable but also something that he seems initially to have resisted. He has referred to the decade, or its identification with him, as an "albatross." Eventually, he seems to have embraced the association, if only somewhat. He narrates the documentary *Hollywood Rocks the Movies: The 1970s* (2002) and he sings, on "Bring Me the Disco King" (from the album *Reality*, released in 2003, but the song was apparently composed in 1992), about "marking time in the seventies." Bowie's aptitude for knowing when to adapt to the times and take advantage of his various cult statuses perhaps brought him to reconsider his reluctance. In any case, the decade would live on as dominated by Bowie and become for him the past that he would always have to top. One might argue that he learned everything in the seventies—especially in terms of approaches to making music and designing concerts—and merely replayed these lessons in different forms throughout the eighties and nineties, and perhaps beyond. For people who came of age in the eighties, Bowie would certainly be associated with that decade, though Bowie himself was at best indifferent to the period and later has actively distanced himself from his work in that decade, never to embrace it as he did his seventies work. The decade began for Bowie with his taking a break from his usual schedule of recording and touring. Though active in 1981–82 in film roles and even in some hit singles, most notably "Under Pressure," he reemerged from this quiet time with the album *Let's Dance*.

Whether by accident or on purpose, *Let's Dance* would become Bowie's best-selling album, earning him a great deal of money and propelling him, for a time, into the arena of superstardom. The title song and the album were international hits and the tour that accompanied them epic. Bowie not only stamped his name on the music of the decade, but his album became emblematic of it. Bowie seemed on *Let's Dance* to turn away from the seventies, distancing himself from his albums made then by utilizing a new producer (Nile Rodgers rather than Tony Visconti) and a new guitarist (Stevie Ray Vaughan). The album's production was especially influential and distinctive. Given the way that "Ashes to Ashes" had closed off the seventies, it is not surprising that Bowie would not return to it overtly, though in many ways *Let's Dance* has more in common with his seventies production than one might think and the differences between it and the seventies may have been more inadvertent than cynically arranged. The enormous public reaction to the album, however, sent Bowie on a new trajectory that did not serve him well artistically. The follow-up album to *Let's Dance*, *Tonight* (1984), was overproduced and contained a dearth of new material. Bowie seemed guided by the pressure of *Let's Dance* and produced his first disappointing album. This was followed a few years later by *Never Let Me Down* (1987), which seemed to Bowie to contain some stronger songwriting but was equally hampered by mismatched production. Sales for Bowie continued to be strong, thanks to an elaborate concert tour and the expectations still riding in the wake of *Let's Dance*, but Bowie fans were left somewhat confused by Bowie's work in the eighties, which other than *Let's Dance* seemed to be comprised of a few significant singles—"Under Pressure," the original version of "Cat People," and "Absolute Beginners"—and a number of very un-Bowie-like musical projects, such as *Labyrinth* (1986) and the single "This Is Not America." The move away from avant-garde projects toward those that were clearly of a more popular nature was splitting his fan base and creating a dissonance that threatened to erode his artistic credibility.

Bowie's somewhat unusual reaction to this threat was to form a new band, Tin Machine, and to record two albums with them, rounding out the decade by erasing his own identity while still making new music. The result was to further split his fan base, who could neither see what Bowie was doing for himself that might have been musically rejuvenating or what sort of audience the new music was for. One has to exert a great deal of willpower to hear the two Tin Machine albums as they were probably meant to be heard—on their own terms and not as David Bowie projects. If one can, then there is much to like in their grunge-like sound. Within the trajectory of Bowie's overall career, however, they are still difficult if not impossible to place except, in some instances, as opportunities for Bowie to test some material that would not properly be used until the nineties. Working with the Sales brothers on the album, Bowie was looking back to *The Idiot* (1977) and *Lust for Life* (1977) that he had made with Iggy Pop in Berlin— connecting punk with grunge to create a new guitar- and drum-heavy stripped down

Figure 1.1   Iggy Pop, the 1977 "The Idiot" tour, Boston.

sound. Unfortunately, it was a sound that seemed to disappoint everyone, and though it was certainly a contrast to his earlier eighties albums, it did not seem immediately to lead into an alternative direction that was any more promising.

The nineties began for Bowie with a second marriage, to supermodel Iman, and the release of his first solo album in several years. *Black Tie, White Noise* (1993), which saw him reteamed with Rodgers and exploring the interstitial space between rock music and free jazz. Another underrated album, its slick production was expansive and the album showed Bowie making new homages, this time to Scott Walker and Lester Bowie. It contains two extremely important new songs by Bowie, "Jump They Say," about Terry Burns' suicide in 1985, and "Pallas Athena," an inspired, mostly instrumental, sax-centered work. Unsupported by a tour, the album was left to live or die on its own, and though something of a return to form by Bowie, it also underlined the problem Bowie would have in the nineties: if he did make engaging music again that he would also be seen as having to outrun the expectations for ceaseless invention and cutting-edge futurity that people associated with his seventies work. Perhaps in an effort to match these expectations, Bowie went on to record the intriguing (if critically overrated) *Buddha of Suburbia* soundtrack and arguably his last great album, *Outside*.[9]

Originally planned as a multi-album response to the fin de siècle, *Outside* was an ambitious one-off affair that brought Eno and Bowie back together again to create an album full of asymmetrical soundscapes, cinematic vignettes, and voice-overs by a cast of characters loosely connected by an elaborate backstory that touched on murder, art, and ritual. A paean to modern primitivism and the body-centered art of the 1970s, it was an attempt by Bowie to channel the atmosphere of millennial anxiety while also finding a way to rethink his own Ziggy-era approach to personae, here literalizing the characters as separate entities rather than embedding them in one on-stage character. Because the sequence of albums was left unfinished, it is difficult to know what to make of the storytelling elements of the album, but the music created for the album remains refreshingly unlike anything else Bowie has ever done and certainly maintains his reputation for unique sonic work. Owing a debt to Eno's own seventies work, especially *Here Come the Warm Jets* (1973) and *Taking Tiger Mountain (By Strategy)* (1974), the album overcomes its elaborate trappings to create songs that, while overwhelmingly dark and idiosyncratic, nevertheless pull you in to a worldview that bristles with paranoia and musical invention. Bowie seems to be self-consciously attempting to find a way to connect the dots between the visuality of his music and his actual visual performances of it. A long-time painter, Bowie was, in the nineties, especially interested in the work of a new generation of young British painters (Damien Hirst, et al.) and of the potential of the Internet. In a way, this album fuses media through music, containing, in its original release, an elaborate booklet and a series of doctored photographs in which Bowie poses as the whole cast of characters. Bowie seems to be attempting to find a way to expand the possibilities for linking the aural and visual arts that he discovered in the seventies and early eighties.[10]

While *Outside* seems like an elaborate experiment, it was followed, like *Ziggy Stardust* was by *Aladdin Sane*, by a road album, *Earthling* (1997), that attempted to catch the sound of a great road band. While doing more with samples and loops than ever before, the album was indebted to jungle sound and the British drum and bass movement. Containing, as it does, a number of intriguing cuts—"Little Wonder," "Looking for Satellites," "Telling Lies," and "I'm Afraid of Americans"—the album would, to some, ultimately sound derivative and suggest that Bowie was trying too hard to sound like younger bands he heard around him. In that sense, *Earthlings* was the last attempt on Bowie's part to try to capture the present and represent it as the future. His prescience perhaps coming to an end, he turned, at last, toward the past, releasing *Hours* in 1999. Though songs on the album were written for the French computer game "Omikron: Nomad Soul," the album contains numerous nods to Bowie's past and a fairly straightforward singing style that would become the staple for his albums in the twenty-first century. The everyman persona that Bowie adopts for the album is unconvincing, but the first song, "Thursday's Child," is moving and contains lush orchestration and singing that set it apart from the album as a whole. The overall conservative, even religious nature of the songs on the album is yet another shocking change after the experimentation with recapturing the past that Bowie evinces on *Outside* and *Earthling*. Bowie was never again to return to experimentation of the type that he had known before and would finally, in the next century, turn toward the role of rock's elder statesman that he had resisted.

In 2004, Bowie suffered a heart attack on a stage in Germany where he was performing on tour for his latest album, *Reality*, which had followed *Heathen*. Both albums represent Bowie settling into the role of someone who, while not attempting to replay his or her past, is also not attempting to lasso the future. Both albums emphasize Bowie's singing, his voice, over other instruments and keep the instrumental experimentation to a minimum. Though the albums are a reunion of Bowie with his primary seventies producer, Tony Visconti, they are not a return to the increasingly flashy, thick production of Bowie's seventies albums, which reached its peak with *Scary Monsters*. While Visconti brings plenty of tweaks to the sounds on *Heathen* especially, overall, both albums continue the approach first previewed on *Hours* and even includes the use of the stylophone (on *Heathen*), which Bowie used on "Space Oddity." Both *Heathen* and *Reality* suggest classic rock of a bygone era—solidly constructed with ample hooks, but eschewing either trendiness or elaborate invention. After a ten-year break from touring and, seemingly, recording, Bowie emerged from his recovery with the album *The Next Day*, which picks up where *Reality* left off, though with a slyer, more winking sound that references his seventies heydays while staying firmly entrenched in the present by offering commentary on contemporary events of a non-musical nature. The songs deal with school shootings ("Valentine's Day"), the horror of warfare ("I'd Rather Be High"), and Bowie's own brush with mortality ("The Next Day"—"Here I am/not quite dying"). In some songs ("Boss of Me," "[You Will] Set the World on Fire") Bowie seems to be making the late-eighties album he never perfected. Most of the songs contain sympathy, especially for youth, and do not appear to be obviously autobiographical. In some ways, they are a continuation of the mid-sixties songs on *Toy* in which Bowie sings what seem to be slices of life, songs about everyday people (like *Sgt. Pepper*, 1967) but often with a twist. Like everything in Bowie's canon, there is distance, yet complexity. Songs on the album can seem both nakedly confessional ("Where Are We Now?") and not, upon closer look, and vice versa. Musically, Bowie references only himself, by now having become his own repertoire of musical history, finding little of interest musically in the present, and realizing that the best way to be yourself is to make the music that you most want to hear.

Performance art

With this overview in mind, we face the difficult task of tracking Bowie's immense output, one that now covers almost fifty years of production (at least since 1964), with only the past ten years constituting anything like a real break (and how much of one it was is yet to be seen as new music may continue to be released). Because of the variety and the volume of production, it is also difficult to conceptualize the many eddies and connections among works. And while there are certainly some repeating motifs, there is also a great deal of new invention. The one common denominator within Bowie's oeuvre may well be the notion of performance. In a sense, Bowie has always been performing himself—as Davy Jones performing David Bowie performing one of his many personae. The self-consciousness of his performances, which call attention to themselves as performances, threads through his work and unites his music with his visual art.[11] As Bowie himself said in the early seventies, he is to some extent at heart an actor, one who is playing a role whether it is before the microphone, on the stage, or in front of a camera. These performances are often, though not always, narratively based, character driven, and at some level dependent upon psychological complexity. As Carter Ratcliff and others have noted, Bowie's attitude toward performance seems patterned after a Romantic notion of art, one that attempts to bring to rock music an approach that is essentially based on rock not as a commodity but as an art form.[12] That is to say, Bowie eschews the usual dictates of rock as purely a commodity—which can control its form, content, and distribution—in favor of an older Romantic idea that a popular form can be treated like "high" art. In this, Bowie shares many similarities with Oscar Wilde and other figures in the previous fin de siècle. Certainly Bowie shares Wilde's proclivities in terms of experimenting with gender, sexuality, Orientalism, and self-invention. But Bowie perhaps comes closest to Wilde in his rejection of the notion that there is no distinction between art and commerce.[13] Though Bowie comes of age as an artist during the era of Andy Warhol and the collapse of the work of art as a form distinct from commercial art, Bowie in some ways pushes back against this idea—at least for rock music. Given rock music's trivialization as a crude popular form, Bowie's resistance is, in fact, a bit startling.

Warhol's approach to art was to dismiss the separation between art and commerce by arguing that all art, once exposed to the effects of the market, was co-opted anyway and that the only response was to treat art—even "high" art—as though it were already a commodity. The problem with this approach is that it removes any sense of resistance on the part of the artist and leaves only the possibility, which Warhol ultimately embraced, of measuring artistic success solely with money.[14] Ironically, or perhaps paradoxically, Bowie and his ilk—Iggy Pop, Brian Eno, and Brian Ferry—injected a Romanticist notion into rock. Pop art, in their hands, became a serious art endeavor—what Warhol would call "real" art.[15] The border between art and life that was partially dismantled by Wilde in his astute performance of self vanished entirely by the time pop art mavens like Warhol and David Hockney pursued it. Bowie was to carry this aspect to an extreme with the complete interpenetration of his art and life via the creation of characters that he would act out in real life and, throughout much of his career, the mystique that has surrounded him, which began before the Ziggy period as the illusion of wealth and fame (riding in limos, having an entourage) even before he really had either. This was a strategy given to Bowie by his first serious manager, Kenneth Pitt, who borrowed it from Wilde's 1882 tour of North America in support of a production of Gilbert and Sullivan's operetta *Patience* (1881), complete with Bowie's elaborate costumes and sailing, à la Wilde, on a steamship to America.[16] Bowie's approach was not the only one, as can be seen in Eno's pursuit of anonymity in musical production—ultimately resulting in the creation of an artistic version of

Muzak in the form of ambient music.[17] In this sense, the democratization of art that Warhol argued for made sense. Bowie was certainly the pop musician who took the idea of the image to new heights. His emblematic appearance on the *Aladdin Sane* cover, for example, was a sort of self-iconization such as Warhol supplied to others: Marilyn Monroe or Elvis Presley. Bowie becomes both subject and object—pop art artist and the best subject of his art. Bowie is not an everyday object like a soup can, but rather a star, like one of Warhol's "superstars" or, say, the way that Jasper Johns uses himself, literally plaster casts of his own body in his target series. The difference, again, is that Bowie is not supposed to be everyday, but extraordinary.

In addition to being a part of the visual-art tradition that resulted in Warhol and pop art, Bowie was also a self-conscious member of the performance art tradition. As noted earlier, Bowie mentions the body art tradition of the seventies on his album *Outside*. More pointedly and personally, he dresses in a costume inspired by Hugo Ball in his 1979 performance of "The Man Who Sold the World" on NBC television's sketch comedy revue, *Saturday Night Live*.[18] By placing himself within the tradition of avant-garde theater and performance, Bowie allies himself with Dadaist, Futurist, and Surrealist artists who combined the street-level aesthetics of vaudeville and the music hall with those of artists who were interested in revolutionizing the arts, removing barriers between media, and creating an art that was a new form of total theater. While the tradition of performance often focuses on the performer and the performer's body,

Figure 1.2   Cover of *Aladdin Sane*, 1973.

in all of its physicality and virtuosity, the Dadaists and their ilk blend or replace the body with the machine, the puppet or automaton.[19] This merging of the body with architectural space is the hallmark of Bowie's performance that night, which begins with his entombment in the suit and then moves on, finally in the last song of the evening, to the replacement of his body entirely by a puppet. The artistic movements Bowie references, while creating their own anti-art traditions (noisescapes, for example), also combined ballet, poetry, set design, and what we now call special effects. The mechanistic or totalizing aspects probably reached their peak with Oskar Schlemmer. What is arguably different about this tradition from how it was used by Bowie was its tendency to emphasize the group over the individual, to make performers one more cog in the assemblage, one more part of the overall functioning machine.[20] While Bowie subordinates himself somewhat on *Saturday Night Live* to his accompanying performers who provide their own simultaneous performances and actions—Klaus Nomi and Joey Arias—he is still the literal center of attention, a still center in the case of the first number. It may be important to remember that the body-oriented performance tradition of theater was not the origin of Dadaism or of other more recent performance art traditions such as Happenings (Allan Kaprow) or FLUXUS. These traditions come out of other media traditions, mostly the visual arts, and can often be traced back to the conceptual art of Marcel Duchamp.[21] Duchamp's work is often bodily oriented—from the notorious *Fountain* (1917), a repurposed urinal, to *The Bride Stripped Bare by Her Bachelors, Even* (1915–23)—but comes from a very different context than that of the historical notion of performance. While performance can mean everything from the performance of everyday life to the extraordinary performances of talented individuals to the context-specific performances of artists, the reality is that Bowie straddles all three, combining and recombining aspects of all three, perhaps seemingly contradictory, approaches to performance.

The notion of performance as an avant-garde tradition can be said to reach from the second decade of the twentieth century, the era of the Futurists and Dadaists, to the 1970s, perhaps even ending then right when Bowie was peaking.[22] English performance traditions in particular were more open to the mixing of the vernacular with the "high" art pretentions of this first generation of modern performance artists, who could not have emerged within the more cloistered confines of the Continent.[23] Bowie's tutelage in mime under the gay Scottish mime artist Lindsay Kemp, which did so much to provide Bowie with a core for his later performances, could not have taken place in another place or time. The notion of performance as the performance of the body was peaking in the late sixties and early seventies, to be replaced, in the 1980s and beyond, with a different orientation to performance that emphasized spectacle and multimedia and moved toward a disembodied experience to be replaced yet again in the 1990s by a turn toward language and the performative.[24] In a sense, theater comes back with a vengeance and the aspects of performance that are not dependent upon the body—the theater of lighting, setting, and mood music that is Robert Wilson's neo-operas, for example. Or perhaps the theater of the European avant-garde never really goes away in Europe, instead finding itself reignited in a US context (Wilson and Laurie Anderson, say). Britain stands alone as an example of the fusing of the individual and the bodily, the artistic and the vernacular, as something like an alternative performative paradigm. Indeed, one might argue that avant-garde performance, for all of its fascination, is at base a style of performance, one whose various aspects are easy to predict in advance. As Richard Schechner argues, "One has to go to popular entertainments—pop music, sports, movies and TV—to find arts conditioned by the rough-and-ready economics of the market. However 'vulgar' these entertainments, they are also often both lively and innovative, especially in the development of physical techniques (lighting, sound, ways of including the audience, 'special effects')."[25] In that sense, Bowie's, and rock music's, low-art status has its advantages, especially in terms of vitality.

Bowie's theatrical approach to rock music, especially in its visual form, is dependent upon a mixture of Brechtian minimalism and Asian theater gesture. Roland Barthes' description of the *Bunraku* puppet theater tradition of Japan could easily apply to Bowie's own use of concision, of the gestural vocabulary of mime, to get the meaning and ideas across in a stylistic way:

> A total spectacle but a divided one, *Bunraku* . . . excludes improvisation: to return to spontaneity would be to return to the stereotypes which constitute our "depth." As Brecht had seen, here *citation* rules, the sliver of writing, the fragment of code, for none of the action's promoters can account in his own person for what he is never alone to write. As in the modern text, the interweaving of codes, references, discrete assertions, anthological gestures multiples the written line, not by virtue of some metaphysical appeal, but by the interaction of a *combinatoire* which opens out into the entire space of the theater: what is begun by one is continued by the next, without interval.[26]

Bowie's gestures are matched, at times, with the purposeful inexpressiveness of his face—the album cover of *Aladdin Sane* or the blank, cocaine face of the Diamond Dogs period. Even the demure smile of Ziggy or the perpetual sneer of the Thin White Duke acted, to some extent, as masks behind which he would hide, wiping out emotions, or disdaining them. The effect, as one might see in Japanese theater, was to force the audience to look elsewhere for emotion, or the signification of emotion, and to read the surface in a counterintuitive way.[27] As Barthes says of Japanese theater, an actor's face might be "offered to the spectators to read; but what is carefully, preciously given to be read is that there is nothing there to read; here again we come to that exemption of meaning (that exemption *from* meaning as well) which we Westerns can barely understand."[28] He concludes: "In *Bunraku*, the puppet has no strings. No more strings, hence no more metaphor, no more Fate; since the puppet no longer apes the creature, man is no longer a puppet in the divinity's hands, the *inside* no longer commands the *outside*."[29] Finally, in Bowie's performances, gender is not erased but merely "absented," to use a phrase from Barthes. In the Japanese tradition:

> The transvestite actor (since the women's roles are played by men) is not a boy made up as a woman, by dint of a thousand nuances, realistic touches, costly simulations, but a pure signifier whose *underneath* (the truth) is neither

clandestine . . . nor surreptitiously signed (by a waggish wink at the virility of the support, as in Western drag shows: opulent blondes whose trivial hand or huge foot infallibly give the lie to the hormonal bosom: simply *absented*; the actor, in his face, does not play the woman, or copy her, but only signifiers her; if, as Mallarmé says, writing consists of "gestures of the idea," transvestitism here is the gesture of femininity, not its plagiarism.[30]

Performance art, as a concept, can be said to be presentational—to begin, in a sense, with its own ending, its own dematerialization, absence, and death.[31] Ever since photography, this essentially presentational aspect has heralded the fact that art goes beyond the object; that all art is, as Wilde declared, "quite useless"; and that the performer, like any other material part of art, is expendable. Bowie's performances are performances of self, ones in which the self is presented as a character in a fiction, much as Cindy Sherman's famous photographs in which she appears as a film heroine in stills from films that were never made, but ones whose context we think we know—or can imagine. We are implicated in performances such as these, made to feel a part of the manipulation of media, genre, and tradition, but also to understand the constructedness of self, the vampiric interconnection between representation and identity—most especially, perhaps, in terms of gender. Female artists who called attention to their bodies in the seventies, such as Carolee Schneemann, or in the eighties and nineties, such as Karen Finlay, emphasized the materiality of their bodies, the degradation of the female body in art and in life, but its separateness from the male body as well. In some ways, Bowie's attempts to create a feminized body in the seventies, in the Ziggy period especially, were parallel to those of these female artists in that Bowie was exploring, in his own way, the limits of the gendered body. Bowie called into question the limits of our definitions of gender and sexuality, creating not transvestitism or camp, but the defamilarization of the body in a way that can only be compared to that of feminist performance artists. Bowie made the male body new again, removing centuries of encrusted meaning to suggest the possibility of new interpretations of it. Just as French feminist writers such as Luce Irigaray, Hélène Cixous, and Monique Wittig were, in starkly different ways, attempting to write through the female body—to create an experimental new language with which to represent the female, feminine, or lesbian—so, too, did Bowie attempt to create a new vocabulary for a language of the body of the future.

As Henry M. Sayre notes, "The tableau is the visual embodiment of contrast and difference."[32] This theatrical, or now cinematic, technique is the essence of Bowie's concert presentations. The body is stylized and becomes a part of the overall plastic meaning of what is framed on stage. From the time of Ziggy, Bowie's presentations of his performative selves have referenced a long range of avant-garde performance, from the "noise music"[33] of the Futurists to the various mechanical ballets, cubist costumes, and increasingly abstract choreography of the Constructivists, Dadaists, Surrealists, and Bauhaus school. Reaching a peak in the mid-1990s with his work for his album *Outside*, Bowie performed "Andy Warhol" (from 1971's *Hunky Dory*) as a puppet on stage in the accompanying concert tour with Trent Reznor. The music video for the first single from the album, "The Heart's Filthy Lesson," specifically referenced the ritualized art of Hermann Nitsch. In a music video, Bowie and a crew of helpers use body parts taken from casts to assemble a Minotaur, one of the characters in the album *Outside*. Bowie claims to have chosen the video's director, Sam Bayer, because he was good at creating a "distressed" feel; was himself, like Bowie, an artist; and was tuned in, like Bowie, to "fragmentation."[34] What is perhaps most striking about the video, however, is how much the actions of the participants seem to echo a Nitsch "Aktion" from the seventies such as *48th Action* (1974), which included the skinning and disembowelment of a goat on stage.[35] The Viennese school of actioners, moving on into Native American rituals and others, attempt to reconnect with primal energies and to strip the participants and the audience of preconceived emotional reactions to their experience of art and performance. Bowie attempted to connect this seventies school with the millennial anxiety of the late 1990s—the sense of paranoia, decadence (among the very wealthy), and return of an interest in the primal in the form of the "modern primitivism" movement. This last was signaled in the popular culture at large by the popularity of tattoos and piercings, which eventually became an almost generational marker of identity. Bowie makes much of this redeployment of the body away from a seamless surface and toward a marked, scarred, and altered one. To some extent, one might argue that Bowie is seeing an alternative version of the future at work, the dark retro future of, say, a cyberpunk sensibility as opposed to the gleaming *Star Trek*-like future imagined as late as the early or mid-1970s.[36] Mixed in with the album's own imagery is the looming specter of HIV disease and the ritual turn toward body modification as one logical reaction on the part of a generation that has been told never to break the boundary of the skin for fear of death. In the video, Bowie and his acolytes revel in bodily fluids, body parts, and death: though coming indirectly from the seventies, the imagery contains a new meaning in the 1990s. Bowie obviously references not only the overt sexuality of Trent Reznor's video "Closer" from his album *The Downward Spiral* (1994), but also his own body modification in the 1970s, first with gender and second with technology, both of which are displaced here with their opposites. First codified in the magazine *Re/Search*'s special issue on "Modern Primitivism," the movement might be said to have a long and rich postwar history in the United States—from Fakir Musafer, who hung from hooks in his skin in an attempt to achieve an out-of-body experience, to Genesis P-Orridge who has engaged in a series of body modifications to create an amalgam of male and female physical traits he calls "Pandrogeny." Primitivism reminds one that one has a body, which in a hypertechnologized, anesthetized world, allows some people, via what amounts to ritual self-mutilation, to feel at one with their body again—no longer modern, but never generally primal as well. This approach to the body, while it has now become quotidian, had its roots not only in Fakir and the 1950s, but in performance art of the 1960s and 1970s as well. Not only Nitsch and the Viennese school, but Rudolf Schwartzkolger, who nailed his scrotum to a board, and Chris Burden, who was nailed to a VW Beetle and shot with a twenty-two-caliber rifle, were among the many artists who were involved in the mutilation of their own bodies in an effort to, among many things, test the limits of them via art.

Mark C. Taylor argues that body modification in general, and perhaps tattooing in particular, represent an ultimately modernist stance toward the body and is part and parcel of the movement away from ornamentation and toward abstraction that takes place during the early modernist period in both painting and architecture.[37] In that sense, the interest in body art since the 1990s is a return to ornamentation, but at the level of the body itself. It is also, for him, connected to the body art of the sixties and seventies. As he says, "Body art represents, among other things, a sustained effort to reverse the dematerialization of art by making the body matter."[38] People who alter their bodies are doing something similar. For Taylor, tattooing allows people to imprint art onto their bodies, or make their bodies into canvases of art, stems especially from the full-body tattoos of Japan or the rich traditions of the South Pacific such as those of Polynesia. These traditions were mingled with "images from the world of 'high' art" such as those from "the cubists, surrealists, Kandinsky, and Lissitzky" to "erasing the line between elite and popular culture."[39] Looking at the modern resurgence of these traditions in a Western context, one might say that with tattoos "postmodernism becomes incarnate. When the sign becomes a body, the body becomes a sign."[40] The ultimate result of tattooing, ironically, may be the collapsing of the body into virtual space. As Taylor argues:

> As the media invade every aspect of life and electronic networks extend their tentacles to create webs that appear to be virtually seamless, reality itself hides behind screens that are infinite. The postmodern world of images translates the modernist project of dematerialization from the world of art into sociocultural processes. In this way, the culture of simulacra becomes the ironic realization of the avant-garde's dream of bringing art to life. When reality becomes virtual, the body disappears.[41]

While one might look at this process as the dematerialization of the body, one might also say that the body is imprinted on the virtual. If the "human mind and body are prostheses that extend to the net" and "if the body is an extension of the electronic networks that increasingly constitute our world rather than the reverse, then the body's reality becomes virtual."[42]

Rather than seeing this process as a positive one or symptomatic of the fusing of the body with technology, as though "modern primitives" were really both, one could just as well argue that, rather than celebrate the body, modification degrades it. While Taylor focuses on particularly elegant abstract designs to illustrate his text, the reality of most tattoos is that they represent a failed, stylized realism. Rather than celebrating the skin, they disrupt the smooth surface of it—its virtuality, in Taylor's schema—to de-eroticize it by writing over it with a glyph that all but vanquishes its physical and erotic properties. The semantic disruption of tattoos is extreme; their permanence is alarming, freezing into place a moment, but one that is placed on a body that changes while its work of "art" does not. At the same time, whatever celebratory aspects of tattoos may represent rebellion or resistance has long since been superseded by the ordinariness of tattoos, the quotidian way they have become bourgeois and lost whatever ability to shock they might have once enjoyed. The exclusive club is no more, and the effects of the popularity of body modification are now, post-nineties, doubtful.

Bowie's interest in other people's body art after the 1970s took other forms as well, such as the dandies Gilbert and George, whose own performance of themselves as puppets or automatons was an extreme version of Bowie's use of seventies personae, especially in terms of creating a total overlap between art and life. For Gilbert and George there is no difference; they are never not performing. Whether singing on a street corner or making room-size photomontages of their faces and their obsessions—they fuse art and life more completely (and intimately) than Bowie. Their motto, "Art for all," could be said to encompass Bowie's approach to bringing the high art of performance art to the masses, or of meeting it half way in the middle transition between the two. Bowie's studied use of spectacle throughout his concert career was one of the most pointed ways in which he made it clear to his audience that his performance was not just about casual entertainment but in its extreme planning and precision, which extended to its choreography, set design, set list, etc., a Bowie concert was closer to performance art than the usual rock show, more about art than pop, theater than music. In this sense, Bowie was closer to performance artists who were themselves, like Gilbert and George and others, interested in making art popular. Though a figure like Laurie Anderson might be a natural point to which all of Bowie's experiments might lead—someone who went from the performance art tradition toward the popular—Bowie also shared space with Robert Wilson, whose works became, after the seventies, increasingly more operatic and spectacular, but whose goal was to bring it to the masses. Bowie was scheduled to perform as Abraham Lincoln in Wilson's multi-country performance piece *The Civil Wars: A Tree Is Best Measured When It Is Down* in 1984, but it was never completed. Wilson has said, "I think T.V. is the future."[43] In a sense, Wilson and other multimedia artists bring us back to Bowie's origins in the most middle class of mediums. A meta-pop artist for the latter half of the twentieth century, Bowie did more than anyone else of his generation to push at the boundaries of how we define performance, not from the standpoint of the elite arts of opera, ballet, the symphony, but from the bottom and middle, from the dictates, traditions, and unwritten assumptions of the popular form we call "rock and roll." As Bowie has said: "I'm the last person to pretend I'm a radio. I'd rather go out and be a colour television set."[44]

Bowie's connection to the arts reflects an interest in the fusion of art and life perhaps as an escape from the middle-class existence he grew up in and a yearning for a Bohemian life via an immersion into a purely artistic realm. Yet his very middle classness, his exposure to rock music via television and film also allowed him to experience the possibilities of popular art at a young age. Bowie grew up during the fifties and the time of Erving Goffman's influential ideas about the performance of self. As Amelia Jones explains:

> Goffman's book links together the theoretical exploration of the self and the performative bodies of body art (especially in its US manifestations). In the 1960s, a number of artists in the United States read Goffman's book, as well as

some of the work of Merleau-Ponty. Goffman's instrumentalized version of French existentialist phenomenology along with Merleau-Ponty's own writings, among other texts, provided a model for younger-generation artists such as Vito Acconci who came of age after the heroic era of abstract expressionism and within the heroic era of the 1960s.[45]

Along the timeline of Western art, Bowie appeared at the moment when existentialist ideas penetrated popular art and became a part of the artistic realm generally. The performance of self in everyday life became a self-conscious act, denaturalized and defamiliarized. Life itself could become art, and vice versa, in a new way. Goffman's book discusses the way we perform our self for other people, whether it is how we enter a room, stand, talk, or sit. Our performance changes, as well, depending upon our audience—peers, parents, etc. The movement of the notion of self into the everyday is an expression of the sense of otherness, of allocentricity, as it rubs up against our supposed sense of oneness, of self. The fragile existential construct that is the self (and the other) is one of many aspects of performance that is uncovered.

Goffman's was one of many key texts that allowed for the locus of art itself to shift toward performance. The lynchpin in this movement may well have been Jackson Pollack's action painting, which found a unique method to express the movement of the body in space on canvas.[46] Pollack's drips, dribbles, and stains became a way to create a field in which to place the body in space, and to externalize the mind and express its most intimate, personal thoughts in a visual, even grand and heroic, way. While maintaining the abstract power of modernist art at its best (Mondrian, for example, whose own paintings were without frames so that they could extend indefinitely into space), Pollack found a way to gesture toward the postmodern—the return of art to the body, to imagery, and toward a new focus on the performative. In a sense, Pollack leads the way toward Warhol and thus to the entire body of performance-based body art afterwards. Whatever one might say about the political efficacy of postmodernism generally, the fragmentation of postmodern art allowed for experimentation with what makes up the self and others, including gender. Vito Acconci's *Seedbed* (1972), in which he masturbated under a walkway over which people passed, was one of many in which the difference between the artist and his audience could be explored. Likewise, the work of Marina Abramović and Ulay allowed for the fragmentation of the structures that define male and female bodies. Though Jones claims that these performances, such as *Imponderabilia* (1977/2010), where they stood naked at the sides of a door frame, forcing visitors to brush up against them, merely masked "the privileging of masculinity in what is in effect experiences as a bipolar model of gender,"[47] Ulay's early work was in transexuality and was an attempt to "[test] the physical limits of the body, balancing male and female principles."[48] Acconci added the aspect of narrative, which "altered the previously nonverbal orientation of body art."[49] What is perhaps most important in these performances, no matter how limited or provisional, was the attempt to move art toward "the social, embodying and so particularizing and politicizing self/other and self/world relations."[50] In a sense, Bowie's groundbreaking work with Ziggy Stardust was an attempt at such a solution—a way out of the sheer refusal of the modernist avant-garde to engage with the world and the collapsing of art into the commercial field. Bowie recognized the need to perform the body in space, a particular body, engendered and fragmented, but engaged and real.

The recording of a performance that Pollock's work seemed to allow lived on in the work of numerous other artists. As Catherine Wood notes, David Hockney's signature work, *A Bigger Splash* (1967), which represents the aftermath of a swimmer's trail from a diving board into a pristine California pool, is in a way an ironic self-conscious commentary on Pollock's action painting.[51] The drips and dribbles that Hockney uses to represent the splash caused by the body entering the water combines pop art's stylized irony, especially in someone like Roy Lichtenstein's or James Rosenquist's faux-comic book panels, with Pollock's action painting as a commentary on the traces that a body in space leaves behind. The diver is never seen, as though he has plunged into another world, and the painting, in its use of bright, flat acrylic colors, comments not only on the evenness of the waterless Los Angeles atmosphere, but the Mondrian-like architecture of flat roofs and modernist outlines that inhabits it. As with almost all of Hockney's paintings of this era, there is an autobiographical element as well. This work, like many from his 1960s and 1970s California era, calls attention to itself. The haptic dislocation of the figure makes one think as much about who it might have been or what they might have looked like than if the figure were actually present. Hockney's frequent use of his current lovers and friends in his paintings emphasized not only his identity as a figurative artist but the homoerotic fascination he had for the physicality of the culture of Southern California—one that drew him from his native Yorkshire. In the end, the lack of a figure, its disappearance, gestures toward the surreal, as though the scene is finally about a link between the subconscious mind and what might be called, for lack of a better word, reality.

Like the work of Pollock or Mondrian or other primarily abstract painters, the abstraction of the splash itself also suggests the merging of life with art, or the movement of the abstraction off the canvas and into real life, aestheticizing the space beyond its borders. The merging of art and life—of seeing his life as theatricalized and at one with his painting, photographs, sketching, and printmaking—has always been a hallmark of Hockney's work. The problem, for Hockney, has always been for the viewer not to see his paintings as merely snapshots of real life, still images from a life in which all is composed and maintained like a still life. The outward prettiness of Hockney's work adds to the temptation by some to see his work as decorative and merely superficially alluring. Like Francis Bacon before him, however, Hockney's work expresses an interest in the figurative that comes from a desire to document the gay emotional world from which he came. His paintings, in general, go from the overtly surreal, rebellious work of his British youth to the balanced, brighter work of his thirty years in California to the more subdued landscape work of his return to Yorkshire. In each of these phases, his work has expressed not only his life, but his life as art. For all his versatility, Hockney's major preoccupation has remained not only visual media but in some ways an almost old-fashioned belief in painting as it is linked to the Old Master tradition. Fragments of his aestheticized life show up in his paintings, but are rarely the actual topic itself—or not any more than that for other painters. In that sense, Hockney's work stops well short of the merging of art and life that one sees in the work of Cindy Sherman, Eleanor Antin, or Jack Smith. The play with personae that one sees in all three artists—among many others—carries visual art into the realm of *Gesamkunstwerk*, creating a total art form that allows for the intensification of art via life, and vice versa. As with the other dandies who preceded him, Hockney opens up the possibility that life offers to art to find new intensities and to bring to life the excitement of art. The key to this movement back and forth is in the notion of performance—to perform a life as a work of art. While dandies have made this type of performance seem, at times, purposefully frivolous, hiding the work (economic and otherwise) that is required of it, performance artists such as Sherman purposefully blur the line, using their lives as the explicit content of their documented performances of identity, making themselves into something else. In a sense, they are not creating art out of their lives—making their lives artistic—but making art using the material of their lives but, like Hockney, keeping the two areas to some extent separate.

Bowie's work with art and life via personae can be seen as building upon these late-modernist and postmodernist artistic traditions, playing with personae and roles throughout his career—emphasizing and de-emphasizing the theatricality and closeness of the roles to himself and the elaborateness of the roles according to the album he was presenting. From early on in his career Bowie was interested in creating characters for his songs. At the age of twenty, Bowie appeared with Michael Byrne in the artistic short film *The Image* (1967). Directed by Michael Armstrong, Bowie appears as a silent young man who stalks the artist, played by Byrne, first as a muse and then as an aggressive ghostly presence. Filmed in luscious black and white by Ousama Rawi and scored to fusion jazz by Noel Janus, the film reeks of art-house pretension, and yet it is also a prescient forecast of what Bowie was to do later in his career. As a painting that, literally, comes to life, Bowie plays the part of Dorian in a modern remake of *The Picture of Dorian Gray* (1891). As in Wilde's novel, the homoerotic element in the artist's love of his creation is present here, especially in Bowie's preternatural androgyny, a pretty object to be observed and admired by the artist and the audience. The role of the artist with respect to his creation is also at play, as the very object of his creation, the young man, who first appears on the canvas and then at the window, threatens to destroy him. Like Bowie with some of his more jealous and malevolent creations that Bowie ultimately feels threatened by, Ziggy Stardust and the Thin White Duke, say, the character of the Artist ultimately fears the advances of the Boy. The shot ends with the character of the Boy slain by the Artist with a knife. The director leaves unclear whether or not the artist's creation is real or a figment of the artist's imagination until the last shot, which is a photograph of the boy. The very undecidability suggests not only the circuit of artist/creation (art, persona)/ audience that is essential to the rock formula, but also the doppelganger aspects of some of Bowie's creations, most especially the theme of the dark twin that haunts the album *Scary Monsters* and is represented by the shadow on the cover of the album and the repetition of the song's lyrics on "It's No Game, Part One" and "Ashes to Ashes" by two distinctly different voices out of synch with each other, mirroring and reflecting.

The painting of the boy shows him extending his arms as an embrace, though whether or not this is a threatening gesture, it is ultimately read that way by the artist.

The belief that the canvas functions as a portrait, photo, or mirror, reflecting the artist, the audience, or their desires is central not only to Wilde's novel but also to Bowie's aesthetic throughout his career. His other notable creation during 1967 was his contribution to Lindsay Kemp's *Pierrot in Turquoise or the Looking Glass Murders*. Another filmed allegory, Bowie here plays the character of Cloud, a character literally and figuratively elevated above the action on the stage who comments indirectly on the play via songs written by Bowie. The play itself, a pantomime, involves Columbine (Annie Stainer) who is loved by Pierrot (Kemp) and Harlequin (Michael Garrett) but chooses the latter. Pierrot subsequently kills Harlequin and then Columbine. While in its own way *Pierrot* is also a period piece, it is difficult to underestimate Kemp's influence on Bowie, acting as perhaps the second major intellectual influence on him after his brother Terry. While Bowie's contribution to this particular piece is singing and songwriting, Kemp's training in the mime tradition was obviously important to Bowie's developing his own unique gestural vocabulary, one in which he combined choreographed dance movements with hand movements from the pantomime tradition. Bowie was able to utilize these movements for a range of situations, from the smaller more intimate scale of music video to the arena stages of his 1980s concerts. Some of his film performances, most especially his portrayal of Andy Warhol in *Basquiat* (1996), emphasize Bowie's dance-like movements, his carriage and way of holding himself, which seem to capture more of Warhol than any of Bowie's other mimicry—speech patterns and facial expressions, for example. Kemp's openness about his homosexuality was also obviously a major influence on Bowie, who was still, at the time of the film, three years away from discussing his own sexuality in print. Finally, Kemp and Bowie's interest in the tradition of the "white clown"—Pierrot and company—shows up most pointedly, again, in the promotion of *Scary Monsters*, where it influences both the cover sleeve and the video for "Ashes to Ashes." The theatrical influences of Kemp were to be even more decisive for Bowie than the filmic ones of Anderson. Bowie was to take what he learned from Kemp into his work in live concerts, especially, where his ability to connect with an audience live transformed the fundamental aspects of rock music. Bowie was able, via his use of characters and narrative, to reinterpret his music live and to raise the expectations for a rock concert in such a way that it was no longer about the mere live performances of songs, but the multimedia presentation of new interpretations of them.

The final sign in the 1960s of what Bowie was going to transform into in later years can perhaps be seen in the pieces that he put together for his series of music videos for German television that he titled *Love You 'til Tuesday* (1968). What is perhaps striking about the videos now is how varied the production for the songs are—each one receiving its own set, costumes, "look." Working well before the era of music videos, Bowie was already emphasizing the importance of visual performance as a way to sell and package his music. The sheer variety of approaches used in the film—from candid outdoor shoots to stylized interior ones—suggests Bowie's fascination with the pliability not only of his approach to song styles, but to their visual representations as well. As noted before, his sixties music, however limited by the sound of others, is still interesting in its range of styles and in the frequent reliance on characters with which to sing his songs. This basic approach to his working method would never change, only the quality (and the content) of the songs. While the standout number in *Tuesday* is definitely "Space Oddity," a late addition, the performance that perhaps is most prescient is a mime sketch that Bowie includes entitled "The Mask."[52] In voice-over to his own pantomime, Bowie tells the story of someone who buys a mask in an antique shop and is unable to take it off; finally, in performance, he dies from the inability to remove it, his art and life finally becoming one and the same thing. At first, the merging of art and life brings the character success, but its eventual terminal ending seems to be a dire warning that the young Bowie makes to himself about the dangers not only of success, but of art itself. In a sense, this odd bit of mime sums up Bowie's ambitions for himself and most useful lessons from the 1960s under the tutelage of Kemp and others. The mask, in the form of characters and personae, would be the controlling symbol of Bowie's contribution to rock performance, his greatest tool. Yet Bowie seemed to know that he was about to strike out on a path to fame, and that it would provide him with wonderful successes that would test him, perhaps kill him, and make him wish that he had never donned a mask at all.

The centrality of dance-like or mime-like aspects of Bowie's aesthetic raises the question of whether the performance art that we might associate with Bowie is allographic or autographic. In Nelson Goodman's original conceptualization, dance would be classified as autographic, or lacking in its own regularized notational system.[53] Dance, in other words, is not like a musical score or a written language; it exists only as a direct personal expression outside of a symbolic layer of meaning. It is, in other words, "phenomenological."[54] While this distinction is useful, it sometimes breaks down upon further scrutiny. Choreography can be codified, and dance is no less ambiguous than other collaborative art forms such as symphonies or architecture.[55] One might argue, however, that the dancer is both inside and outside of the work at the same time, thus, as Kaprow first points out, Pollock's paintings can themselves be considered to be indebted to dance not only in their form and shape but in the fact that Pollock can be said to be both within his work and outside of it (beside it) at the same time. He is not so much acting on a medium as within it—like a performer. Bowie's performances are similarly acts of both inside and outside, a sort of double consciousness in which he is playing himself and a character simultaneously, his rock performances never represent the performance of an authentic self. As Eda Čufer argues about Pollock, "Instead of reducing the painting to pure form, he activated and expanded the practice of painting through space and movement."[56] The freedom opened up by Pollock led to "body and movement-based art [becoming] the only viable medium for many artists."[57] For others, the opposite became true: "The very blurring of art and life was . . . the only way to disclose how life become irreversibly entwined with and undifferentiated from art."[58] In terms of the latter, one can see the turn toward the use of everyday movements in the choreography of Pina Bausch and Toni Basil, both of whom have worked with or influenced Bowie, and many other modern choreographers. While the interpenetration of art of life seems to be a hallmark of Bowie's work, it is important to keep in mind that his performances, whether on the stage or off, are highly choreographed. Just as we now know that Kaprow's famous Happenings were in fact highly scripted,[59] the performances of Bowie as a rock star are never a mere performance of life. Ultimately the autographic and allographic distinction breaks down since though there can be a blurring of art and life, the artistic side of the equation is never purely without premeditated thought and, at some level, form. Even a concert by John Cage contains a structure, something that separates it from the extreme linearity and variety of life, however it might also be affected by art in a postmodern age. Avant-garde art has been absorbed into society, but society itself is still separate, though the distinction has changed as both art and life have changed as well. The avant-garde won the battle for acceptance and has been so thoroughly assimilated into our culture that its arguments are just assumed to be truths.

At the level of the purely performative, therefore, one might say that Bowie's art crosses boundaries of art and reality, inside and outside, subject and object. He pulls the world into his art, but his art also expands outward to aestheticize the world, a different version of the total artwork. His work is, as he has said, primarily about "fragmentation."[60] But his notion of the fragment is closer to that of Friedrich Schlegel, for whom the fragment is a miniature version of reality, a capsule version of art that takes from any and all genres and creates a new art form that combines all genres within itself. It becomes pure irony in the Romantic sense: both inside and outside at the same time. In Dieter Roelstraete's words, it "is a stage upon which the utopian wholeness of this world can be enacted."[61] Bowie's presentation of the self through his many performances enacts this Schlegelian self-consciousness about art—a sort of proto-avant-garde that sees art as essentially performative. In his lyrics and staging of them Bowie often reverts reflexively to surrealism, arguably an inherently realist aesthetics.[62] He never loses sight of the figure, the psychological interpretation of what he is doing, or of the movement of the body in space. Performance art as a paradigm, therefore, is central to an understanding of him. Performance art is also arguably the best way to approach literature and cultural production now as increasingly we view it as an "event."[63] Artistic production can now be seen as a nexus where artist and audience meet, trading information back and forth. With the advent of immediate and ubiquitous online culture, art is no longer isolated from viewers. The members of subcultures that once were separated from each other (and the works of culture upon which they were based) via time and space are now connected twenty-four hours a day in the virtual space of the Internet. The cultural studies formulation that sees art not as hierarchically organized but as so much democratically created culture has become dominant. Culture can be constantly and almost instantaneously commented upon. The opinion of the artist about his or her own work is but one view among many. Art and culture have become more and more an erotics, another way to the body. The erotics of culture that Susan Sontag asked for in *Against Interpretation* (1966) has come about.[64] Now more than ever before, audiences enact what Foucault called "the use of pleasure." Aesthetics have become about pleasure, though not necessarily simple ones. Bowie has been at the forefront of this shift from the artist to the audience (and back again), encouraging the network of interpenetration and encouraging his fans to interpret his work in multiple ways. The days of the notion of authority as a given are quickly eroding. Having begun in the late Victorian era, the voice of authority has been eroded to the point of breaking in today's user-centered cultural matrix. Bowie remains a content provider, an author of powerful texts, but he has long ago abdicated his role as the sole authority over them. Always taking his cues from street culture, seeing himself not as a futurist but as a canny antenna for what is just forming in the present, Bowie has always been a mixture of heroic artist and ardent follower of others. Bowie's ultimate importance may well be his ability to see that art would be replaced with culture, that the age of the artist was nigh and that the rise of the fan meant that the future would be very different.

Gender studies

The more general problem is one of an absence of difference, bound up with a decline in the display of sexual characteristics. The outer signs of masculinity are bending towards zero, but so are signs of femininity. It is in this conjunction that we have seen new idols emerging, idols who take up the challenge of undefinedness and who play at mixing genres/genders. "Gender benders." Neither masculine nor feminine, but not homosexual either. Boy George, Michael Jackson, David Bowie . . . . Whereas the idols of the previous generation were explosive figures of sex and pleasure, these new idols pose for everyone the question of the play of difference and their own lack of definition. They are exceptional figures. For want of an identity, most of them have gone in search of a "gender model," a generic formula. Some kind of differentiating feature has to be found, so why not look for it in fashion . . . or in genetics? A "look" based on clothes, or a "look" based on cells. Any old gimmick will do, any idiom. The question of difference is more crucial than that of pleasure. Are we seeing here a post-modern version of a sexual liberation that is now past and gone, that liberation as mere fashion, or is this a bio-sociological mutation in our own self-perception, based upon the sexual losing the priority it formerly enjoyed, a priority which characterized the whole modern period?[65]

—Jean Baudrillard

While Bowie's contributions to art and life are numerous and stretch throughout his long career, the highlights might arguably include the early seventies glam era when gender and sexuality were emphasized; the late-seventies Berlin period when Bowie played most explicitly with fusing rock music with the avant-garde; the early eighties when Bowie's synergistic manipulation of image and hype resulted in his most extensive commercialization of his work; and the mid-nineties when Bowie sought to tear down the barrier separating the visual arts from music, attempting to bring the techniques of the former most completely into a musical context. As noted earlier, scholars consider the Ziggy period to be Bowie's most important historically. Certainly, it is the period of Bowie's great career most frequently discussed and analyzed as music critics and performance scholars alike attempt to define what

Bowie accomplished with the album and the concerts in support of it in terms of gender and sexuality. While a number of theories have been promulgated about Bowie's performance of Ziggy and his alien visitation, none quite gets it right, at least in terms of sex, gender, and representation. It is difficult to get at the essence of what Bowie is doing in his performance of gender. On the album, the shifting gender perspectives are confusing at best, with Bowie taking full advantage of the fluidity of gender and sexuality that accompanies any musical performance. While few of Bowie's songs are explicitly coded as gay—"Queen Bitch" and "John, I'm Only Dancing," for example—a number of other songs have been seen as possibly homoerotic, from "The Width of a Circle" on *The Man Who Sold the World*, with its explicit description of oral sex, to the obscure "The Bewlay Brothers," to the barely winking metaphors of "Cracked Actor." On *Ziggy Stardust* Bowie refers to male fans who swoon over Ziggy (or a Ziggy clone). Ziggy himself is sexualized ("god given ass") and is linked with "Moonage Daydream," a cock-rock song that nevertheless is homoerotic in its content. The fan/rock star formula becomes sexualized as Bowie pushes to the fore the fact that listeners of rock songs have to be fluid in their gender dynamics, forcing male listeners to listen as females in love songs sung by a male persona—alternating between identifying with the male voice and with the female beloved. Stable gender identities are almost impossible in sung music and Bowie makes clear here and on many of his albums of the seventies that he is often a male singer singing to another man. On the album after *Ziggy Stardust*, *Aladdin Sane*, Bowie makes "boy" into a repeating chorus on "Time" just as he does "boys" on the song "Candidate" on *Diamond Dogs*. Bowie's destabilizing of gender and sexuality is always present in his music, but the same ambiguity that rock music enables also acts to some extent to obscure moments of queerness, allowing them to float through the ether of gender undecidability that makes up music in general. On stage, however, Bowie made his gender politics more explicit, miming fellatio on Mick Ronson's guitar, or bending forward while he was straddled by Ronson in an obvious reference to rear entry. More subtle was Bowie's performance of songs throughout the show as a mixture of the assertive and the demure. Bowie never plays Ziggy as literal—he never really seems to be an alien from Mars—but he performs parts of what makes up Ziggy and, perhaps, metamorphoses him into a series of performances of gender and sexuality. The most recognizably gay aspect of these performances is probably the torch song, the drag act that, to some extent, accompanies "Rock and Roll Suicide" or, on *Aladdin Sane*, "Lady Stardust." Here most clearly Bowie seems to be a man acting like a man acting like a woman. Most of Bowie's other performances, by contrast, seem to be closer to a pastiche of gender in which Bowie places the codes of maleness and femaleness (or really, masculinity and femininity) next to each other. His own body is reinscribed in such a way that both its male characteristics (strong legs, tall stature) and its female ones (narrow shoulders, large eyes) are called attention to. Not only is the result not drag but it is not androgyny either. The frequently used descriptor *bisexual* is also not correct as that is an identity—or even an activity—that has no correlate with gender presentation or identification. Bowie's presentation of self can be called futuristic, but it is of a future that has yet to happen, that is arguably a utopian project of the (then) present, but that also does not have an actual origin. It is a performance of gender and/or sexuality that is a simulacrum—a "nostalgia for the future," as Bowie was later to call it.

That Bowie's presentation of an alternative notion of gender or sexuality is difficult to define has not kept it from resonating with audiences then and now. Bowie seems to present an alternative to gender encoding as it might exist in the future. To some extent, he presents an alternative mainly to straight male sexuality—one that is not gay, but allows for the possibility of feminine self-expression or of same-sex erotics. As in later Goth music, this openness to the possibility of sex with men might be seen as bisexuality or simply open-mindedness, but in the world of Ziggy this sexuality seems especially marked by Ziggy's seductive powers, his function as the locus of attraction because he is alien, futuristic, or even god-like. In that sense, he functions as the exception, the male figure who is so inspiring, that it is not transgressive for men to be attracted to him. He opens up an alternative terrain where it is possible that his followers, male and female, are both his lovers. His charisma, however, is itself both feminine and masculine as he plays both roles, often a subject and object at the same time. Bowie seems to imagine a universe in which sexuality is no longer a binary choice. To some extent, Bowie simply looks ahead to a more tolerant time, but it is not clear that he is queering straight identity so much as positing an identity that does not yet exist. His performance fractures gender and sexuality, but does not put them back together into a coherent whole. He leaves them as points on a linear continuum that seems to be ever shifting.

From a practical point of view, Bowie's playing with gender might seem to be liberatory for his male viewers, but it was equally as important to his female fans, who also saw themselves reflected in him. Women have, since the highpoint of Bowie's career, embraced and acknowledged the fluidity of their own sexuality, and ability to experiment with it, in ways that straight men have not. For straight men, Bowie might have represented one small blip in time when they were encouraged to sleep with each other, but for women Bowie seemed to represent a different kind of sexual object, one that was less threatening than some other male rockers and one who could be identified with more directly because of his feminine or female characteristics. If gay men felt themselves reflected in Bowie and straight men that they were being given permission to be something else, then for women Bowie represented, to some extent, themselves as they frequently encountered the world—as object and subject together. This mixing can be seen in the reactions of female fans to Bowie, miming his gestures in the D. A. Pennabaker documentary of the last Ziggy concert, for example, or in the fan letters written by women about him.[66]

In reality, of course, Ziggy expressed Bowie's years in and around gay culture, from Lindsay Kemp through his own work with androgyny on *The Man Who Sold the World* and *Hunky Dory*. Ziggy may have reflected Bowie's own fascination with gay or bisexual identity as he encountered them via Warhol and his own wife, Angie, respectively. By the time of Ziggy, he was no longer reacting to the mere fact of gay sex ("took my logic for a ride"), but using it as a central tenant of Ziggy's persona. Orientalization, futurity, and queerness make up these central identities, and for Bowie they are all linked.

The East represents, especially in Buddhist monks, a kind of post-gender androgyny; futurity is science fiction's interest in the alien as the outsider; queerness is the moving into the limelight that which the sixties rejected: alternatives to heteronormative codes and identities. Despite the radicalness attributed to the sixties, gender and sexuality were not a part of it. Women in these movements always took a backseat to men, who were the organizers. Bowie critiques these attitudes and proclaims the seventies as different. Bowie emphasizes the artificiality of all performances, including those of gender and sexuality. He realigns politics so that it is not just about electoral politics but identity politics as well. The personal becomes political in the seventies, and Bowie plays his part in making this fact known.

If those are some of the practical, maybe personal, aspects of Bowie's gender politics, the theoretical possibilities are even more complex. What Bowie represents in his performance of Ziggy can perhaps best be described as Deleuzian. That is, Bowie becomes a rhizome, a line linking different versions of gender and sexuality together to form one complex, ever-changing matrix. As described by French philosopher Gilles Deleuze and French psychoanalyst Félix Guattari in their books on capitalism and schizophrenia, the rhizomatic exists beneath the arboreal structures, running underground to connect via hidden linear, non-hierarchical means. The rhizome is associated with them and with other figures such as gay-liberation theorist Guy Hocquenghem with the deconstruction of centered systems that endeavor to organize knowledge and power in such a way as to privilege some and de-privilege others. In much the way that a tree contains a hierarchy of structures—a canopy, trunk, and roots—so, too, does society's institutions. The hierarchy of the church, for example, is mirrored in that of the state, which reproduces itself in something like Freud's Oedipal complex in which a hierarchy of sexual maturation rules—from the oral to the anal to the genital stages. Patriarchy and heterosexism are based upon the notion of some sort of centralized, organized, hierarchical structure. Deleuze and Guattari put in its place the notion of the rhizome as the simple sub-root that runs beneath the surface, connecting and branching and reconnecting wherever necessary.[67] Much like the development of the Internet, especially in its pre-monetized form, the rhizome branches off secretly underground in a variety of unplanned ways based upon desire, invisible from the structures that are visible above. This almost utopian version of an alternative structure for society, outside of the family structure and the supposedly more visible mode of respectability, one that was epitomized in Hocquenghem's mind by the cruising male homosexual who plugs into desire wherever he meets it, connects to Bowie's modus operandi. Bowie was not only enormously affected by the image of the homosexual male, whether via the Beats or his interest in the work of William S. Burroughs and John Rechy, but it is also a model for Bowie's approach to art more generally. As Paul H. Fry describes, Deleuze and Guattari were interested in "'multiplicity of coding,' thinking that does not just take place in language but careens among the verbal, the pictorial, the musical, the filmic, and yet other codes."[68] The notion of an alternative linear way of thinking means not only decentering the hierarchies of presumed authority but also opening meaning up to possibilities of language that exist outside of the linguistic. Deleuze and Guattari's writing constitute a theoretical version of the sixties revolution, especially the May '68 riots in France. For all that it has done to define, and be defined by, the seventies, Bowie's work also represents an internalization of the sixties, its energy transformed into a radical redefinition of the self and society. The body and identity become for Bowie a site of transformation, much as it was for Hocquenghem or for Deleuze and Guattari's concept of "the body without organs."[69] The manipulation of the body for Bowie became his own version of what Deleuze and Guattari call "lines of flight" or "deterritorialization." Bowie tries in his work, but especially in the character of Ziggy, to escape verticality and to generate alternatives to it. Part of Bowie's almost obsessive self-invention has to do with this aesthetic desire to divest himself of authority, to escape from the preordained mold, whether musically or otherwise. Bowie dissolves the interior and the exterior, making of himself a sort of Möbius strip. As Fry says, "The dehumanization of the postmodern results not in denying the importance of the human but in rethinking the human among other bodies and things." The result of this transformation "stresses a dissolve into otherness, a continuity between subject and object in which the difference, ultimately between what is inside . . . what is authentic or integral . . . and what's outside . . . become completely permeable and interchangeable."[70]

As Lawrence R. Schehr has noted about the world described by Hocquenghem, "It is a world where definitions are multiple, like the space they inhabit, a world in which if something called 'homosexuality' is still believed to exist, it is multiple in nature as it always was, but it is now recognized as such."[71] Bowie helped to bring this world about, especially within the realm of popular music, and in his basic performative paradigm created, like Hocquenghem, an

> eroticized model . . . for the space he constructs . . . a utopia of sexual possibilities of deterritorialized desires, of contacts, flows, couplings, and uncouplings. Organs of pleasure meeting other organs in an eroticized space where these organs, free of any *phallic* order, are free to be organs of pleasure; not only is the asshole made a desublimated public space, but also the penis is freed of its onus of having to serve as a lightning rod for an entire civilization.[72]

As Schehr concludes, "He wants to celebrate this erotic communism in the loudest possible way."[73] Bowie did likewise, not only during the Ziggy period—though perhaps there, "at maximum volume"—but also throughout his career.

Theories of gender and sexuality such as Judith Butler's are helpful in their emphasis on performativity, though the point of her theory is not that people put on genders the way they do clothing, depending upon their mood or the day's function, but rather that gender has no script, no origin story, and therefore must be constantly performed in order to keep up the illusion that it is natural, real, and coherent.[74] Of less use are more recent theories from Judith Jack Halberstam that seek to dematerialize the body as a sort of machine for making gendered meaning that yet reinscribes biology in a new way by insisting on the notion of "female masculinity": as though the only masculinity that counts is one attached to a biologically female body, a formulation that not only ignores male masculinity but requires that the cultural concept of masculinity be attached, once again, to the biology of sex. Although Halberstam has begun to examine some male masculinity in more detail, such as her work on Ashton Kutcher, her emphasis most recently on popular culture—the aesthetics of "failure," as she sometimes calls it—often feels like someone making great claims for popular art that cannot be sustained by the work itself.[75] Richard Rambuss' work suggests another possible direction in which masculinity studies can be rethought in terms of queer theory and may yet provide some tools for better understanding what someone like Bowie is up to. Rambuss emphasizes the failed attempts to describe the erotics of what he terms "male masculinity." How do we find a vocabulary for discussing the "masculinist" aspects of male homoerotics, for example? As he notes:

> I'm reluctant to freight . . . male homosocial bonding perforce with misogyny (or homophobia), in part because it tends to retain such an intimate relation to "the female." Male masculinity sometimes sustains misogyny, but I don't think that it is reducible or has any necessary relation to it. Virility—as feeling, as sentiment, as performance, as manners, as comportment, as role, as position, as power, as hierarchy, as fantasy, as an erotics—need not be coextensive with a patriarchy that enjoins a political gendered inequality.[76]

As he goes on to argue, "As for feminism, I don't think it has ever developed much of a lexicon (apart from terms of censure) for describing and analyzing what's perceived to be indicatively male. Nor do I think that it especially needs to do so. But I don't think that queer theory has been particularly effective on this account either."[77] Rambuss ends his essay with a pointed rejection of androgyny, or more precisely, a post-gendered future of the cyborgian variety.[78] He wants to retain the masculinity of male masculinity (when present) but also to find a way to talk about it. While Rambuss makes a point of defining gay male sexuality, *pace* Leo Bersani, as something more than "cocks" and "asses," he also makes a point that body parts play a major role in gay male erotics. The problem, for him, is how to talk about whatever it is that constitutes male sexuality, especially the specifically masculine component of it.

Bowie comes in here as a decidedly unmasculine man, but more importantly, as an artist who has tried to give us a vocabulary for talking about masculinity—and femininity—in terms of the male body. In other words, What is Bowie doing when he is doing gender? What is he, as a man, performing? As Philip Auslander argues, "Bowie's presentation of his sexuality . . . suggests a perception of sexuality as performative, not expressive. His performance of a gay or bisexual identity did not express some essential quality of her person; it was, rather, a performance of signs that are socially legible as constituting a gay identity."[79] The ultimate target for this deconstruction was not Bowie's own identity but the assumed identity of rock itself as white, heterosexual, and male. The reason that Bowie's subverting of sexual identity in rock is so difficult to pin down is that it is a performance of a performance—a demonstration of how constructed and dependent upon performance that sexuality is within the arena of rock and roll. Bowie is not expressing the self, and he is not creating a representation of a gay or bisexual man (or woman or transgendered person), he is commenting upon the presumed innocence of rock's naturalist pose. As Auslander concludes, "Rather than raising questions about his own sexuality, Bowie threw the sexuality of rock into question, not only by performing a sexual identity previously excluded from rock but also by performing that identity in such a way that it was clearly revealed *as a performance* for which there was not underlying referent."[80]

In the Ziggy persona was the formula for what was going to remain the approach to gender and sexuality that Bowie was to follow for most of his career—at least from the seventies through the nineties. The creation of a stable "I" or ego—for him or for one of his personae—was taken apart. Bowie did not represent a stable identity or body, but was something closer to Jacques Lacan's notion of the mirror stage when the slippage between what one thinks one is and what one sees in the mirror creates desire. The notion of the "I," however, creates a false notion of completeness, the illusion that one's multiple identities are somehow working together, that this identity is somehow complete. The result of this illusion, this mirror, is to alienate one from one's allocentric or other identities. As Jeremy Tambling describes it, "The alienation makes identity other to what I am, in other words, the 'ideal I' that I identify with and desire to be is not me."[81] One is subsequently alienated from one's own identity, or "identity is truly an alienated identity."[82] Bowie makes this idea literal by positing an identity that is always made up of shards of discourse, parts of different people's realities, and frequently characters that try, but can never completely, see themselves. They exist as a collection of their own desires—whether the messianic powers of Ziggy, "who takes it all too far," or the fascist leanings of the Thin White Duke, who also wants a "word on a wing," they are characters desperately "searching and searching."

For Bowie, these characters embody a notion of the self as other, or of otherness as the central metaphor for life itself. His interest in and attraction to gender and sexuality reflects this outsider notion—whether it is the sexually marginalized or the overlooked identity of women as the silent majority. Sex and gender are not ends in themselves but a means to an end—to a presentation of self that includes the body politic as made up of a number of disparate individual voices that are all contained within one central character or concept. Bowie becomes a reflection of desire, reflects others' desires, but also elicits desire from the observer. He becomes their mirror, thus solidifying the promise of rock music to its fans to represent the unrepresented, or even unrepresentable. The Ziggy moment defined Bowie, not because it made clear to rock that it was, up until that moment, an elite boys' club, but that it did that while also upholding the cultural meaning that rock wants to believe about itself—that it is made up of the desires of its fans to be noticed, known, and heard. Ziggy, as an ersatz rock star, plays out the meaning of the music you are listening to and, rather than questioning its power to move you, congratulates you for getting it right, for understanding that your desire is the correct one for this particular genre or taste in music. The album creates a feedback loop in which the desires of the fans for the album further legitimate the album and hence the mythos of rock itself.[83]

Bowie was to go on to write about gender and sexuality in different ways, but his latter forays avoided the self-congratulating aspect of Ziggy, often making the gender and sexuality either secondary to the character he was portraying or marked as more conventionally outside the mainstream with no larger meaning to signify. Sexuality became, later, merely a symbol for itself. This does not mean, however, that his portrayal of either was ever simple or clear. Bowie's original sexual experimentation via the Ziggy persona was part of what Stan Hawkins refers to as the "feminized and effete" nature of British pop stars—from Jagger to Bowie, Morrissey to Doherty and beyond.[84] What was different about Bowie, as I have tried to explain, was the extremely fabricated nature of his sign system, his performance of performances, one that ultimately "afforded Bowie room to regulate his identity well beyond normative codes and assumptions."[85] Bowie's embracing of queerness before we had a label for it arguably also marked a moment of turning away from the oppositional power of gay or lesbian politics in that queerness might embrace straightness or act as a looser designation than the essentialist model of lesbian or gay.[86] One might also say that it is more postmodern, born from the celebrity culture that the dandy tradition turned into in the twentieth century.[87] There is, arguably, something different in what Bowie is doing. But is his performance different "from the performativity of non-heterosexual artists"?[88] Likewise, "is queering a legitimate 'vehicle' for expressing an affiliation with anti-homophobic politics?"[89] While I am not sure that Hawkins' assessment that Bowie is about the straight-queer position of Calvin Thomas and others, he is right to interrogate the oppositional nature of queerness.[90] While it was incubated in reaction to the government's inaction in the wake of the AIDS crisis, its own pointedly political nature was eroded or diluted by its absorption into postmodern alternative culture. Its very success was its own undoing. If all codes of difference become oppositional, then codes simply keep cycling through and no change in the overall structure of transgression is possible.[91] Binaries are replaced, but the binary system is not.

In his resistance to a sixties countercultural stance, Bowie may have been suggesting not that he was apolitical, or that queer politics was not effective, but simply that the problem was more complicated than one might think. He may have intuited as much and attempted to stave off the problems ultimately endemic to identity politics even as he helped to pave the way for them, at least in terms of sexuality. Certainly, Ziggy was not the final word on gender flexibility. All of Bowie's albums after it have, in one way or another, commented on the politics and erotics of sexual undecidability. Bowie was to continue in the vein of Ziggy, however, in not doing the expected when it came to commenting on gender and sexuality. While the character of Aladdin Sane seemed to continue Ziggy, gender and sexuality are placed within an elaborate backstory on *Diamond Dogs*. Similarly indirect was Bowie's interest in dance music on *Young Americans* where comments on gender and sexuality are never made directly after the title song on the first track. Instead, the soulful dance groove that takes over from "Fascination" through the spiky "Fame," a song that shocked Bowie when it became a dance hit. As Andrew Branch observes, dance music allows for an alternative to "phallocentric arguments about the central position meaning-formation holds for particular audiences (invariably white and male) with regard to popular music formations."[92] Ideally, "dance music is embodied as a collective experience, whereby rigid categories of sexuality and gender potentially dissolve."[93] Bowie's contribution to this idea is made again with his albums *Let's Dance* and *Black Tie, White Noise*, where he once again taps into black dance music as not only an embodiment of racial identity but arguably haptic fluidity as well.

Bowie's comments on gender and sexuality are not reducible to the white, middle-class male background that he is from. Much of his music comments either directly or indirectly on female desire and experience—most clearly in the music and videos for *Lodger*—but also in his adopting Marlene Dietrich's male clothing for his costumes for his late-seventies Isolar tours. The effect on Bowie's choice of silhouette on subsequent tours was also clear. Sometimes his clothes morphed into outright gay themes, such as his sailor suit during his 1978 tour. Bowie's feminine clothing, while never as outrageous or baroque as those of his Ziggy period, nevertheless continued as one of the hallmarks of his career, not really becoming particularly masculine until the street clothes of his "Reality Tour" in 2004. Bowie seemed always to be aware of his many female fans, many of whom might have identified with him or as him. Likewise, Bowie's importance to working-class youth is demonstrated in Todd Haynes' version of a Bowie fan in his film *Velvet Goldmine* (1998), where the Christian Bale character identifies with the Bowie-like central character of the movie, Slade, in a series of scenes that demonstrate what Chad Bennett calls "the shame of queer fandom."[94] The courage

Figure 1.3 David Bowie, Isolar tour, Boston, 1976.

Figure 1.4   David Bowie, Isolar II tour, Boston, 1978.

to invest in the identification with glam rock across class lines is a part of the strong power that Bowie had during that time and that the film demonstrates.

Much of Bowie's gender bending and playing with sexuality has obviously been related to his sartorial changes and experimentation with hairstyles and makeup—traits that have marked him since well before his Ziggy career. Bowie's changeableness with clothing and hairstyles, especially, have always marked him as seemingly feminine rather than masculine, his play with personae and frequent redirection in his musical tastes treated as metaphors for the same thing—fashion, not tailoring. That is, rather than appearing to be the staid unchanging authentic self, he seems to present a fluid pseudo-femininity that offers some kind of alternative. Pseudo-feminine because Bowie is not linked directly with the negative, perhaps misogynistic, aspects of female fashion as the reverse of masculine fashion—that is, as throwaway culture meant to be replaced seasonally and to signify, at some level, frivolousness. As Anne Hollander makes clear in *Sex and Suits: The Evolution of Modern Dress*, masculine and feminine fashion are not so easily divided—at least not until the "great renunciation" of the nineteenth century, when the modern suit came into being, and really not after that.[95] As she explains, women and men's dress was originally much the same, with both wearing versions of drapery (the Greek *chiton*, for example). While men moved slowly toward shorter robes to allow for more physical movement, they were essentially wearing the same thing even in the early medieval period in Europe. All that was changed was the addition of leggings to account for the colder temperatures of Northern Europe over the Mediterranean. A gendered differentiation in clothes did not really appear until after the introduction of armor, and even then, the first iteration, chain mail, was essentially heavy drapery—that is, the same costume made out of something else. What we frequently think of as armor today—made of pounded metal and joints—was the beginning of male fashion. The different parts of a knight's armor closely followed the contours of the male body and articulated a relationship between the body's parts and the clothing over them that was not possible with drapery alone. Male clothing slowly evolved new elements—the pants, as we know them today, the shirt, the collar, the waistcoat, etc. Women's clothes eventually adapted many of these ideas. The ultimate modernization of the suit of armor was the business suit, which maintains, to Hollander, the two essential elements of male clothing: that it reflect the male body and that it still act, to some extent, as a form of armor as well, insulating the body's vulnerability and shielding the wearer, allowing him some distance and reserve, at the same time that he appears essentially nude.

For Hollander, then, the great generator of fashion innovation has always been male clothing.[96] In part this has come about by the seriousness accorded to anything male, especially in its connection to the public sphere, but also because women's clothes essentially remained unchanged—a form of the classical gown—until women's clothing began to take on male details and innovations. When absorbing male fashion traits, female dress still remained feminine—the male suit, even, finally making the female wearer seem even more like her sex or gender. But the invention was the result of male tailors. The only two truly female items of clothing, according to Hollander, were décolletage and the skirt, the latter as a separate piece from a gown. By the seventeenth century, women also began to have not only bare necks but also bare arms—the latter still not considered completely seemly for men, the former becoming popular in some situations as early as the late eighteenth century (the French Revolution, for example, or the myth of pirate clothing) and has reached its peak only now when casual wear is frequently open-necked.

Within Hollander's schema, then, Bowie's sartorial excesses can perhaps be more precisely mapped. For Hollander, men's clothing in general, and the suit in particular, is much more multifaceted and changeable than people might imagine. The great renunciation, in which men seemed to turn over the fashion arm of clothing to women, was not quite what it seemed.[97] To Hollander, it was a codification of the neoclassical idea of the expression of the body through clothing. The minimalism of the suit, its abstractness and muted colors, can be read one of two ways: as an attempt to ape classical nude statues of the human male (or paintings that represent the same, such as the neoclassical work of French painter Jacques-Louis David), or as a sort of early modernism—an architectonic removal of anything unnecessary and distracting in order to create one overall effect. Bowie, in this sense, is already heir to fashion as a man enculturated as male. He must work against the codes that Hollander suggests. Throughout his career, one might argue, he has done precisely that. In his Ziggy costumes, he specifically bared his necks and limbs, giving his costumes a feminine nuance usually (but not always) a part of the look of the male suit—especially in the renunciation of the phallic tie, needed, according to Hollander, when the coat is buttoned and the crotch occluded. The addition of a décolletage has been a part of many of Bowie's stage costumes, even when the more outrageous Ziggy costumes had long been retired. According to Hollander, one thing that makes male clothing appear more classical and unchanging (positives to her) is the fact that men rarely mix codes—the suit is, by its very name, meant to be worn as an ensemble made out of the same material. Bowie, in the late sixties and early seventies, confounded that expectation by purposefully wearing designs and bold colors that were much more likely in women's clothing. He has periodically returned to this practice throughout his long career. What he has maintained from the land of masculine dress is some connection to the idea of the suit—to the unified silhouette and the overall effect, which he emphasizes with his use of one-piece outfits on stage. The effect, however, is again often subversively feminine. Bowie scrambles the codes of the body, the body's expected clothing, and uses the costuming to add another dimension to his songs' complex commentary on gender and sexuality.

While Hollander has less to say about hair than about clothing, she makes the point that long hair is often, depending upon the era, associated with male virility, though often in a free-flowing, even slightly disheveled state. Women, too, can use long hair for sexuality, though it was, until recently, expected to be kept kempt. While hair length can, now, change for women and men, with short hair on women, like men's suits, often emphasizing femininity, what men often do not have is elaborately styled hair. To complete his ensemble, Bowie has always maintained meticulous hairstyles. Whether the copper-top of the Ziggy period, which gets referenced again during his *Earthling* phase in the mid-nineties, to his slicked back Germanic look in the late seventies, Bowie's hair style, color, texturing, even part, has always changed with each album, and even if it remains relatively fixed during an era, still undergoes metamorphoses. His hair, that is, like his dress, calls attention to itself in a specifically feminine way. The earliest television footage we have of him is as a member of the "Society for the Prevention of Cruelty to Long-Haired Men" in which he sports long, straight sandy hair. His hairstyles changed as often as the cover bands he was in in the sixties, culminating with the long pre-Raphaelite hairdo of *The Man Who Sold the World* and *Hunky Dory* pre-Ziggy era. It was also at this time that Bowie wore dresses that he called "men's dresses." While he would go on to fracture gender codes more completely with Ziggy, producing a jagged, darker postmodern edge to his gender performance, in this immediately earlier period he was still not doing drag—not dressing as a transvestite—but dressing as a man wearing clothing that men (still) rarely adopt. He was forging his own approach to gender while calling attention to the scope and limits of how it is usually constructed by history and culture.

Bowie's last major foray into gender and sexuality is perhaps his influence on Goth. While his album *Scary Monsters* introduced, or really reintroduces, the character of Pierrot, Bowie uses that figure as, to some extent, a doppelganger for his own life as an artist, a made-up figure or clown. He also taps into the notion of the playacting of gender—Pierrot is a strikingly feminine "white clown" of the commedia dell'arte tradition, made slightly futuristic and Asian in Natasha Korniloff's version of the makeup for Bowie. Clearly, on the album cover and accompanying stills, Pierrot could be a man or a woman, a fact made clear on the cover where we see Bowie sans hat, smoking a cigarette in what looks like rumpled post-drag. While Bowie's own subtle references to his gender-bending past are made much of here, the album's songs present a newer approach to gender and sexuality, ones that carry over from its immediate predecessor, *Lodger*. "Scream Like a Baby" references gay men hounded by police and the album's first song, "It's No Game (No. 1)" features female Japanese poet Michi

Hirota in her own gender-bending performance. Bowie attempts to keep things real and connected to actual street-level politics.

While *Scary Monsters* and the Berlin trilogy before it may have influenced New Music or the New Romantics movement, the most important influence that Bowie had during that period on other musical styles may well have been Goth, or the Gothic movement.[98] By the late seventies, Bowie was being blamed by the media for spawning a variety of new styles of music, a claim that was intensified in the 1980s when *Let's Dance* seemed at first to lay claim to another decade whose sound Bowie was credited with having an undue influence over. The Goth sound, however, was one that Bowie seemed glad to claim, appearing with Susan Sarandon and Catherine Deneuve in Tony Scott's 1983 film *The Hunger* as an aging vampire (John Blaylock). The film's music, by Bauhaus, set the Goth template. Bauhaus had covered Bowie's song "Ziggy Stardust" and the original song they sing here, "Bela Lugosi's Dead" (1979), is about an actor who plays a vampire in the presence of actual vampires (Bowie and Deneuve). The multiple levels of media references point to the elaborate number of in-jokes the film makes, but also to the extent to which Goth is itself an ekphrastic construction of art about other art. That it gets its start in a film only to then become an actual movement parallels the origin of punk, which was also originally a joke, a fashion created by Malcolm McLaren's boutique in London, that actually did tap into a real movement of disaffected youth who identified with it and made the fantasy a reality—or saw their reality in its fantasy. In its references to Oscar Wilde, fin-de-siècle decadence, vampires, bisexuality, and sadomasochistic sexual practices, Goth became one of a number of countercultural pop music subcultures. Mainly a force in American high schools, it came to symbolize, like the subcultures before it, resistance to what Dick Hebdige calls the "parent culture." What separates Goth from the fads that predate it is its emphasis on gender and sexuality.

That this understanding of gender and sexuality might be trite still does not take away from the fact that any alternative to mainstream versions of it may in fact provide young people with some source of resistance and some place for their identity to reside, however temporarily. In fact, by making connections between the late Victorian period and the millennial period of the twentieth century, Goth was actually doing something critically to our sense of culture, making connections and offering a simulacrum for the present constructed of various fictions from the past—Bram Stoker, Romanticism, etc. One could also argue that Goth made this process self-conscious by quoting not people, but texts, images, and purposefully blurring the real with fantasy. Bowie's participation in the film, therefore, might have been, as Kimberley Jackson has argued, an attempt by Bowie to acknowledge Goth's imitation of him, a deconstruction of his myth, and acknowledgment that the notion of his influence was about to change, that the notion of the rock star was about to be different and that Bowie was aware of the transformation.[99] Goth's references to gender and sexuality were references to Bowie's characters' gender and sexuality, which became stand-ins for the real thing at the same time that they were acknowledged to be fictions or performances. As Michael du Plessis argues, Goth references to gender and sexuality are finally not to gender or sexuality but to Goth itself. That is, "as a style, goth evokes depths of expression but, in actuality expresses nothing but itself."[100] Goth represents for him a type of melancholia, a loss that acknowledges the giving up of conventional gender and sexuality but that is so taken up with the signifying of that loss that it is finally all consuming: "Goth plays up melancholia, looping it through all manner of conventional gender performances in ways that always refer to goth's own distinctiveness."[101]

In some ways Bowie's participation in Goth in the early eighties signifies a sort of end point of gender and sexuality. He was, however, to return to Goth in 1995's *Outside*, which presents a neo-Goth future in which the movement becomes, in a way, the defining mood for the end of the century again. While in *The Hunger* the vampires are bisexual, choosing a mate once every century, alternating male and female to avoid boredom, on *Outside* Goth is used not as a way to reference sexuality but as a way to suggest violence, especially the notion of the potential artistic side of ritualized murder. Goth takes a turn away from a fake darkness—Bela Lugosi's Dead—toward a real one, taken from the visual arts but also from the headlines.

The many references to Bowie's play with gender and sexuality are too numerous to discuss in toto, but his attention to these topics shows a profound attempt to stick with the issue long after it may have had relevance to him personally. While he was not taking the notion of a gay identity or transvestitism literally, he opened the way for gender-queer performances and identities. Whether the pangender living performance of Genesis P-Orridge or the popularity of San Francisco's porn and performance sensation "Boychild," Bowie's constant experimentation with gender and sexual alternatives and interrogation of what we mean by those concepts, has resulted in one of his most remarkable and misunderstood legacies. Bowie recodes the body for the future.

Notes

1   In the summer of 2011 the New York Museum of Arts and Design held a show on Bowie as an artist. In the fall of 2012 the University of Limerick held a David Bowie Symposium, the call for papers for which far outstripped that anticipated by the conference organizers. The Victoria and Albert Museum show on Bowie's career featured 300 curated objects from Bowie's personal archive of costumes, notes for lyrics and music videos, designs for live concerts, and never-before-seen films of performances. Entitled "David Bowie Is," the show sold over 70,000 tickets in what has been the most popular show in design history. The exhibit went on tour to the Art Gallery of Ontario in Toronto, Sao Paulo, Chicago, Paris, the Netherlands, and Berlin.

2   Qtd. in Nicholas Pegg, *The Complete David Bowie*, 6th ed. (London: Titan Books, 2011), 209–10.

3   Over the years, Bowie has been called both a "modernist" and a "postmodernist." The truth is probably somewhere in the middle in that he contains elements of both eras of cultural history. Using Ihab Hassan's "table of differences between modernism and postmodernism." http://en.wikipedia.org/wiki/Ihab_Hassan, Bowie seems to be both a modernist in his use of "Romanticism" and a postmodernist in his use

of "Dadaism." Likewise, "Totalization" and "Deconstruction," "Genital/Phallic" and "Polymorphous/Androgynous." While his music has always been made up of echoes of the work of others—a fact that can be seen in the echoes of fifties doo-wop and the Beatles on *Ziggy Stardust*, for example—as his career has matured, Bowie has arguably become more postmodern. Again using Hassan's vocabulary, Bowie has shifted more and more from "Finished Work" to "Process/Performance," from "Distance" to "Participation," from "Centering" to "Dispersal," and from "Root/Depth" to "Rhizome/Surface."

4   David Buckley describes "Songs of the Silent Age" from *"Heroes"* as "another futuristic nostalgia song." David Buckley, *Strange Fascination: David Bowie, The Definitive Story*, rev. ed. (London: Virgin, 2001), 321.

5   Hugh Wilcken, *Low* (New York: Continuum, 2005), 35. Wilcken continues: "This nostalgia for a future that never happened was something that Bowie also picks up on; it's the sadness that informs the second side of *Low* but also its successor *'Heroes.'*" (35).

6   Wilcken, *Low*, 35.

7   Marc Spitz, *Bowie: A Biography* (New York: Crown), 20. Spitz claims that mods and rockers were the first young people to be seen on TV (118).

8   David Bowie Is, Art Gallery of Ontario, Toronto, November 20, 2013.

9   *Buddha* does act as an intriguing link between the jazz-inflected instrumentation of *Black Tie, White Noise* and the extreme experimentation of *Outside* all the while recalling Bowie's own instrumental B-sides on *Low* and *"Heroes."*

10 According to David Buckley, Eno always intended the project to include "interactive material, even an operatic performance at the Salzburg Festival in December 1999." Buckley, *Strange Fascination*, 499. He quotes long-time Bowie pianist Mike Garson as saying that all of the recording sessions for the material for *Outside* was recorded on camera (500).

11 Bowie was always interested in total design and in mixing media. As early as his group The Kon-Rads, in 1962, he was in charge of the set designs. He also designed the costumes by taking green jackets and decorating them with black cartridge ink pin strips. Bowie was always a total artist, something which could always be seen in the meticulous details of his concerts and his music videos up until now. Even *Young Americans* was to be filmed as a movie in 1975. David Bowie Is, Art Gallery of Ontario, Toronto, November 20, 2013.

12 Carter Ratcliff, "David Bowie's Survival," *Artforum* 21, no. 5 (January 1983): 39–45.

13 For more on the connection between Bowie and various Romanticist precursors, please see Shelton Waldrep, *The Aesthetics of Self-Invention: Oscar Wilde to David Bowie* (Minneapolis: University of Minnesota Press, 2004).

14 Simon Frith and Howard Horne, *Art into Pop* (New York: Methuen, 1987), 109–10.

15 Frith and Horne, *Art into Pop*, 116.

16 Kenneth Pitt, *Bowie: The Pitt Report* (New York: Omnibus Press, 1985), 211; Paul Trynka, *David Bowie: Starman* (New York: Little, Brown, and Co., 2011), 217.

17 Frith and Horne, *Art into Pop*, 118.

18 According to the organizers of the exhibition "David Bowie Is" the costume design for the first number of the night can be traced to Tristan Tzara's avant-garde anti-play, *The Gas Heart*, 1923, especially Sonia Delaunay's costume designs for it, and to Ball's recitations. David Bowie Is, Art Gallery of Ontario, Toronto, November 20, 2013.

19 According to notes at the Bowie exhibit, "Nine foot-high puppets moving in a choreographed sequence were initially planned for the *Station to Station* tour. He later dropped such complex props in favour of a simple set bathed in stark bars of white light." The final set design was influenced by Man Ray and Judi Dench's performance in *Cabaret* in London in 1968. David Bowie Is, Art Gallery of Ontario, Toronto, November 20, 2013.

20 Marvin Carlson, *Performance: A Critical Introduction* (New York: Routledge, 1996), 91.

21 Carlson, *Performance*, 97, 101.

22 Richard Schechner, "The Five Avant Gardes or . . . or None?," in *The Twentieth-Century Performance Reader*, ed. Michael Huxley and Noel Witts (New York: Routledge, 1996), 313.

23 Carlson, *Performance*, 106.

24 Carlson, *Performance*, 108, 116.

25 Schechner, *The Twentieth-Century Performance Reader*, 312.

26 Roland Barthes, *Empire of Signs*, trans. Richard Howard (New York: Hill and Wang, 1982), 55.

27 In further contrasting Western theatrical traditions to Japanese ones, specifically the puppetry tradition of *Bunraku*, Barthes writes:

> The basis of our theatrical art is indeed much less the illusion of reality than the illusion of totality: periodically, from the Greek *choreia* to bourgeois opera, we conceive lyric art as the simultaneity of several expressions (acted, sung, mimed), whose origin is unique, indivisible. This origin is the body, and the totality insisted on has for its model the body's organic unity: Western spectacle is anthropomorphic, in it, gesture and speech (not to mention song) form a single tissue, conglomerated and lubrified like a single muscle which makes expression function but never divides it up: the unity of movement and voice produces *the one* who acts; in other words, it is in this unity that the "person" of the character is constituted, i.e., the actor. As a matter of fact, beneath his "living" and "natural" externals, the Western actor preserves the division of his body and, thereby, the nourishment of our fantasies: here the voice, there the gaze, there again the figure are eroticized, as so many fragments of the body, as so many fetishes. The Western puppet, too (as is quite apparent in our Punch and Judy), is a fantasmal by-product: as a reduction, as a grim reflection whose adherence to the human order is ceaselessly recalled by a caricatural simulation, the puppet does not live as a total body, totally alive, but as a rigid portion of the actor from whom it has emanated; as an automaton, it is still a piece of movement, jerk, shock, essence of discontinuity, decomposed project of the body's gestures; finally, as a doll, reminiscence of the bit of rag, of the genital bandage, it is indeed the phallic "little thing" ("das Kleine") fallen from the body to become a fetish. (Barthes, *Empire of Signs*, 59)

28 Barthes, *Empire of Signs*, 62.

29 Ibid.

30 Barthes, *Empire of Signs*, 89.

31 Henry M. Sayre, *The Object of Performance: The American Avant-Garde since 1970* (Chicago: University of Chicago Press, 1989), 2.

32 Sayre, *The Object of Performance*, 129.

33 RoseLee Goldberg, *Performance Art: From Futurism to the Present*, rev. ed. (New York: Henry N. Abrams, 1988), 20.

34 David Bowie Outside, January 2, 2014. http://www.youtube.com/ watch?v=spb8bhuKDdQ.

35 Goldberg, *Performance Art*, 164.

36 For more on the seventies as a paradigm shift in popular and generational approaches to culture, see the introduction to Shelton Waldrep, ed., *The Seventies: The Age of Glitter in Popular Culture* (New York: Routledge, 2000), 1–15.

37 Mark C. Taylor, *Disfiguring: Art, Architecture, Religion* (Chicago: University of Chicago Press, 1992), 103.

38 Taylor, *Disfiguring*, 111.

39 Taylor, *Disfiguring*, 121.

40 Taylor, *Disfiguring*, 123.

41 Taylor, *Disfiguring*, 127.

42 Taylor, *Disfiguring*, 143.

43 Robert Wilson, "Interview," in *The Twentieth-Century Performance Reader*, ed. Michael Huxley and Noel Witts (New York: Routledge, 1996), 396.

44 David Bowie Is, Art Gallery of Ontario, Toronto, November 20, 2013.

45 Amelia Jones, *Body Art/Performing the Subject* (Minneapolis: University of Minnesota Press, 1998), 39.

46 Jones, *Body Art*, 62.

47 Jones, *Body Art*, 141.

48 Kristine Stiles, *Theories and Documents of Contemporary Art*, ed. Kristine Stiles and Peter Selz (Berkeley: University of California Press, 1996), 690.

49 Stiles, *Theories and Documents of Contemporary Art*, 690.

50 Jones, *Body Art*, 205.

51 Catherine Wood, "'Painting in the Shape of a House,'" in *A Bigger Splash: Painting after Performance*, ed. Catherine Wood (London: Tate Publishing, 2012), 11.

52 For more on this video, see Waldrep, *The Seventies*, 1–15.

53 Eda Čufer, "Don't," in *A Bigger Splash: Painting after Performance*, ed. Catherine Wood (London: Tate Publishing, 2012), 23.

54 Čufer, *A Bigger Splash*, 23.

55 Ibid.

56 Čufer, *A Bigger Splash*, 25.

57 Ibid.

58 Ibid.

59 Čufer, *A Bigger Splash*, 27.

60 David Bowie Outside, January 2, 2014. http://www.youtube.com/ watch?v=spb8bhuKDdQ.

61 Dieter Roelstraete, "Painting (the Threshold of the Visible World)," in *A Bigger Splash: Painting after Performance*, ed. Catherine Wood (London: Tate Publishing, 2012), 32.

62 Roelstraete, *A Bigger Splash*, 34.

63 Jonathan Culler, *Literary Theory: A Very Short Introduction* (Oxford: Oxford University Press, 2011), 132.

64 As Sontag noted about the fragment:

There's a reason why the fragment, starting with the Romantics, becomes the prominent art form that allows for things to be more true, more authentic, more intense. There are privileged moments of pleasure and of insights, and some things can be more intense than other things because we live in many different places in our lives and consciousnesses. But the fact that you can distinguish a certain moment as being privileged—and not just because it's memorable but because it's *changed* you—doesn't mean that it's a fragment. It could mean that it's the culmination of everything that's gone before it. (Jonathan Cott, *Susan Sontag: The Complete* Rolling Stone *Interview* (New Haven: Yale University Press, 2013), 55)

Sontag goes on to argue that the form of the fragment is itself decadent, not morally, but because it comes at the end of an era:

The fragment presupposes that one knows and has experienced a great deal, and it's decadent in that sense because you have to have all that stuff behind you so that you're making allusions and commenting on things without having to spell it all out. It's not an art form or a thought form of young cultures that need not make things very specific. But we know a lot and are aware of a multiplicity of perspectives, and the fragment is one way of acknowledging that. (56)

65 Jean Baudrillard, *America*, trans. Chris Turner (New York: Verso, 1988), 47.
66 See also letters from actual fans in Fred and Judy Vermorel, *Starlust: The Secret Fantasies of Fans* (London: Comet, 1985).
67 For Deleuze and Guattari's theories, see their *Anti-Oedipus* (Minneapolis: University of Minnesota Press, 1983) and *A Thousand Plateaus* (Minneapolis: University of Minnesota Press, 1987). For more on Guy Hocquenghem, see his *Homosexual Desire* (Durham: Duke University Press, 1993).
68 Paul H. Fry, *Theory of Literature* (New Haven: Yale University Press, 2012), 198.
69 For more on this concept, see chapter 3 of my *Aesthetics of Self-Invention: Oscar Wilde to David Bowie.*
70 Fry, *Theory of Literature*, 197.
71 Lawrence R. Schehr, "Defense and Illustration of Gay Liberation," *Yale French Studies: Same Sex/Different Text?* 90 (1996): 152.
72 Schehr, *Yale French Studies*, 150.
73 Schehr, *Yale French Studies*, 150.
74 Butler puts forth her idea about the performance of gender in *Gender Studies: Feminism and the Subversion of Identity* (New York: Routledge, 1990) only to have to explain how her theory is misunderstood in *Bodies that Matter: On the Discursive Limits of "Sex"* (New York: Routledge, 1993).
75 See *The Queer Art of Failure* (Durham: Duke University Press, 2011).
76 Richard Rambuss, "After Male Sex," *South Atlantic Quarterly* 103, no. 3 (Summer 2007): 585.
77 Rambuss, *South Atlantic Quarterly*, 586.
78 Rambuss, *South Atlantic Quarterly*, 587.
79 Philip Auslander, *Performing Glam Rock: Gender and Theatricality in Popular Music* (Ann Arbor: University of Michigan Press, 2006), 135.
80 Auslander, *Performing Glam Rock*, 135.
81 Jeremy Tambling, *Literature and Psychoanalysis* (New York: Manchester University Press, 2012), 91.
82 Tambling, *Literature and Psychoanalysis*, 91.

83 The most profoundly important change to the work of art during Bowie's time, and one that he was uniquely qualified to take advantage of, was the opening up of our concept of the text, especially in terms of the interchange between artist and audience. As Roland Barthes famously decried "the death of the author," cultural studies opened up the interaction between the author and the audience. As texts expand, the roles once played between producer and consumer of texts blurs—eventually seeming almost to change place. As Williams describes:

> The new object is intertextual: held between other texts, it is a multi-dimensional space, a methodological field, in which discourses circulate. When text is understood in this way, authorial control is reduced and the immanent meaning of a text becomes less distinguishable from what readers make of it. These thoughts, which have become standard for poststructuralism, show Barthes the structuralist becoming Barthes the poststructuralist, acutely aware that there are no meta-codes with which to stabilize interpretation. Originality and authority cannot be attributed solely to the text and derivation and subservience entirely to the critic, since both produce texts that interact and signify. (Williams, *Constructing Musicology*, 35)

84 Stan Hawkins, *The British Pop Dandy: Masculinity, Popular Music and Culture* (Farnham, Surrey, England and Burlington, VT: Ashgate, 2009), 97.
85 Hawkins, *The British Pop Dandy*, 101.
86 Hawkins, *The British Pop Dandy*, 104.
87 Hawkins, *The British Pop Dandy*, 105.
88 Hawkins, *The British Pop Dandy*, 106.
89 Ibid.
90 See, for example, Calvin Thomas, ed., *Straight with a Twist: Queer Theory and the Subject of Heterosexuality* (Urbana: University of Illinois Press, 2000) and Richard Fantina, ed., *Straight Writ Queer: Non-Normative Expressions of Heterosexuality in Literature* (Jefferson, NC: McFarland, 2006).
91 Hawkins, *The British Pop Dandy*, 108.
92 Andrew Branch, "All the Young Dudes: Educational Capital, Masculinity and the Uses of Popular Music," *Popular Music* 31, no. 3 (2012): 39.
93 Branch, *Popular Music*, 39.
94 Chad Bennett, "Flaming the Fans: Shame and the Aesthetics of Queer Fandom in Todd Haynes's *Velvet Goldmine*," *Cinema Journal* 49, no. 2 (Winter 2012): 37.
95 Anne Hollander, *Sex and Suits: The Evolution of Modern Dress* (New York: Kodansha International, 1995).
96 As Roland Barthes and others have pointed out, the male dandy has played an important role in the evolution of fashion: "Though slower and less radical than women's fashion, men's does none the less exhaust the variation in details, yet without, for many years, touching any aspect of the fundamental type of clothing: so Fashion, then, deprives dandyism of both its limits and its main source of inspiration—it really is Fashion that has killed dandyism." Roland Barthes, *The Language of Fashion*, ed. and trans. Andy Stafford (New York: Berg, 2006), 69.

97 Here and elsewhere, Hollander references the "Great Masculine Renunciation" outlined in J. C. Flügel's, *The Psychology of Clothes* (London: Hogarth Press, 1950). First published in 1930, Flügel's famous thesis:

> If, from the point of view of sex differences in clothes, women gained a great victory in the adoption of the principle of erotic exposure, men may be said to have suffered a great defeat in the sudden reduction of male sartorial decorativeness which took place at the end of the eighteenth century. At about that time there occurred one of the most remarkable events in the whole history of dress, one under the influence of which were still living, one, moreover, which has attracted far less attention than it deserves: men gave up their right to all the brighter, gayer, more elaborate, and more varied forms of ornamentation, leaving these entirely to the use of women, and thereby making their own tailoring the most austere and ascetic of the arts. Sartorially, this event has surely the right to be considered as "The Great Masculine Renunciation." Man abandoned his claim to be considered beautiful. He henceforth aimed at being only useful. So far as clothes remained of importance to him, his utmost endeavours could lie only in the direction of being "correctly" attired, not of being elegantly or elaborated attired. Hitherto man had vied with woman in the splendour of his garments, woman's only prerogative lying in *décolleté* and other forms of erotic display of the actual body; henceforward, to the present day, woman was to enjoy the privilege of being the only possessor of beauty and magnificence, even in the purely sartorial sense. (Flügel, *The Psychology of Clothes*, 110–11)

98 To be clear, I am talking here about Goth as a musical and sartorial movement of the late seventies and early eighties, not as the anti-social youth culture of the nineties.

99 Kimberley Jackson, "Gothic Music and the Decadent Individual," in *The Resisting Muse: Popular Music and Social Protest*, ed. Ian Peddie (Farnham, Surrey, England and Burlington, VT: Ashgate, 2006), 186.

100 Michael du Plessis, "'Goth Damage' and Melancholia: Reflections on Posthuman Gothic Identities," in *Goth: Undead Subculture*, ed. Lauren M. E. Goodlad and Michael Bibby (Durham: Duke University Press, 2007), 162.

101 du Plessis, *Goth*, 162.

2

The Persistence of the Dandy:
Subcultures and Resistance

Throughout his long career, singer-songwriter David Bowie has functioned as an arbiter of taste not only in music but in fashion and lifestyle as well. His long reign as pop's glitter king has created not only legions of devoted music fans but also a number of influences that are perhaps not as easily noticed, especially his direct impact on visual artists of the late twentieth and early twenty-first centuries who have attempted to respond to and absorb Bowie as a musical (and general performative) influence on their art.[1] Whether responding to him personally as a fan or attempting to come to terms with his funneling of eighteenth- and nineteenth-century versions of dandyism into the present, these artists (Leon Johnson, Yinka Shonibare, and others) make clear that they see him as someone who has fundamentally helped to change our notion of the relationship between high and low art. In his own work, Bowie helped to usher in this change for rock music—vastly expanding what might be considered appropriate material to sing about. Likewise, his music has now become material for the next generation of artists. In this sense artists who use Bowie in their work are a part of a long history of subcultures that have spun off Bowie's global influence. Bowie has left his mark, especially, on the resistant strain of subcultures as they have been theorized by Dick Hebdige. Bowie's successive waves of "Bowie damage," as the *Village Voice* once termed it, is related to his success with middle-class media, especially television, which became the perfect form for him to represent both the influences on him and the ambitions he had for impacting other fans like him.

* * *

The representation of pop music in much of contemporary art—and the particular fascination of photography, for musicians throughout its history—suggests an affinity between visual artists and pop musicians. In many ways, pop and rock musicians are our closest living exemplars of the nineteenth-century dandies. From Mick Jagger dressing up as Oscar Wilde in the 1960s to Jim Morrison fancying himself a latter-day Rimbaud to David Bowie's Ziggy Stardust, the classic era of rock music often references dandies in general and Wilde in particular as examples of resistance to bourgeois authority. The tradition has continued up to the present with bands that tap into the sexual side of the Wildian tradition—the Smiths, Pet Shop Boys, Suede, Blur—and those who continue to see it as retaining the power for general disruption and rebelliousness. To some extent bands now seem to have absorbed glam rock impulses thoroughly enough to recognize Bowie and his ilk as the origins of their own (distant) historical moment. Emo bands represent the mainstreaming of glitter (Panic at the Disco, for example) while figures like Marilyn Manson, Beck, and even Trent Reznor have created their personae from the offshoots of seventies glitter culture.[2]

The references to New Order, the Pretenders, Kraftwerk, Roxy Music, Iggy Pop, Blondie, Patti Smith, and any number of other artists from the seventies and eighties whose images are reproduced by contemporary artists show the generational interests of the artists and function as a part of nostalgia, especially nostalgia for something lost. Many of the visual artists that work in what we might consider the dandical style blur the sixties and seventies together into one period. For artists born between 1955 and 1975 the past can be seen as malleable—something into which you may reinsert yourself, to fantasize different outcomes, different histories, alternative childhoods. For some artists, this reinsertion is connected with the manipulation of history and the materiality of art—texts, magazines, photos—the fetish of the real, even as a copy. It is not unusual to see album covers, photos of teen stars, or portraits of rock stars used to create personal or generational iconic images or *aides-mémoire*.[3] In some ways this tendency is connected to the art of collecting. While these artists celebrate the pop detritus of our culture—rock stars, film icons, teen heartthrobs—they are also engaging in a similar accretion of culture such as one finds in J.-K. Huysmans' *À Rebours* (1884) or chapter 11 of Wilde's *The Picture of Dorian Gray* (1891). They carry Jack Smith's idea of trash as art a step further into a positive realm where "the idea of culture" is "necessarily redemptive and therapeutic, instead of an entity that eternally dismembers and consumes."[4]

The artists that I refer to are heirs to the revolution in pop art begun by Andy Warhol, James Rosenquist, Jasper Johns, Roy Lichtenstein, Claes Oldenburg, Tom Wesselmann, Robert Rauschenberg, and David Hockney and continued into another generation by key figures like Jeff Koons. The pop art movement not only focused on art as surface and symbol, but also famously removed the line separating it from advertising and distinguishing artistic aura from commercial appeal. Pop artists also allowed a place for sexual desire to be expressed unabashedly and for those emotions to intermix with fan worship and personal and public displays of iconicity. Nowhere is this clearer than in Warhol's own interest in stars—including rock stars—a lineage that is picked up on by Koons and other artists, leading to the generation of younger artists I am talking about.[5]

The artists that I am most interested in focus specifically on David Bowie, who has often used himself as a self-conscious pop-art symbol from his Ziggy Stardust period to his later "Berlin Trilogy" of albums from 1977 to 1979. Both of these eras in his career seem to be especially conducive to the imagery of other artists, and in his own most recent album, *The Next Day* (2013), he seems to make reference to this fact by turning the cover of one of his most iconic albums, *"Heroes"* from 1978, into a pop-art joke by obscuring it, negating the album photograph and name, and replacing it with a nondescript square that seems to suggest a number of possible ideas: what now

Figure 2.1   Jeff Koons, *Michael Jackson and Bubbles*, 1988.

constitutes David Bowie? What is his relationship to the past? How does one negate it
or live up to it?

Some of the artists whose generation is coterminous with the Young British
Artists have been trying to parse these relationships for a long time, asking how one
acknowledges one's own nostalgia while resisting it at the same time. Or how one
makes art out of those materials that have formed one's own obsessions—rock stars,
other art—while also recasting it to make new art. This sort of ekphrastic effect is the
basis of the work of Tracey Emin, Gavin Turk, Mat Collishaw, and Douglas Gordon,
identified, along with Damien Hirst, with the Young British Artists, and others who
have worked with some of the same strands of influence that connect with the dandy as
the self-conscious pop artist: Steven Shearer, Meredyth Sparks, Babak Ghazi, Christoph
Schmidberger, Joan Morey, Slater Bradley, John Bock, T. M. Davy, Mark Leckey, Iris
Van Dongen, Hernan Bas, Zak Smith, Lisa Tan, T. J. Wilcox, Rachel Harrison, Carlos
Pazos, Francesco Vezzoli, Piero Golia, Ignasi Aballi, Pierre Bismuth, Carol Bove, Dora
Garcia, Juan Luis Moraza, Ryan McGinley, Leon Johnson, Yinka Shonibare, Marcus
Muntean/Adi Rosenblum, and Mickalene Thomas, to name a few. What this list of
varied and often exemplary artists have in common is the references in their work
to pop culture, especially music fan culture, but, to varying degrees, to a dandified
past.[6] The latter might take the form of seeing the self as a star or recreating tropes
from nineteenth-century painting or attempting to reproduce styles that seem vaguely
Pre-Raphaelite or Symbolist or might make explicit references to Charles Baudelaire,
Wilde, or other writers connected to the dandy tradition. Pornography, fashion, and
eroticism show up as frequent tropes as do some of the influences acknowledged
by the musicians themselves: William S. Burroughs, Edvard Munch, James Ensor,
Huysmans, and others. The interconnection between neo-pop and Victoriana is linked
via androgyny, which seems to act as the thread that connects these strains from the
present to the past.

In an attempt to theorize the dandy, Roland Barthes argued that men's fashion has for a long time existed only as a series of subtle details ("discreet *signs*"[7]) that could be emphasized by the wearer but that this possibility evaporated with the coming of machine manufacture and standardized clothing. The dandy was the master of the detail and turned his entire life into a detail. He was a perfect object.[8] Giorgio Agamben's Marxist perspective carries the concept of the dandy and self-objectification even further. In a discussion of Baudelaire and Beau Brummel, Agamben argues:

> The greatness of Baudelaire with respect to the invasion of the commodity was that he responded to this invasion by transforming the work of art into a commodity and a fetish. That is, he divided, within the work of art itself, use-value from exchange value, the work's traditional authority from its authenticity.[9]

The process by which artists become the shock troop of the avant-garde is through the dandy, specifically the transformation of the body into an uncommodifiable substance—an object so objectified that it becomes a subject. As he continues:

> But what gives his discovery revolutionary character is that Baudelaire did not limit himself to reproducing within the artwork the scission between use-value and exchange value, but also proposed to create a commodity in which the form of value would be totally identified with the use-value: an *absolute* commodity, so to speak, in which the process of fetishization would be pushed to the point of annihilating the reality of the commodity itself as such. . . . Baudelaire understood that if art wished to survive industrial civilization, the artist had to attempt to reproduce the destruction of use-value and traditional intelligibility that was at the origin of the experience of shock.[10]

Agamben summarizes his thoughts on Baudelaire in another context, saying, "This is the sense of 'art for art's sake,' which means not the *enjoyment* of art for its own sake, but the *destruction* of art worked by art."[11] Brummell comes into the picture in his extreme emphasis on becoming himself an object. As Agamben argues, "The redemption of objects is impossible except by virtue of becoming an object. As the work of art must destroy and alienate itself to become an absolute commodity, so the dandy-artist must become a living corpse, constantly tending toward an *other*, a creature essentially nonhuman and antihuman."[12] Or, as Agamben concludes, a puppet or automaton—essentially the living dead—a trope in the work of Baudelaire, Rimbaud, Kleist, Lautréamont, Mallarmé, Klee, Eugenio Montale, Paul Celan, Grandville, and Gautier, among many others. The uncanny Freud theorized is ultimately popularized by the surrealists. Brummell's bon mots, which were often tied to objects—"Do you call that thing a coat?"—are described by William Hazlitt as "founded on a single circumstance, the exaggeration of the purest trifles into something important . . . their significance is so attenuated that 'nothing lives' between them and nonsense: they are suspended on the edge of the void and in their shadowy composition they are very close to nothingness."[13] The description of this trajectory and this tradition partially explains Bowie's use of the dandy as a signifier for the modern avant-garde, his own collapsing via Warhol and pop art of the subject-object distinction, and his penchant for surrealism—or, at least, realism that shades that way.

Of the many artists who illustrate this interest in the dandical tradition, Shonibare arguably stands out as someone who has made it the centerpiece of his oeuvre. Though a visual artist, he has long been attracted to art that utilizes narrative functions.[14] He remade William Hogarth's *A Rake's Progress* series as a set of photographs entitled *Diary of a Victorian Dandy* (1998). More tellingly, he has staged his own series of photographs based upon Wilde's *The Picture of Dorian Gray*. His work, published in 2001, is based in part upon the film version from 1945. In the film, an Orientalist influence on Dorian is given more space than it has in the novel. Dorian's soul seems to be fought over by influences from both the East and the West.[15] Shonibare restages scenes from the novel and the film, but, as Robert Stilling notes:

> By removing the East Asian, South Asian, and Egyptian iconography from [Albert] Lewin's film, Shonibare heightens the contrast between his own presence as black dandy and the background image of white, Victorian London. In swapping the threat of reverse colonization from one corner of the empire for that from another, Shonibare enacts not one but two substitutions: the black dandy substitutes for the white, and an oppressive Englishness substitutes for an oppressive Orientalism.[16]

Figure 2.2   Yinka Shonibare, *Diary of a Victorian Dandy*, 1998.

Shonibare's creation of himself as the exotic "other" of the text is of a piece with his frequent use of one of his signature materials—Dutch wax cloth in bright colors and baroque patterns. Meant to seem "African," they are actually a European invention, one now frequently sold in Africa as a symbol of "Africanness." In the *Dorian Gray* series, Shonibare is himself the symbol of otherness, but with the same confused cultural heritage—raised in Nigeria he lives in London. Seemingly, an outsider within his own adopted culture, he is the consummate insider, like Wilde, who deconstructs empire from within. Shonibare has said that he is attracted to the dandy in general and Wilde in particular because of the seriousness of the frivolity, the mobile signifier that could "progress within English society."[17]

Wilde acts as a similar signifier for the artist Leon Johnson, whose *Remembering Wilde* (2000) documents a trip to the Père Lachaise Cemetery in Paris to restore the stone penis of the art-deco male figure that decorates his tomb. Removed at some point in an act of violence, Johnson replaces it with an exact replica made of metal. The Jacob Epstein monument, built in 1914, symbolizes Wilde's plight as a gay man, even beyond the grave. In a discussion of Steven Shearer's work, Bruce Hainley notes that Shearer's

> indexing of every picture of Left [*sic*] Garrett or Shaun Cassidy presents the sign (if not the actuality) of the fan's all-encompassing obsessive collecting, the dandy's highly edited arrangement Shearer's blatant wish, in fact may be to circulate the *imponderability* of Cassidy, Garrett, and Kiss as embodiments of nonbeing resistant to theorizing . . . the idea of culture as necessarily redemptive and therapeutic, instead of an entity that eternally dismembers and consumes.[18]

For Shearer, like Johnson, the act of remembering offers an alternative to the economic system that insists that art is always about profit, novelty, and the future. Meredyth Sparks' collages of covers from Joy Division, New Order, Prince and others mix that iconography with Soviet Constructivist architecture, art, and design to pull out the revolutionary potential of seemingly ephemeral art. She focuses especially on the years 1972–78, when the potential to resist conservatism and the rising neoconservatism was at its peak.[19] Art about popular culture, in other words, not only makes visible subcultural desires such as looking at the world as a particular fan, or from, say, a queer perspective, but also highlights the latent potential lurking in what might seem, on the surface, as mere nostalgia.

The Bowie-esque art highlighted here includes a great deal that focuses on the artist as subject. Koons often includes his own image in his works of art, much as Warhol did, including elaborate photographs taken with his porn-star wife in a series of mock billboards (*Made in Heaven*, 1989). But Warhol's subject/object play is also picked up in Gavin Turk's *Piss Painting* (2008), which apes Warhol's series of the same name, Babak Ghazi's *Andy Warhol* (2006) and Pierre Bismuth's *One Thing Made of Another On Thing Used as Another—Andy Warhol* (2003), both of which play on Warhol's use of the Brillo box as sculpture and framing of found objects generally. Mat Collishaw's *Narcissus* (1991) shows the artist taking a photograph of himself while looking into a muddy puddle on the road. Some artists reflect their interest in glitter culture literally, creating paintings or sculpture that is covered in gold or has a gold background, such as Dora García's *I Read it With Golden Fingers (J.D. Salinger)* (1999), which is a gold-covered copy of *The Catcher in the Rye*, and *Le future doit être dangereux* (2005), or Slater Bradley's *Gold All of this for you* (2007). The use of gold flattens out the background of paintings, much as pounded gold leaf did in the Middle Ages, and calls attention to the work as an object of worship.

Still some artists (Joan Morey, Babak Ghazi, Douglas Gordon, Slater Bradley) incorporate rock stars such as Bowie, Brian Ferry, Kurt Cobain, and others, directly into their art as subject matter, while others (Lisa Tan, Christoph Schmidberger, John Bock, Rachel Harrison) do the same with nineteenth-century dandies such as Baudelaire. Others reference nineteenth-century decadence more indirectly—either as design, such as Carol Bove's *Untitled* (2008), whose peacock-feather wallpaper suggests James Whistler's peacock room, or as subject matter, especially the beauty of youth in sexually suggestive poses and situations (Steven Shearer, Iris Van Dongen, Hernan Bas, Zak Smith, Muntean and Rosenblum, T. M. Davy). The past that is remembered or recreated in many of these works is not, of course, a real one.[20] Beck's *Midnight Vultures* (1999), for example, could be called a seventies album because it creates not the seventies, but a simulacrum of the period, a seventies and early eighties album as it might exist in or for the nineties.[21] All pop music or cultural work in nostalgia really reflect the present, but some act as self-conscious constructs that examine just what nostalgia is or might actually be.[22] The use of the sixties and seventies pop culture since the nineties has, if anything, only intensified, though the nineties stands as the decade for which there was the first wave of serious seventies revisionism. While the nineties deserves its own attention as a decade of genuinely original creative currents, whether the grunge scene in music or the return of paranoia in television, it also acts as the beginning of a sustained analysis of the seventies that we still have today.

In many ways the tributes to rock music that appear in some of this work are a part of the notion of subcultures as places not just of nostalgia and history but also of resistance. As Meredyth Sparks notes, the period 1972–78 was one when art and social change seemed not just possible but even inevitable.[23] It is not surprising, therefore, that many of the artists who work in the general vein of the dandy seem to privilege rock stars over other artists or media celebrities. While there may be several possible reasons for this, one may be the inherent instability of identity in rock music. That is, the typical pop song creates a situation in which the star and the fan become fused in a complex mutual performance. The star needs the fan as an audience, and the fan wants to be the star, but both subject positions have to be occupied separately. The essential erotic aspect of this relationship is compounded by the fact that pop songs complicate normal norms of identity. If one listens to a typical pop song centered on a boy/girl romance in which a male performer is singing about his long lost love, does a male listener imagine himself as the boy or the girl? Or both? The slipperiness of the gender identification carries over into other aspects of pop singing that complicate the usual notions of identity. If in watching narrative film and television we agree with Laura Mulvey's famous dictum that the normative gaze is always gendered male, in music this formula might be even more complex.

While most of the nostalgia for rock heroes is for male rock stars, the stars themselves are often androgynous. The reproduction of their images or their work by various artists often seems to reference their ability to be both male and female at the same time, to allow for identification across genders and across sexualities—a function the dandies knew well and that has allowed for a further magnification of the gender undecidability of music. No musical artist has explored this trend more than David Bowie. Not only does he exemplify the notion of the artist as transgressive figure, but his work from the late 1970s, the so-called "Berlin Trilogy" of albums (*Low, "Heroes,"* and *Lodger*), seems to be an especially rich locus of interest among many of these artists. Certainly in terms of musical form these albums are his most experimental and are, within his oeuvre, the albums that have been the most influenced by visual artists. The cover of *"Heroes"* was based on the frequent visits that Bowie and his Berlin roommate Iggy Pop made to Die Brücke museum in then West Berlin. The first of Pop's own Berlin albums, *The Idiot* (1977), echoes the same style. Though Bowie would not return to such an intense interest in art until *Outside* in 1995, it is worth noting his influence on visual artists throughout his forty-year history of experimenting with the interpenetration of visual art and music in the form of costuming, stage design, album covers, music videos, and film. His songs are themselves often evocations of visual landscape and, whether futuristic, dystopian, or otherwise, suggest either a theatrical or, more often, cinematic effect.

One nexus for the intersection of the visual and the musical can be found especially in Bowie's influence on subcultures. Certainly the emergence of extremely

Figure 2.3   Cover photograph of *"Heroes,"* 1978.

expressive and effective subcultures in the 1970s parallels not only an essentially linear development from the 1950s until then, in which various subcultures vied for dominance one after the other, but also indicates the extent to which subcultures played a part in the development of major historical movements related to social change. That is, the seeds of change that were laid by the 1960s became institutionalized in the 1970s where the hard work of the sixties revolution was adopted by governments and became a part of the matrix of society and, arguably, changed our notion of social progress. In this sense, subcultures might be said to function as the superstructure to the base of political change and to be a part of the permanent progressive transformation that has developed in Western society despite repeated attempts by conservative forces to reverse, slow, or imagine away these changes. Subcultures now, of course, would likewise have to be imagined quite differently from Dick Hebdige's original model.[24] The history of subcultures would have to be updated to include the changes brought about, especially, by the rise of the Internet and virtual technologies generally. From an historical point of view subcultures are now a part of the extreme fragmentation of culture that has taken part during postmodernism. Identities for individuals have become multiple and many-sided. Political movements have likewise become less about one dominant theory that provides unity of purpose—class or Marxism on the Left—than about the unification of disparate causes and movements—ecology, feminism, gay and lesbian marriage rights, etc.

Theorizing subcultures

At a general level the dandy is synonymous with rebellion and can seem to be roughly parallel to the resistance of youth culture to adult culture, or what Dick Hebdige calls "child" and "parent" cultures. The rise in youth culture could come about in the United States and ultimately in Europe only after the increase in industrialization after the world wars allowed enough economic prosperity for young people to have their own money to spend on entertainment—on record singles, concerts, clothes, etc. As Hebdige argues, the result was the creation of a mode of symbolic resistance in which young people, perhaps for the first time, registered their discontent with dominant culture by resisting it in their tastes in music, clothes, hairstyles, films, etc. One can see the origin of this type of image in James Dean's performance in *Rebel without a Cause* (1955). The red leather jacket, white t-shirt, and blue jeans express a working-class solidarity while also suggesting the danger and non-conformity of biker gangs. The famous knife fight outside the Griffith Observatory in Los Angeles solidifies the connection between delinquency and external threat. Dean's character fits neither into his family, where his father has become an emasculated figure unable to provide a role model or stable gender, nor with friends at school, who have become actual physical threats. The alternate family at the end of the movie—the younger gay character, Plato (Sal Mineo) and the strong girl (Natalie Wood)—represent the fantasy of escape into another social reality.

While these images connect to a number of other aspects of the film, most especially to the interrogation of masculinity that is perhaps now seen as the film's greatest legacy, they are also attached to the notion of a stratum of resistance that hides in plain sight: young people who have developed their own codes and means of identification, their own social groupings, and their own way of commenting on the fissures, stresses, and contradictions of their lives under capitalism. Somewhat ironically, the primary means for resisting homogenization is to use capitalism against itself. Youth subcultures are, perhaps, one of the purist examples of *bricolage* in that young people use the detritus of popular culture as a way to resist dominance. That is, they take signs and symbols from popular culture and give them new meanings by taking them out of their original context and placing them within a new one with other signs with which they were not originally associated. While Hebdige tracks a rich history of music-based British subcultures, from Rockers and Teds to Mods and Rastafarians, he ends his conversation with the example of the punk rock scene that rises in Great Britain in the mid-1970s. The punks are, for Hebdige, the masters of signification—at creating a new sign system out of old materials. They are the point to which all post-youth subcultures lead. Within the punk system, therefore, a baby pin is taken out of its original context and used instead to hold worn out clothing together or to pierce ears. What was innocent and benign becomes its opposite and takes on associations of primitivism and sado-masochistic sexuality.

The codes of the structuralist layers of punk arrange themselves, according to Hebdige, as a "homology." The music (short, pithy, simple, anarchic, imprecise) is homologous to the clothing (simple, cheap, falling apart), the hair (spiky, unkempt, brightly colored), to the drugs of choice (generic beer), to the public displays (visible, public, rude, rebellious, thrash dancing, vomiting), etc. In a similar way other subcultures such as the American Hippie culture (or, say, the followers of jam bands such as the Grateful Dead) formulate a subculture out of different signs plucked from other parts of the dominant culture that are equally homologous: long, jam-like, frequently technically difficult songs; handmade, natural, hemp clothing; long hair and facial hair; marijuana; "Love ins"; etc. The homologous system of the punks is united by an overarching philosophy or logic that might be described as nihilistic—anarchy and what Hebdige calls "semantic disruption" are designed to have the most devastating effects on British culture at the time. In many ways, nothing could be more disruptive to the gentrified, class-stratified world of British society than the emergence of the punks. It is not surprising that for a time people in Britain, and a couple of years later, the United States, thought that the world was indeed coming to an end. The hippies, less than a generation before, were by contrast interested in peace, love, and understanding.

Punk culture resisted absorption into the mainstream for a couple of years. During this time it was able, according to Hebdige, to actually mount symbolic resistance to the ruling class and create "subversion." This moment, however, was eventually (and inevitably) followed by the style's "incorporation" in which the parent culture, like an amoeba that has encountered a grain of irritation, absorbs the offending particle and moves on its way. Incorporation usually produces the "freezing" of the subculture's traits. That is, it stops evolving. The reason that we can talk about punk now (or hippies or mods) is because we recognize characteristic traits (in the music, fashion, attitude, etc.), which also allow the subculture to be more easily commodified. In punk's case, it wasn't long before you could find t-shirts torn by designers selling in boutiques in New York for considerably more than if you had torn them yourself. Everything can become high fashion, even that which supposedly in its essence resists it. Punk's evisceration proves how limited the power is for subcultures to change their parent cultures. It is, however, possibly the only weapon many young people have with which to resist. More importantly, symbolic resistance clearly goes beyond teenage subcultures and is used by most members of society as a way to register dissatisfaction, even if only through the notion of taste and style. Depending upon one's view of life, the incorporation of a subculture can seem like a way to eliminate it, or, by absorbing the subculture, one might argue that the parent culture is changed in some essential way and will never be the same again.

The one aspect of the development of subcultures that has perhaps remained stable and offered the most rewarding opening for artists and critics alike has been the reorientation of cultural production away from authorial intention and toward the interest in the audience and the use that it makes out of culture no matter what the intended object of its original idea. The most famous example of this effect at work may well be the "K/S" or "slash" fiction of the 'zines of the 1990s. This subculture created scenarios in which the characters from the 1960s television show *Star Trek* are made into the objects of fantasies by putatively straight women. A typical plot might find Kirk and Spock reimagined as gay male lovers, not only disrupting the function of the original series but providing an opportunity for the women to cross not only gender but sexuality to create satisfying sexual scenarios. In a sense, the whole notion of a fan base allows for this same sort of active creative involvement with works that seem, on the surface, to be finished or final. The critical act, therefore, is also creative and involves changing the object of one's affection. The Internet makes this type of loop extremely easy by providing for fan sites, blogs, and comments on every episode of every television show, new movie, album release, etc. The opportunity to become a part of the audience, in other words, has never been easier. Slash fiction has branched out into Gale/Peeta of *The Hunger Games* or even Snape/Harry/Ron/Malfoy of the *Harry Potter* series.[25] Whether "shippers" or "bronies," there is now every possible stripe of romance slash and porn slash as the audience takes on the content of television, film, and novels to create parallel worlds for the characters that build upon, exaggerate, and expand the author's original universe.

Hebdige's essential theory remains as influential today as it ever was, though it has been challenged and criticized both for its gender bias, by Angela McRobbie and Jenny Garber, and by Susan Willis for its insistence that symbolic action occurs outside of the dictates of class.[26] Willis specifically postulates that the study of subcultures has to refer to capitalism. That is, she would not maintain that "interpreting the semiotics of subculture constitutes a political understanding of the subculture."[27] For her and other Marxist theorists, whatever the semiotics of subcultures may teach us should always lead back to the materialist reality of capitalism itself. Subcultures are mainly the articulation of the stressful contradictions of capitalism or come about as young people try to find ways to deal with them.

Willis' approach to subcultures as barometers of class offers a useful model for understanding the complexity of influence that Bowie has exerted on subcultures especially in terms of the Birmingham School's definition of "parent" versus "dominant" culture—the former being one's class, the latter one's relational position as seen in one's basic activities.[28] In this sense, one may be working class, for example, yet practice a cultural position equivalent to someone in the middle class. The complex interdependence of these two levels might help to explain the complexity of Bowie's first major group of fans: the copycat carrot-topped Ziggy clones who would show up at his concerts. Perhaps Bowie was the first major middle-class glam artist—a non-working man's Gary Glitter—or perhaps he actually spoke across class lines. After all, both Bowie and Brian Ferry—though often expressing aristocratic fantasies—were working class (though for Bowie, only barely by British standards). Yet, to claim that Aesthetes or aristocrats are fantasies only of the middle or upper classes is to miss the point of what makes rock music fandom function. Likewise, Bowie's use of television—a medium he quickly took to—may have been possible only with the rise of a postwar middle class in Britain, though it was not the only way—or perhaps even the primary way—that knowledge about him was disseminated.

Hebdige has himself noted that Bowie is responsible for the development of subcultures based on gender and sexuality rather than class in Great Britain. Bowie and other glitter rockers, according to Hebdige, did offer subcultural resistance to the adult world, "and they did so in singular fashion, by artfully confounding the images of men and women through which the passage from childhood to maturity was traditionally accomplished."[29] While mainstream youth culture subsequently divided between Bowie, Lou Reed, and their circle and their more pop alternatives, Bowie's fans challenged the authenticity and puritanism of working-class youth subcultures. As Hebdige argues, "We can now begin to understand how the Bowie cult came to be articulated around questions of gender rather than class, and to confront those critics who relate the legitimate concerns of 'authentic' working-class culture exclusively to the sphere of production."[30] Hebdige goes on to enumerate the ways they did this by "challenging the traditional working-class puritanism so firmly embedded in the parent culture"; "resisting the way in which this puritanism was being made to signify the working class in the media"; and "adapting images, styles and ideologies made available elsewhere on television and in films . . . , in magazines and newspapers . . . in order to construct an alternative identity which communicated a perceived difference: an Otherness. They were, in short, challenging at a symbolic level the 'inevitability', the 'naturalness' of class and gender stereotypes."[31]

In some ways, this distinction explains the extreme importance of a figure such as Bowie, who was able to get his message across via television and who displayed so much adept attention to the multiple platforms through which he would deliver his messages, with music acting as the originary but not final text. The division between classes and how they utilize subcultures goes back to a difference noted in *Resistance Through Rituals*, where the authors claim that "middle class youth tend to construct enclaves within the interstices of the dominant culture."[32] That is, "Working-class sub-cultures reproduce a clear dichotomy between those aspects of group life still fully under the constraint of dominant or 'parent' institutions (family, home school, work), and those focused on non-work hours. . . . Middle-class counter-culture *milieu* merge and blur the distinctions between 'necessary' and 'free' time and activities." Indeed: "Working-class sub-cultures are clearly articulated, collective structures. . . . Middle-class counter-cultures are diffuse, less group-centered, more indivisualised."[33]

Bowie came onto the scene, as *Resistance* notes, at the moment when the middle class was supposed to move from "thrift" to "consumption."[34] This disorienting change meant a new lifestyle, one in which much of what had been held as gospel was suddenly upturned. Work was replaced with play. "Sexual repressiveness and the ideals of domesticity" were challenged by permissiveness.[35] The world of advertising has already begun this change, but the breakdown in morality, in the line between pornography and everyday life that we see so exaggerated today, had already begun and was acting similarly to erode what had been seen as the natural social fabric. Inevitably, panic over these changes centered on young people themselves. Whereas "working-class youth groups were seen as symptomatic of deeper civil unrest," "middle-class groups, with their public disaffiliation, their ideological attack on 'straight society', their relentless search for pleasure and gratification . . . were interpreted as action, more consciously and deliberately, to undermine social and moral stability: youth now, as the active *agents* of social breakdown."[36] Perhaps no one eventually came to symbolize that threat more than Bowie, at least after his megastardom as Ziggy Stardust, and perhaps via no other more middle-class medium than television.

* * *

In much the same way that Bowie tried to stretch the medium of the video clip, he also attempted to do more with televised performances than merely advertise a new song or album. Coming in the same pre-MTV era of his best videos, two of Bowie's guest appearances on network TV—from 1973 and 1980, respectively—neatly bookend the decade he would help to make famous as well as comment self-consciously on his own performance style. In the first, he appears on NBC's *The Midnight Special* in his final performance as Ziggy to perform songs from *Ziggy Stardust* (1972) and its sequel, *Aladdin Sane* (1973).[37] Bowie had not performed these songs for some time, but for this event he reassembled the core of the Ziggy band for what was to become a cabaret-style send off for Ziggy that surpassed in theatricality—if not in content—the live concert versions of his creation. The show begins with Bowie dressed in a cobweb costume, essentially a crocheted cat suit, designed by Natasha Korniloff based on the costumes for Ballet Rambert's 1967 *Ziggurat*. This emphasis on his skin was made real when he in fact "shed" one skin to reveal another. Bowie's outer costume broke apart to reveal underneath a legless one-piece suit. The startling spectacle—especially for a US television audience—intensified the song's already melodramatic explorations of theatricality. The costume had stick-on hands placed strategically over Bowie's breasts and, in the original version of the costume rejected by censors, there was a third hand on Bowie's crotch.[38] Bowie was transformed into a glamorous but desirable monster while the costume also allowed his well-built physique to show through even as it emphasized his feminine aspects as well. Perhaps most effectively, Bowie sang "Time" dressed in a green lizard-like costume while being supported by a chorus of male dancers. Bowie's alienness was belied somewhat by the hands of the male dancers who loft him up in the air like a female star in an MGM musical. Perhaps nowhere else does Bowie make clear the effectiveness of his performance of gender than in this well-choreographed and flawlessly executed number. The show ends, appropriately, with Bowie and Marianne Faithful singing "I Got You Babe"—she, in a strapless nun's habit.

Over six years later, on a live broadcast of the US television show *Saturday Night Live*, Bowie referenced his earlier floor show as well as his concert and video production in general. In the performance of three numbers from different points in his career, Bowie provided a neatly compact overview of his oeuvre in order to suggest that even though his work as a whole had not left the arena of gender politics, his ways of signifying his stances had become more aestheticized and pointedly political than they had been before.[39] For his first song, Bowie was brought out onto the stage inside a box-like costume based on Dadaist performance artist Hugo Ball, from which only his hands and face were visible.[40] He was removed from the box only for the duration of the song, "The Man Who Sold the World," which he sang dispassionately, though in an arrangement that made this selection from 1971 sound fresh and even startling given the theatricalized treatment.[41] The performance proved not only the staying power of his earliest arrangements but also referenced his early glam period by his presentation of himself as a person who comes from another world—or from within a box like a performing automaton. The significance of this was further emphasized by his including Klaus Nomi as one of his two backup singers (the other was Joey Arias, who worked for Fiorucci design clothing store).[42] Long a footnote to queer performance, Nomi was a German singer and performance artist, a friend of both Bowie and Eno, who carried the aestheticizing of life even further than Bowie by dressing every day in a tuxedo and full makeup. Indeed, Nomi's carefully created persona was mainly fashioned from the discards of Bowie's earlier mythologies: part science fiction, part Oriental, with a hefty portion of gay high-camp glamour. Nomi went on to record two albums before dying from AIDS-related disease in the early eighties. His songs—camp remakes of fifties "girl-group" tunes mixed in with Purcell arias and parodies of gay disco styles—were mostly notable for his use of singing traditions that he learned from Chinese opera—piercing falsettos that are as dissonant as they are resolutely queer. Bowie's inclusion of Nomi, therefore, acknowledges where his earlier work would—and could—go as an influence, as well as simply updating some of the themes as the choreography displayed by Nomi and friend was important to the performance of the song.[43]

At the end of "The Man Who Sold the World," Bowie was put back into the box/costume from which he had been disentombed. He was to reemerge again later in the show for two more numbers that were, if anything, even more spectacular. Appearing as relaxed as he had earlier appeared theatrical, Bowie took the stage in a British

Figure 2.4   Cover of *Klaus Nomi*, 1981.

WAC uniform—a gray top and long matching gray skirt. Except for the dress, Bowie appeared conventional—his hair, for instance, was closely cropped and naturally blond. The effect of his "normal" haircut and the sleek dress, though certainly disconcerting, did not necessarily signify as drag. Bowie had pulled off the same effect that he had managed with the original album cover for *The Man Who Sold the World*, where he appears in a "Man's dress"; as Bowie claimed then, he wore the dress because it was one that he looked good wearing.[44] He did not, as a drag performer might, attempt to suggest to the audience that there was a slippage being performed between himself as gendered male and a female character he was performing. In fact, the gender code of his outfit only really signified from the waist down, though it was here—in the shapely lines of his skirt—that Bowie's point was being made: the dress looks good on him, yet it is not what he normally wears; it is a theatrical prop meant both to reference his earlier gender-bending costumes and to update and prepare the audience for the last number of the night.

Entitled "Boys Keep Swinging," Bowie's next song, from the album *Lodger* (1979), reflected anew the political message of the video. As the former interpretation made clear, the song is not a paean to fond memories of boyhood—as its jaunty sound might suggest upon an initial hearing—but rather an indictment of male privilege: "When you're a boy/you can wear a uniform/when you're a boy/other boys check you out/ you get a girl/these are your favourite things/when you're a boy." The lyrics are sung against a musical background whose sinister grind sounds like it is about to break apart. Indeed, the song was recorded using instructions that Eno, the album's producer, turned up randomly from a special deck of tarot-like cards. One of the results of using this method to construct the song was to have all of the recording musicians switch instruments. Quite literally, the music is a fragile "medley" of sounds—some innovative and some simply dissonant. For Bowie's final performance on the show, he sang this song while wearing a body suit whose particular physical qualities caused it not to register in front of a camera. Bowie's body disappeared and was replaced with a twitching puppet of a boy's body, but with Bowie's head—the only part of his body not covered with the material. Though always one to exploit technology, Bowie was here also making a point: should anyone be confused, this song is at least a put-on, at best one with a serious point to make. Bowie's album—one of his most political—was to give the lie to the idea that his music up until then had been apolitical, as some on the left have claimed.[45] The album's politics concern gender inequity. The penultimate song, "Repetition," deals quite realistically with wife battering, while the album's first song, "Fantastic Voyage," is a plea for nuclear disarmament. His point on this particular television show was at least in part to carry over the theme from that album and wed it to his past personae: though he had done much with gender bending, and still could, he now wanted to make the political aspects of these actions clear. That is, the music was put to a political use—specifically, a feminist one. Bowie's performance had matured from one in which shock was used to open up new territory for redefining the self to one in which he realized that one must be specific about what is possible. That is, Bowie acknowledged and commented on the fact of male privilege and that gender is not just an act to be performed. His understanding of the potentialities of the performance of gender in a theatricalized venue had changed and was, more or less, to disappear from his work after his next album, *Scary Monsters (and Super Creeps)* (1980).

Bowie's function as a subcultural figure changed a great deal in successive phases of his career as his fans also changed.[46] Bowie may never have lost his core English fans, but he did gain others: German fans, during his years of living in Berlin, and US fans after the successes of *Young Americans* and then again, later, after *Let's Dance*.[47] In each of these instances, generational and geographic differences are markedly played out by the distinct subcultures that arise around Bowie's stardom. His significant appearances on US television, for example, have their own history just as did ones on British television such as his 1972 performance of "Starman" on BBC One's Top of the Pops. Adding to this the vicissitudes of his sexual symbolism and his already self-conscious approach to the relationship of fan and star (as can be seen in many of his songs, from "Rock and Roll Suicide" and "Candidate" to his noting in "Modern Love," "I'm standing in the wind, but I never wave bye bye"), the subcultural matrix operating around Bowie is especially complex. As a sort of late-Mod, Bowie is definitely of the order of "intentional communication," to use Hebdige's distinction, one that "stands apart—a visible construction, a loaded choice." Bowie took seriously the dictates of the Mod—"*obviously* fabricated" they "*display* their own codes" and "in this they go against the grain of a mainstream culture whose principal defining characteristic, according to Barthes, is a tendency to masquerade as nature" to help create a series of personae that did anything but become a part of the background.[48] In a sense, Bowie's frequently changing characters, looks, and musical styles functioned to heighten the effect of subcultures, to make himself a constantly evolving subculture-of-one. In that sense Bowie emphasized in his own creative slipperiness the basic idea at the heart of subcultural meaning, that "it depends . . . on consumer abilities to make value judgements, to talk knowledgeably and passionately about their genre tastes, to place music in their lives, to use commodities and symbols for their own imaginative purposes and to generate their own particular grounded aesthetics."[49]

For most young people, perhaps especially those of the middle class, subcultures themselves have become fodder for other subcultures as "only a small minority of young people adopted the complete uniform of youth subcultures, large numbers drew on selective elements of their styles creating their own meanings and uses from them."[50] Subcultural young people become performers, and the performativity on display in someone like Bowie establishes a paradigm for not only subcultural resistance at the level of youth culture but art as well. Bowie comes along at the moment of postmodern fracture when, as John Mowitt explains, "the grand historical narratives" have been "derailed." Performativity of the type that Bowie represents "emerges as the sole criterion of epistemological legitimacy. Legitimation through performativity implies that if what one does works to enable other performance, it not only deserves to be done, it is valid. Theory, as a generic 'fellow traveler' of the grand historical narratives, submits to their fate regardless of its practitioner's intentions."[51]

This model of dandyism as subcultural practice places it within an historical time frame that includes roughly the era after the Second World War and does not take into account the dandy's potential precursors and rich historical dimension. Central to this argument would be the period between the Enlightenment and the onset of modernism—the eighteenth and early nineteenth centuries. The persistence of the image of the dandy in modern culture perhaps no longer needs to be explained. The dandy, aesthete, or decadent figure has, to some extent, become ubiquitous, either as an ideal or an influence. One can argue that postmodernism itself is predicated upon the dandy in its connection between commerce and performance, self-consciousness and the pastiche of history. For all of its seeming importance and pliability, however, the concept of the dandy is not well understood—its definition and history still contain the ability to generate shock and resistance.

The work of this historical dandy is on display in the paintings, sculptures, films, and mixed-media installations in the work of various visual artists who track and deploy the original concept of the dandy. There seem to be different strains of influence or ways that the dandy gets reproduced in contemporary art. One is by imitating the effects from the dandies of the past—using realism or the figure as a way to suggest the nineteenth century. The other is to update the dandy to a contemporary setting and find equivalents for them, often in media icons in general and rock stars in particular. Artists who fall into the former category might quote from the work of fin-de-siècle Vienna, Expressionism, Ensor, Munch, or perhaps Manet or Caravaggio, preserving at least some of these artists' use of figuration (however, at times, abstracted or flattened out) as perhaps a necessary way to preserve the emphasis on sexuality and the body, which is certainly a major part of decadent art of the original period. This second tendency is to approach the influence of the dandy via performance art, interdisciplinary art, films, and a tendency toward the breakdown of formal barriers between arts. Andy Warhol seems to be a major catalyst here, especially in his call for the manipulation of celebrity culture by mimicking the proliferation of media that feed off other media. Both approaches may involve the use of abstraction or conceptualism—not as an obvious stylistic reference to the dandiacal style, but a use of its conceptual tools to comment on our own age (Jeff Koons via Marcel Duchamp, for example).

The desire to celebrate the celebrity of others is of course often related to the notion of making oneself the star. Throughout much of the neo-dandies art is the notion that the most suitable subject for the artist is the self. In many ways this sort of approach to art mirrors the one that was begun by Bowie in the early 1970s when he signed with the management company MainMan and acted like a star—complete with limos, security detail, etc.—before he really was one. Artists who work in this area now seem self-consciously to pick up on the dandy idea that one's life is a work of art, that one is always becoming, not being. This blurring of art and life is key to the aestheticist doctrine that critiques the notion of materiality, of art as essentially moral and life as utilitarian. As Wilde did over a century before in his "Phrases and Philosophies for the Use of the Young," these artists insist that "to love oneself is the beginning of a life-long romance."

Notes

1   While one might claim that Bowie's glitter period was fairly short-lived and contained to the early 1970s, the effect of Bowie's glitter or glam period lingers and resurfaces from time to time both within his work and without and is key to the powerful influence he has had on successive generations of performers.

2   Michael Jackson and Kurt Cobain update this paradigm for the eighties and nineties, respectively. Specifically, Jackson represents the instability of gender and race, an iconic stature that has only grown in the time since his death. His face, which Jean Baudrillard once referred to as a hologram, functioned for decades as an unstable signifier of fame and wealth. Cobain was perhaps our last rock star—self-mythologizing, whether intentionally or no, he represents the last truly anti-theatrical rock moment. Though his fame is based upon his music, his death recreated him as a link to late-sixties culture, another martyr to the rock cause.

3   A particularly potent literary parallel to this effect is the early poetry of Dennis Cooper such as *Tiger Beat*, from 1978, and *Idols*, from 1979, in which Cooper queers male pin-up stars of the seventies.

4   Bruce Hainley, "Steven Shearer," *Artforum International*, September 2003 to July 18, 2009. http://www.thefreelibrary.com/Steven+Shearer-a0108691825.

5   One might say that some of these artists build on the notion of an anti-futurity as it is expounded in Lee Edelman's controversial book *No Future* (2004). As David Buckley notes:

> Many gay critics deride the heterosexual fascination with history, connections and antecedents which give the illusion that history matters and that a future

exists. Writer Bertha Harris argues that the privilege of the homosexual sensibility is "to make things stop happening. Reality is interesting only when it is distorted, and second . . . reality lacks interest because it is controlled by usefulness which is pertinent only to the heterosexual continuum. The positive decision our hypothetical artist makes is to attach himself to the inexpedient and the impertinent." (David Buckley, *Strange Fascination: David Bowie, The Definitive Story*, rev. ed. (London: Virgin, 2001), 503)

6   For more on these artists and the influences on them, see Rocío Gracia Ipiña, Sergio Rubira, and Marta de la Torriente, eds., *Sur le dandysme aujourd'hui: Del maniquí en el escaparate a la estrella mediática* (Santiago de Compostela, Spain: Centro Galego de Arte Contemporánea, 2013).

7   Roland Barthes, *The Language of Fashion*, ed. Andy Stafford and Michael Carter, trans. Andy Stafford (New York: Berg, 2006), 66.

8   Barthes, *The Language of Fashion*, 66.

9   Giorgio Agamben, *Stanzas: Word and Phantasm in Western Culture*, trans. Ronald L. Marinez (Minneapolis: University of Minnesota Press, 1992), 42.

10   Agamben, *Stanzas*, 42.

11   Agamben, *Stanzas*, 49.

12   Agamben, *Stanzas*, 50.

13   Qtd. in Agamben, *Stanzas*, 52.

14   Paula Rego, "The Artist's Progress: Hogarth's Legacy in the 21st Century," *The Guardian*, January 13, 2007 to March 23, 2013. http://www.guardian.co.uk/artanddesign/2007/jan/13/art.classics1.

15   Robert Stilling, "An Image of Europe: Yinka Shonibare's Postcolonial Decadence," *PMLA* 128, no. 2 (2013): 312.

16   Stilling, *PMLA*, 313.

17   Qtd. in Stilling, *PMLA*, 313.

18   Hainley, *Artforum International*.

19   "Meredyth Sparks, We Were Strangers for Too Long at Elizabeth Dee Gallery," *Art Fag City* September 1, 2008 to August 19, 2009, http://www.artfagcity.com/2008/09/09/meredyth-sparks-we-were-strangers-for-too-long-at-elizabeth-dee-gallery/.

20   According to Sigler, theories of nostalgia are often unable to locate the source of pleasure in nostalgia. During the postmodern theoretical period, Fredric Jameson and others suspected it of being the dupe of postmodernity—of functioning with the same internal logic to remove history from consciousness. Sigler claims that nostalgia functions like Jacques Lacan's "petit objet a," the excess that can never be located, the time period that never really existed, can't be recovered, and therefore is the object of intense longing. (Cf. Slavoj Zizek's Madeleine in *Vertigo*.) David Sigler, "'Funky Days Are Back Again': Reading Seventies Nostalgia in Late-Nineties Rock Music," *Iowa Journal of Cultural Studies* 5 (Fall 2004), July 30, 2009. http://www.uiowa.edu/~ijcs./nostalgia/sigler.htm.

21   Sigler, *Iowa Journal of Cultural Studies*.

22   David Sigler argues that "nostalgia is most frequently studied as a form of commodity."

23   Paddy Johnson, "Meredyth Sparks, We Were Strangers For Too Long at Elizabeth Dee Gallery," *Art Fag City*, August 19, 2009. http://www.artfagcity.com/2008/09/09/meredyth-sparks-we-were-strangers-for-too-long-at-elizabeth-dee-gallery/.

24 In *Subculture: The Meaning of Style*, Dick Hebdige investigates and interprets the subversive power of punk style. First published in 1979, it has been reissued annually since, which indicates its theoretical and political significance within the study of youth subcultures. The book looks backward to earlier theorizations of youth cultures (Center for Contemporary Cultural Studies' *Resistance Through Rituals*, which stressed social class as the basic framework shaping subcultural groups), and forward to theories of discourse and semiotics (especially Roland Barthes' *Mythologies*, which is referenced throughout the text).

25 For more on recent examples of slash fiction and its queer history and context, see Catherine Tosenberger, "Homosexuality at the Online Hogwarts: Harry Potter Slash Fanfiction," *Children's Literature* 36 (2008): 187–207.

26 See, for example, Angela McRobbie and Jenny Garber, "Girls and Subcultures," in *The Subcultures Reader*, ed. Ken Gelder and Sarah Thornton (New York: Routledge, 1997), 112–20.

27 Susan Willis, "Hardcore: Subculture American Style," *Critical Inquiry* 19, no. 2 (Winter 1993): 379.

28 John Clarke, Stuart Hall, Tony Jefferson, and Brain Roberts, "Subcultures, Cultures and Class," in *The Subcultures Reader*, ed. Ken Gelder and Sarah Thornton (New York: Routledge, 1997), 100–01.

29 Dick Hebdige, *Subculture: The Meaning of Style* (New York: Methuen, 1987), 62.

30 Hebdige, *Subculture*, 88.

31 Hebdige, *Subculture*, 88–89.

32 Stuart Hall and Tony Jefferson, eds., *Resistance Through Rituals: Youth Subcultures in Post-War Britain* (London: Routledge), 60.

33 Hall and Jefferson, *Resistance Through Rituals*, 60.

34 Hall and Jefferson, *Resistance Through Rituals*, 64.

35 Ibid.

36 Hall and Jefferson, *Resistance Through Rituals*, 72.

37 Called "The 1980 Floor Show," the performances were filmed from October 18–20, 1973, and broadcast on November 16.

38 Ken Scott, *Abbey Road to Ziggy Stardust: Off the Record with the Beatles, Bowie, Elton, and So Much More* (Los Angeles: Alfred Music, 2012), 181.

39 This show was broadcast live on NBC on December 15, 1979.

40 Bowie's performance that night emphasized the way that puppets can comment on the human body and its expressiveness by transferring the characteristics of the animate body to the inanimate object. In this way, Bowie is able to make the viewer self-conscious about the body's performance. As Ed White says about Roland Barthes' discussion of the Japanese puppet tradition of *Bunraku*, "By foregrounding the human-puppet relationship, we focus on a composite attempt to capture elements of expressiveness, seeing, instead of persons or things, 'fragility, discretion, sumptuousness, extraordinary nuance, abandonment of all triviality, melodic phrasing of gestures,' all *qualities* of the body without the full body." In Bowie's performances, every hand gesture or facial expression seems calculated and choreographed—as indeed it is. Ed White, *How to Read Barthes' Image-Music-Text* (London: Pluto Press, 2012), 147.

41 The song was performed in an acoustic version by the band Nirvana in 1994 and turned out to be the selection from the CD of that concert, *Nirvana Unplugged in New York* (1994), most often played on radio.

42 For more on Bowie's relationship to Nomi, see David Bowie, "Journal for 20th Feb 99" davidbowie.com March 8, 1999.

43 Nomi was in Munich in December 1982 to deliver Purcell's strange aria "The Cold Song" from the English seventeenth-century baroque opera *King Arthur*. In 1695 Purcell died from incurable tuberculosis at age thirty-six. Nomi dies in 1983 and this would be his last public performance. For more on Nomi, see *The Nomi Song*, 2004.

44 "I went to America to promote 'The Man Who Sold The World' and, as I was going to Texas, I wore a dress. One guy pulled out a gun and called me a fag. But I thought the dress was beautiful." Reprt. in *Bowiepix* (New York: Delilah Books, 1983) from an interview April, 1971.

45 See especially Simon Frith's, "Only Dancing," *Mother Jones* 8, no. 7 (August 1983): 16–22.

46 Bowie's fan base continued undaunted even when he was mostly invisible during the first decade of the twenty-first century. Simon Jacobs', *Saturn* (Tucson: Spork Press, 2014) imagines scenes from Bowie's life with his family as he muses on fame, art, and the everyday, while Dana Johnson's novel, *Elsewhere, California*, chronicles a young African-American's girl's coming of age in Southern California in the 1970s. As Johnson writes:

> To me, Bowie sounded black when he sang a song, which made him like me. And when he was Ziggy Stardust, he seemed to be something I couldn't name. He wasn't a man or a woman. He wasn't even from this planet. Because he was anything that we wanted him to be, he would be with anything and anyone he wanted to be with, with someone who was whatever she wanted to be, somebody like me, so many things rolled into one. (Dana Johnson, *Elsewhere, California* (Berkeley: Counterpoint, 2012), 85)

47 "As Frith and Horne say of him, 'the biggest and most influential stars . . . are precisely the ones who design their own *fans*." Allan F. Moore, *Rock, The Primary Text: Developing a Musicology of Rock*, 2nd ed. (Aldershot: Ashgate, 2001), 187–88.

48 Hebdige, *Subculture*, 101–02; emphasis in original.

49 Paul E. Willis, *Common Culture: Symbolic Work at Play in the Everyday Cultures of the Young* (Boulder: Westview Press, 1990), 60.

50 Willis, *Common Culture*, 87.

51 John Mowitt, "Performance Theory as the Work of Laurie Anderson," *Discourse: Theoretical Studies in Media and Culture* 12, no. 2 (Spring-Summer 1990): 50.

3

Avatars of the Future: Structuring Music

As Simon Frith and other theorists of rock have pointed out, many of us like to talk about rock music, but many of us do not really have a vocabulary for discussing it. That is, we do not have available to us either a musicologist's technical vocabulary or a cultural critic's expressive one. While I am not equipped to provide the former, I would like to begin to try to discuss how best to approach rock music as a cultural critic. Toward this end, we need to understand that though many of us might be looking for a more detailed—or articulate—way to express why certain pieces of music have meaning, there are actually many areas of inquiry tied to even a simple discussion of rock music. To name only a few, we might wish to discuss or theorize such things as the audience for this kind of music, the marketing of it, the production of it, its ties to ideas about performance, gender, and technology—in addition to whatever biographical and archival knowledge we might want to bring to a study of rock.

It is perhaps important to acknowledge at the outset that what we are discussing is, at least in part, a cultural practice. That is, we are not just looking at the music itself—as intricate and interesting as that might be—but also at the ways in which we integrate the enjoyment of rock music into our everyday lives. Rock music exists for many of us as a subculture, an obsession, a hobby, a social discourse—as various practices that can be read as having meaning either for us personally or for others. It is paramount, therefore, that we see the study of rock as the study of a kind of cultural production that involves understanding the social and political coding that both the music and the practice of making or interacting with the music might contain. We need to let go of our concept of high art and learn to take seriously the analysis of activities that we might think of as everyday or ordinary, but which are actually important activities to analyze in order to understand the culture of rock and roll.

I would also like to say a few words about what rock and roll is for me—and what it is not—and why this meaning is perhaps always a personal one. Although I am interested in some bands for just a short period of time—like anyone else might be—more typical of my own tastes is for me to follow just a few bands or musicians for a very long time. That is, rather than taking a broadband view of the world of rock, I tend to focus vertically on just a few bands or sub-movements of rock. I like to think of these interests as a snake-like line that goes through the history of rock music from the late 1960s to the present, and that includes performers whom history will ultimately deem as truly great artists. But the truth is that I was a nerd in high school who did not buy a non-classical album until my senior year. To make matters worse, I never listened to

Future Nostalgia

the radio. So, my own interest in rock is somewhat retrospective in that I have had to learn a lot of what my contemporaries simply lived through, and I have stuck to certain artists not out of stubbornness or a sense of their innate superiority, but because I do not have the scope that some might. Having said that, however, I do not feel that the approach I was destined to take was necessarily a limited one in that one can see the vibrations and currents in styles that occur in the larger rock realm reflected in most major artists' work over the course of a career. This is not to say that knowing a lot about a lot is a bad thing, but that knowing a lot about a little is okay—and is certainly one version of the dominant style of fandom in general.

I should also confess that my own interests in rock, while primarily sensuous, also contain some fairly cerebral components about which I try to stay self-conscious. Namely, I tend much more toward those performers who posit artificiality over authenticity, and those who are actively interested in playing with the intersections between "high" and "low" forms of cultural production. The first dichotomy constitutes the difference between the United Kingdom and the United States in the sense that rock musicians in the United Kingdom frequently have a much more vaudevillian approach to their music and performance styles than do their US counterparts. But then, just as one begins to set up a binary system like that, one can see where the differences in the two sides might easily break down: who is to say that a rock pioneer like Little Richard is not highly artificial? Or that heavy metal is not, from a slightly skewed perspective, high camp? And what about the authentic style of someone like Bob Dylan: he had to teach himself to sound so terrible, and the owner of a clothing boutique assembled the Sex Pistols. The point is, one cannot be too sure about absolute categories when talking about something as multifarious as rock, but also that one need not be too exclusive about what one thinks one knows about one's own tastes because they are just that. Instead, one needs to understand rock and roll as a complex nexus of needs, wants, desires, erotics, ideas, and, above all, feelings that are often very difficult to explain or convey to another person.

Of the many different ways to talk about popular music, one may ask, what, if anything, can be learned by comparing and contrasting different kinds of music? Is it possible to like styles of music that seem radically at odds with each other? If so, how? What is the difference between describing an erotics of surface versus explaining how something works the way it does? Why do critics so often become involved in questions of worth—or value? Do you have to believe in axiology to enjoy popular music? How do critics also bring in questions of social worth? Why do they bother to stay attentive to questions of history: class, politics, etc.? Of the many major theories of rock music, much of our approach to the analysis of rock music still goes back to Theodor Adorno and the Frankfurt School approach to discussing popular music. However controversial or disputed, Adorno was the first to ask many of the questions that we still grapple with.

Adorno famously wrote about popular music as the horrible "standardization" of music. Among other things, he felt that popular music (he really had in mind something more like 1940s big-band jazz than Elvis/Beatles/Stones/Bowie) created predigested identities, experiences that could not be authentic.[1] His work is often misunderstood as a classical versus popular debate with the deck stacked for the former, but he was actually making an argument against mindless repetition (the Blue Danube waltz, say, versus the use of the Turkish march by Beethoven). He also tried to theorize the notion of "the listener," an idea that was way ahead of its time. He was a fan of Schoenberg, and what he (Adorno) most disliked about popular music was its lack of attention to detail—the part's relationship to the whole (or the note to its context). The problem with Adorno (and his work is complicated and there are many facets, so I am compressing here) is that he wants to judge popular music (or jazz, which may have more standardization than popular music) by the standards of the Western classical canon. While there may be some aspects of popular music that would be explored through this comparison—structural aspects, say—one has finally to ask if classical music is at all what popular music is trying to do. Indeed, maybe it is trying to do the opposite—that is, to emphasize rhythm, percussion, and movement (of the body, for example) over melody, structure, and the cerebral. Of course, this distinction can be broken down in many ways (especially, for example, around the guitar tradition), but the point is that we have to ask to what extent do we need a new definition of music when we discuss popular music—and to what extent can we use the tradition of musicology?

"On Popular Music"

Adorno begins his famous essay, from his book from 1941 entitled *Studies in Philosophy and Social Sciences*, with the idea that music can be divided into two groups: serious and popular. One has to accept this division in order to understand his argument even if it is one that should not be recognized. That is, why should this division be used as the primary basis of comparison? Why is not popular music also serious? Adorno goes on to note that there are two ways to specify the comparison—"musical" and "social." Adorno next considers the idea of charting the two "spheres" historically—especially the idea of musical production. He argues that the split between popular and serious music occurred in Europe ages ago. The American approach to this phenomenon is to accept it as "pre-given." He finally says that his essay will attempt to examine the current popular music scene in the United States rather than attempt an historical analysis of its origins because history does not mean anything in America because American newness indicates a new era. Note that this might be a very autobiographical argument that Adorno is implying here, but not making.

Adorno moves on to make his first famous claim in the essay: "The whole structure of popular music is standardized."[2] Remembering that Adorno is probably thinking of jazz here, one might wonder what exactly Adorno means by this. He attempts to include everything under the rubric of standardization: the characters or personae of the songs; the musical structure of a piece; the "whole" versus the "details" or parts of that structure, etc. The concept of standardization covers a great deal. The effect of standardization is to offer only a preordained form; one can only experience the song in a prefabricated way. Every song is interchangeable, and though one might notice a detail—if it is placed strategically—it does not matter because all is subordinated to the overall effect of the song, which is in itself generic.[3]

Adorno goes further to define standardization to mean replaceable parts—as in an automobile or, say, certain types of television shows (a soap opera, for example). All of this is read in contrast to classical music, specifically the example of Beethoven. Though Adorno does acknowledge that some types of classical music, such as the Viennese school (re: Johann Strauss), is dance music, which seems to require repetition, he defends Beethoven's use of dance music (though, by implication, not Strauss').[4] For Adorno, "details" mean something in serious music—they are the music—while they mean nothing in popular music, where they are supposedly completely interchangeable.

Adorno backs off his own sweeping statements a bit in the next section, where he acknowledges that some jazz is better than "Viennese classicism" and that some work by Tin Pan Alley composers is better than some Haydn. That is, he does not like classical music that might be characterized as being composed of generic repetition of phrases and musical ideas.[5] Adorno's next move is to call popular music dangerous to a free society. Why he makes this move and how it helps him to make his argument is probably related to his escape from Nazi Germany, equating repetition and standardization with the mechanistic and repetitive movements of German propaganda. Adorno finally begins to address the concept of audience. First, he argues that popular songs listen for you and that fans of popular music are taught to listen only one way. Second, that the music is "pre-digested." One is not encouraged to think, but to listen passively. Of course, we still hear these arguments today, though mainly in other contexts, mainly in relation to television, but also to popular culture generally.[6]

Adorno next dips a bit into musical history and says that popular music in this country at one time was competitive and changeable, but that eventually the conventions of popular music froze or formed a style or genre that remains unchanged. Adorno seems to suggest that then-current music has to appear to sound "natural"—that is, to follow the conventions (which also are based on older music, music like hymns, which he considers to be "primitive") while giving the illusion that it deviates from this naturalness just a bit. Perhaps it is here that Adorno comes closest to understanding what we now call rock music. We can never know if, within Adorno's concepts, rock-and-roll music that attempts to break free from the notion of the natural would ever be labeled good music to him, or if Adorno would say that rock music is simply the newest form of jazz.

In the next section, on "pseudo-individualization," Adorno gives us a clue as to how he would answer that hypothetical question by saying that it is the job of standardization to give the listener the illusion that she is getting that which is not natural as well as that which is, while what she is really hearing is simply the perfectly oiled mass-produced illusion of rebellion. Indeed, Adorno posits the concept of pseudo-individualization to underscore the paradox at work when one consumes popular music: the buyer thinks she is choosing one group or sound over another when in fact she is simply choosing one predetermined option over another in a closed system in which all the choices are non-choices. She might think that choice equals self-definition, but actually, one either chooses to buy or not to buy as all the selections are the same. Standardization, in other words, extends to the buyers themselves, who are duped into becoming interchangeable consumers. Capitalism—or mass production—makes cogs of us all. Adorno's famous example here is jazz improvisation, which acts as a summary metaphor for all the effects he has been talking about. One might make the argument that he is right about jazz improvisation, that what is happening in jazz is the idea that music is all style or technique and no substance. Jazz has become a fairly standard thing (hence the phrase, "jazz standards"), and even jazz improvisation is predetermined, limited. That is, when a genius like John Coltrane writes a piece that takes a tune like "These Are a Few of My Favorite Things" and makes a song out of it, he is saying that the music does not matter, but the genius of the jazz musician does. Jazz, originally a malleable form, has become calcified and rigid. Jazz might be fundamentally different from rock because there are fewer markers of an individual artist—the music was designed that way—but pop tunes can be endlessly reinterpreted. Rock still has the ability to change. Though perhaps right about some aspects of jazz, Adorno was wrong that popular forms necessarily limit the freedom of interpretation.

In the section entitled "Theory about the Listener" Adorno shifts registers again, and here posits a listener—or audience—for the product he is deconstructing. According to his formulation, the typical pop audience is in need of distraction, but too tired to have to work at it. The listener helps to create the limitations of the music that she gets by wanting the familiar, because that is what is easy. The listener gets music that is boring in order to ease her boredom. She buys music that reproduces, in the entertainment realm, the same characteristics that mark her existence in the realm of work: imitation, repetition, standardization, and easy replaceability. Another inescapable paradox is introduced. But one might argue that Adorno underestimates the role of the listener and seems to attempt to shift the blame from the listener to the system. One could say that Adorno is deterministic, that he thinks all listeners are the same.

The final piece in Adorno's theoretical puzzle is the concept of "social cement," which also functions as a way out of the problem of the listener. That is, the listener listens not because she really likes the music, but because it acts to bond her with others—specifically, via the recapitulation of her own wishes, hopes, desires, and fears. Popular music acts as a storehouse of archetypes—specifically, those that might be decoded by the young. The young are more susceptible because "they are more susceptible to a process of masochistic adjustment to authoritarian collectivism" and they listen to the radio more.[7] It is here that Adorno makes his boldest—and perhaps most off-the-mark—arguments. He goes on to say that "the uses of inexorable popular musical media is repressive *per se*" and that if you respond to rhythm in music you are part of a fascist movement because you are allowing yourself to become part of a "mechanical collectivity."[8] The other type of consumer—gendered female, by Adorno—is the "romantic" who listens to music for the "scant liberation that occurs with the realization that at last one need not deny oneself the happiness of knowing that one is unhappy and that one could be happy."[9] This second listener is considered a "type" who is not only obviously considered female, but also a "late romantic." Adorno is obviously not interested in emotional release—he does not see it as helpful because it does not act as a form of resistance. One might wonder, though, how Mozart's and Beethoven's music does. Or why "Slavic melancholy" gets lumped into the same unhelpful category.

There is obviously much to criticize in Adorno, such as the sexism, but it is also important to begin with what he gets right. For one, he hits on many of the primary issues in the study of rock music—audience, reception, production, musical structure, etc.—that still occupy the center stage of debates about music. Though we should no longer feel that we need to justify the enjoyment of listening to rock rather than to classical music, the question of just how seriously to take "low" art forms still comes up, and lyrics are rarely considered a part of the literary canon of classics. Adorno writes from the perspective of the Second World War, and his concern for the social aspect of music should be read within that context. We all think some forms of popular music are better than others (most of us do, anyway). If so, how might our own justifications run along some lines similar to Adorno's? Might we all argue that complexity is part of what is going on—that Adorno's arguments are accurate, but that he simply underestimates the extent to which popular music replicates effects from "serious" music? Adorno considers the aping of serious music by popular music as proof that the latter is inferior. But should we take a different approach altogether? At any rate, Bernard Gendron offers one possible response.

"Theodor Adorno Meets the Cadillacs"

While not the final word on Adorno's piece, Gendron's essay does raise some interesting questions and, by attempting to deconstruct Adorno's argument, perhaps allows us to understand some of its strengths. To begin, the author argues that Adorno was not against standardization per se, but against its new capitalist formation. Gendron writes, "Part interchangeability results from the drive to minimize the cost of production; pseudo-individualization results from the imperative to maximize sales. The system of advertising seduces us into believing that differences in packaging reflect differences in essence. Pseudo-individualization glamorizes style over the real inner content."[10] One might think of NASCAR: either Ford or Chevy. One cannot even choose Chrysler. It is a manufactured difference, but then only one difference. Musical groups like the Cadillacs were, like the car, interchangeable. At this point Gendron seems to support Adorno—mainly by explaining his ideas through analogy.

The author goes on to apply some of Adorno's ideas to rock music to conclude that most subgenres of rock—whether doo-wop or heavy metal—do function with what amounts to interchangeable parts. When he finally gets to his critique of Adorno, he begins by saying that Adorno underestimated the differences between "functional" and "textual" artifacts, and that he did not understand diachronic standardization in reference to record production. Adorno's political critique, therefore, does not really hold up. More specifically, he thought that record production was backward—a "handicraft"—and that new technology was focused on marketing. He did not understand completely that standardization could not apply to music production because it was not like automobiles—a new type of production line technology does not sweep aside older forms, they just keep getting added. As with a literary genre, we now read the relatively new form of the short story, but we still read epic poems. Some people erroneously feared that television would get rid of reading, but it did not, etc.

The extent to which standardization may have happened in the record industry vis-à-vis production is probably a good thing, as the author notes, in that new technologies (or other ideas) just allow more kinds of new music. But Gendron is wrong about Adorno's take on oligarchy. Indeed, Gendron presents a neoconservative viewpoint when he thinks that government and industry work together to further the development of new ideas through some sort of symbiosis. Adorno's bleaker, and wiser, take may be factually wrong (there does not seem to be any one form of popular music now, as there may have been in his day), but his essential explanation of one of the pitfalls of capitalism is accurate. It is not clear that Gendron's example of the different versions of a song getting recorded, but only one making it to vinyl, is really germane to Adorno's argument that the songs all sound the same (to him).

Gendron next shifts to a discussion of consumption rather than production to conclude that buying an album because it sounds like another is not a bad thing. But is Gendron playing into Adorno's hands by saying that this impulse is a conservative one? Or is he pointing out something that Adorno never acknowledges: that liking one kind of something, and wanting more of it, may not mean that one is a dupe of capitalism and no longer a selective buyer, but rather, that you have made a choice, that that choice is for this kind of product, and that that can be seen as an intelligent decision (one might choose Schoenberg, for example)? But what is at the heart of this particular debate is the question of aesthetic value, not shopping.

Gendron comes back to the question of diachronic standardization to say that Adorno posits the idea that popular music never changes, which Gendron says is wrong. He attempts to extend this point by questioning Adorno's structural model for how popular music functions—part to whole—and says, correctly, that rock music should be analyzed for "timbre and connotation" rather than "melody and harmony." The problem with this argument, however, is that Adorno did not have rock music as an example. Yet, it is true that Adorno's assumptions are Eurocentric, and surely Adorno would have known about non-Western music, though he may have thought that it was not germane to a discussion of American music.

Does rock music change, or do the styles simply come and go? Rap, for example, comes out of rhythm and blues but also marks a different kind of music. Perhaps Adorno was simply not thinking far enough ahead, though popular culture had already offered plenty of examples that change was inevitable. Even what we think of as postmodern cyclical change—what the author here calls "nostalgia"—is on display in the nineteenth century (the Pre-Raphaelites, for example). Why did Adorno fail to recognize that the standardization of cars, while it has not changed, would not apply to developments in music? How do these changes come about if the rock industry mainly reproduces the same thing for a while—what is perceived as popular—but then oversaturates and forces there to be another new thing? Does change come about from this market-driven process, or from somewhere else?

This line of questions leads to Gendron's final point about the auteur theory in rock. Does rock leap forward on the backs of a few great composers/performers? Or, via its audience (Dick Hebdige)? Or, via the industry? That is, to what extent does the composer, the audience, or someone else create a rock song? Where should rock theory go? How might we reintegrate Adorno's productionist stance with theories of reception? Just what kind of theory is the author calling for, and what might it look like?

Musicology

How we might approach the analysis of Bowie's musical output, then, is as complex as tracking his influence. Combining high and low, he proves that Adorno's rejection of the popular in preference for the avant-garde need not be the only solution to the split between high and low, or artistic and vernacular, culture that Adorno bemoaned. If we attempt a musicological analysis of Bowie's music, we can see his effort to fuse avant-garde experimentation with popular forms and the extent that his music is successful gives the lie to Adorno's conclusions, at least about the structure of popular music.

From a primarily musicological standpoint, during the 1970s Bowie moved from well-crafted songs with chromatic changes, an approach that perhaps reaches its peak on *Hunky Dory* (1971), to songs characterized by sudden jumps, where, as in *"Heroes"* (1978), jarring bits of musical texture are slammed together to create an avant-garde dissonance in which a song's twists and turns are often unheralded. On *Hunky Dory* Bowie puts acoustic instruments to the forefront—the piano and the guitar, for instance—creating musical spaces in which it is clear to the listener where we are in space in reference to the instrument and to the singer. The album's somewhat folkie appeal makes it one of Bowie's most traditional (if still innovative) musically, the sense of acoustic space the most conventional or realistic in his oeuvre.[11] The plaintive melancholy of the album offers an English twist on the Dylan-esque lyrics and coffeehouse aesthetic of the album as a whole. That does not mean that Bowie did not imbue his album with his own characteristic obsessions, whether the references to Nietzsche and fascism in "Quicksand" or to H.P. Lovecraft and the neo-Gothic on "Bewlay Brothers." Likewise, one of the themes of the album is the almost ekphrastic use of technologically based art as the basis for some of the songs—whether film in "Life on Mars" or photography in "Andy Warhol." That is, Bowie does not really make a folk album, but does his own take on the singer-songwriter tradition to comment on rapid changes in the contemporary world. In this sense, it is, despite its many homages, a commentary on the folk tradition—the songwriter as troubadour and one-man band.

As Allan F. Moore argues, most rock music is held together by the percussion, which usually determines the rhythm of the song and acts as the skeleton upon which the song hangs. Repetition can be used by the drum kit either discursively or musically, the latter, similar to structuralism, forming the smallest unit of music, perhaps a phrase, that gets repeated. An example of the latter would be the word "who" in "My Generation" (1965) by The Who. On "Life on Mars" Bowie takes this idea and complicates it. He introduces the notion of sequence, "a standard discursive technique"[12]:

> In this case, the . . . process is one of growth from the first (harmonically static) phrase of the verse to the second (harmonically modulatory) phrase Bowie employs sequence through the verse's first eight bars: the first, third, fifth and seventh have the same melodic rhythm and counter, but raised one step higher on each occasion, introducing motion towards the second phrase.[13]

Or as Moore argues later, "Bowie consistently employs, and often mixes, both open-ended and period structures: the standard example of the latter is probably 'Life on Mars' (1971), whose piano-dominated sequences are inventive in their modulations."[14] The song "Ziggy Stardust," an album later, "combines a standard gentle periodic structure for the verse with a power chord open-ended chorus structure . . ." while the song "Five Years" "makes use of an open-ended repetitive sequence (Ionian I-VI-II#3-IV), but instead of allowing the song to remain on one level, Bowie uses it to generate tension by, in the first verse allowing the vocal range to get ever higher, and in the second thickening the texture."[15] The hard rock sound, as Moore goes on further to note, disappears from Bowie's work in the mid- and late seventies where the drum kit is replaced by the synthesizer. Likewise, Bowie's delicate alternation between "parody and pastiche"[16] of other rock songs and references disappears as well. Both of these elements start to come back after the soul and funk experiments of *Station to Station* (1976) and the avant-garde electronica of *Low* (1977) and *"Heroes"*[17] and to continue from *Scary Monsters* (1980) to *Never Let Me Down* (1987) to the Tin Machine era to be picked up again in the early 2000s.

In *Young Americans* (1975) and *Let's Dance* (1983), he creates a rapprochement between rock and dance, employing self-consciously hackneyed music in some instances, such as "Panic in Detroit" or even "Ashes to Ashes" (doo-wop, nursery rhymes, etc.). On something as seemingly innocuous as "Starman" from *Ziggy Stardust* Bowie "focuses on acoustic guitar but breaks into a boogie bridge from chorus to verse; a boogie pattern also underpins the strange chromatic sequence."[18] References to other work, in other words, are typical. Bowie's fondness for his first instrument, the saxophone, is clear as early as "Soul Love," which prefigures *Young Americans* by three years.[19] Some of his music is known for its use of piano (Mike Garson) or for horns (in the 1980s and early 1990s, especially), but, true to most rock tradition, the electric guitar gets a lot of attention. The guitar choices range from the cut-strum work on *Station to Station* and elsewhere to the dissonance and progressive off-key sound of Robert Fripp's work on *"Heroes"* and, especially, *Scary Monsters*.[20] *Lodger* (1979) and *Scary Monsters* retain the thick, dense textures that Bowie developed in the mid-seventies in his mixing of rhythm and blues and German bands, but begin to return to true rock hardness. As Moore explains of the music on *Lodger*: "This density is formed by all the arrangements being constrictingly tight, with straight rhythms and a preference for simple sequences, each chord tending to last two bars, not being rounded out to 4- or 8-bar phrases. This avoidance of rock's normative grouping prevents a clear sense of orientation."[21] He offers as one example, the opening number, "Fantastic Voyage," whose "Lydian I-II-#V" is "representative." On the album, "only the voice syncopates, and the opposition between voice and frantic backing . . . remains strong, as on 'Look Back in Anger.'"[22] In later albums, like *Let's Dance*, more pop-song crafting and outside influence is apparent.

One way to look at the changes in Bowie's approach to music is to see how difficult it is to separate his music's compositional structure from studio production. As Theodore Gracyk argues, rock music in general is impossible to separate from its link to the studio.[23] That is, rock music may be the first type of music to be made for sound recording. It is impossible to divorce a rock song from its literal origins on magnetic tape (or hard drive). Rock concerts are an attempt to play live music that was created in the process of mixing. Acoustic depth, musical harmony, singing—all of the parts of a rock song are actually created via the studio, or can be. The actual recording of the music itself is but one part of the total finished product that we might consider the album version of a song. While obviously composition and skill at playing and singing are extremely important to the creation of the work itself, they are also, depending upon the song, not necessarily central to it. Rock recording does not usually attempt an accurate recording of a finished acoustical work. It is not field recording, which is what most classical, blues, or jazz records are. It is the attempt to synthesize musical instruments with studio production techniques to create a whole that is greater than its parts.

It is clear that Bowie realizes this fact especially with the transition to his "Berlin" period of albums (that is, *Low*, "*Heroes*," and *Lodger*). Using the studio as an instrument, Bowie learned from Brian Eno and others—especially the synthesized Krautrock of Edgar Froese (Tangerine Dream), Klaus Dinger (of Neu!), and La Düsseldorf—that the studio could be used to create a democratizing of effect in which instruments, sounds, and voice could be made equally central to a song's structure.[24] Electronic music, whatever it might take away from skill and solid songwriting technique, brought to music a sonic landscape that allowed the rock musician (or creative producer) to work with a far larger palette via the studio. Arguably, for the first time, rock musicians had available to them the vast landscape of effects available heretofore only to classical composers. It is not surprising that Bowie was increasingly drawn during the initial Berlin phase to writing lyric-less instrumentals and pieces that combine stately "serious" writing, whether influenced by Japanese or European classicism. Bowie felt free to combine effects in a new way—not toward the end point of a hit song, but as a way to test the bounds of creative expression. If the songs on *Hunky Dory* are a pastiche of references to other artists—Dylan, the Velvet Underground, et al.—on the albums of the latter half of the twentieth century, Bowie's references to musicians and artists in other media expanded greatly to include new cultures, new types and modes of music historically, and attempted to place rock music in dialogue with many other types of music than it normally ever intersected. While the "prog rock" music of the sixties and seventies could certainly be said to take itself seriously, Bowie's "art rock" of the late seventies pushed beyond classical music to search for a way to create effects that were not only genuinely personal and idiosyncratic, but innovative as well.

While much of Bowie's music is comprised of effects associated with the studio—one might say producers' manipulation of sound, from Phil Specter to George Martin to, of course, Eno's ambient systems—Bowie was reversing tape loops and guitar parts since before Eno's influence on him. Bowie's work obviously builds on Steve Reich and Philip Glass (and others), but it seems to take on a different character in rock music, where it is rarely used as a serial end point. Eno tends to use music as atmosphere—in a Cage-like way, no sound is really in the foreground, none is more important than another—but ultimately Bowie does not. He uses ambient techniques for more traditional rock-and-roll purposes. Eno, perhaps, does seem to make Bowie focus more on music without lyrics—the B-sides of *Low* and *"Heroes,"* for example—but it would be inaccurate to say that any one of Bowie's albums is purely ambient. What he perhaps gets most from Eno is the importance of studio production to the composition of the album as a whole. That is, in considering his work as well as that of any other rock musicians, one must, to some extent, dislink performance from production. One might ask who the author is: Bowie, the producer, the musicians, or the studio (Sigma is supposed to have had a big effect on *Young Americans* and Hansa on *"Heroes,"* for example)?

That the synthesizer would be the instrument at the forefront of this change might seem counterintuitive at first. It could be seen as the antithesis of traditional music—a machine aping the effects of acoustic instruments but without their materiality, their warmth, imperfection, and personality. Synthesizers shift music from place to space, removing music from architecture and instrumentality to complete the transition to a virtual format that is promised by rock music's essentially electronic form.[25] The seeds of the synthesizer are there in the electric guitar and the taping booth. The synthesizer is the logical conclusion of rock music. For Bowie and Eno and other avatars of the future, the synthesizer was exciting because of the plastic possibilities it seemed to open up. Tony Visconti, Bowie's frequent producer, exclaimed that the Eventide Harmonizer synthesizer used on the album *"Heroes"* "fucked with the fabric of time."[26] Certainly, the synthesizer opened up new possibilities for Eno to reproduce the work of Steve Reich and to create loops and systems through which to process acoustic and electric instruments and to combine them with synthesized ones as well. Before the advent of digital recording and the use of personal computers to manipulate voice and sound, synthesizers represented a new way to create an almost infinite number of sounds and to utilize delay and playback possibilities that would have been cumbersome, if not impossible, without it. With the invention of the Moog synthesizer in the 1960s, the synthesizer as an instrument slowly came into its own. If one remembers the wheezy electric organ used in early Doors songs like "Light My Fire," the synthesizer was a much-needed keyboard update. By the early 1970s it had become an important instrument of its own in the hands of Wendy (Walter) Carlos, who wrote not only "A Fifth of Beethoven" but translated several baroque and classical pieces into arresting synthesized "futuristic" music for Stanley Kubrick's *A Clockwork Orange* (1971).[27] In this case, the novelty of combining classical music with the then cutting-edge technology of the synthesizer allowed for the juxtaposition of old content with new form to show the sturdiness of the former and the clean, hard-edged possibility of the latter. The harshness of the synthesizer could be used as a foil to bring out the brightness of baroque music, especially the architectonic structure of Bach's music as can be seen in Carlos' *Switched-On Bach* (1968).

Bowie's use of the synthesizer moved from the somewhat spare use of it on *Low*, an album, for all of its influence, that combined electronic techniques such as the gated snare and the synthesized back beat with harmonica and other instruments that emphasized the imprint of the human body. This high/low approach gives the album warmth, almost as though we are hearing American country or road music reinterpreted as modernist shards. The recurring theme of alienation on the album is belied by the extremely emotional content of the songs—not so much in the lyrics as in the music itself. Much of this effect can probably be credited to Visconti, who had the biggest influence on the sound of *Low*, *"Heroes,"* and *Scary Monsters*. (Eno seems triumphant on *Lodger*.) Though many critics have often debated who was really calling the shots, Eno's role, except on *Lodger*, seems to have been more conceptual or compositional rather than in terms of production. Like Eno, Visconti was interested in the manipulation of the synthesizer with other instruments and the addition of treatments and found sound. This sort of Musique Concrète reaches its peak of complexity on Bowie's recordings on *Scary Monsters*, where the layers of sounds made up of textures and devices, from recording an acoustic piano through an Eventide Instant Flanger or a guitar synthesizer in a stairwell, the production lends the album a complicated, subtle sonic density that becomes as important to an individual track's success as any other aspect of it.[28]

While Visconti was the key producer of Bowie's albums after Ken Scott and other than the important contribution of Nile Rodgers on *Let's Dance* and *Black Tie, White Noise* (1993), Eno's influence was significant and reaches a peak with Bowie's *Outside* in 1995. More than anything, Eno may have changed Bowie's approach to making new music. He brought with him an alternative tradition of music that dates back at least as far as French composer Érik Satie, who introduced the idea of "furniture music," music that would be ignored or purposefully talked over by the audience—like a backdrop to the main action or like furniture in a room.[29] Satie's idea seems to owe a great deal to Claude Debussy, the most famous of the "Impressionist" composers, whose compositions were criticized for their static nature, for staying still as though they were musical versions of still-life paintings.[30] This failure to advance the melody, of leaving a work to function like a still-point in time, always returning to the same spot, was shocking for its day. Satie took this direction further by creating music that he purposefully wanted to be ignored. He had already created an early version of Muzak, and in that sense had laid the foundation for what would later be termed *ambient* music.[31] A crucial element in this new type of music was boredom. His work *Vexations* (1893) consisted of eighty seconds of music repeated 840 times.[32] Like Andy Warhol's *Empire* (1964) where the audience spends eight hours with one stationery shot of the Empire State Building, Satie forces the audience to think seriously about what constitutes music and what constitutes environment, architectural and social.

Perhaps Satie's greatest work was his collaboration with Pablo Picasso and Jean Cocteau for Sergei Diaghilev's ballet *Parade* (1917), which incorporated "found" sounds such as automobile horns, and a later ballet with Francis Picabia, *Relâche* (1924), which included a silent film as a part of the performance.[33] Both productions were collaborations that were prescient examples of avant-garde *Gesamkunskwerke*. The latter seemed to look ahead to multimedia events such as Bowie's own use of Luis Buñuel's *Un Chien Andalou* (1929) on his Isolar tour in the mid-seventies, while the former emphasized the Dadaistic chance operations ten years before there was a name for them. In both instances, Satie's work with environmental sound and chance operations paved the way for the monumental vision of John Cage, who also worked with collaborators from other arts at the Black Mountain College in North Carolina in the 1950s. By then, Cage had already experimented with music "composed" of multiple radios in 1942. He went on to work with magnetic tape in 1952 and televisions by 1959.[34] He was, in other words, the first composer to create truly electronic music. In a speech in 1937, he prophesied that one day there would be an electronic music that could create any possible sound—what we might today call the synthesizer.[35] As he noted in 1954, "If the word 'music' is sacred and reserved for eighteenth- and nineteenth-century instruments, we can substitute a more meaningful term: organization of sound."[36] It is precisely this movement from music to sound that inaugurated a true revolution in how we might think of music, from structure to soundscape. Increasingly interested in Asian philosophy and musical traditions, Cage eventually ignored structure completely, creating works, such as *4' 33"* (1952), that suggested the total absence of generated sound in favor of the chance operations of the aural environment. Cage famously blamed Western music's lack of growth on Beethoven, who championed and perfected the notion of melody. In its place, to his mind, should be put Satie's much superior notion of time.[37]

In the work of Debussy, Satie, and Cage, music finally achieves a completely egalitarian dimension. No one element of a musical piece is any more important than another. As Mark Prendergast notes, they allowed for a movement from music performed in a space "towards music as an immersive, environmental experience."[38] By the time of Eno, tape machines, and now computers, altered our notion of time—all music becomes present once it is recorded. In a sense, Eno's work takes music out of time and places it in space instead.[39] It spatializes time. His experiments with technology ultimately resulted in "generative" music (such as "Bloom" for iPad and mobile phones) in which computer algorithms could generate music on their own or in response to random human interactions. One logical continuation of this experimentation is the notion of DJs as composers. Already working the postmodern pastiche of found sounds, they have morphed into major authors of their own music constructed almost completely from the work of others—whether Moby or, more recently, Girl Talk.[40]

Like Cage, Eno claimed not to read music. What he brought to Bowie generally, as Cage's inheritor, however, was more than just philosophical or conceptual. By pushing at the notion of the studio as an instrument, Eno arguably displaced live music altogether in favor of machines. At the very least, live music was made clearly only one component of the total system that was involved in the making of recorded music. As Eno wrote for the back of his influential album *Discreet Music* (1975), "Since I have always preferred making plans to executing them, I have gravitated towards situations and systems that, once set into operation, could create music with little or no intervention on my part. That is to say, I tend towards the roles of planner and programmer, and then become an audience to the results." In the case of this album, an actual "group of performers" perform portions of the Pachelbel Canon, which is played through a synthesizer, manipulated via a graphic equalizer and echo unit, and then recorded on two tape recorders, one with a delay line that feeds back to the first recorder. The resulting mix is the main output. Technologically, Eno developed numerous similar systems that would defamilarize sound and music and create ghostly senses of landscape or mindscape that often seemed familiar—as topography or memory, for example—but that was genuinely startling in its lack of cognates within the world of Western music. From a purely musical standpoint, the key to Eno's development is as an inheritor of Serialism. He combined the notion of stripping away any unnecessary material with the repetition of minimalism such as one finds in Reich's music and that of Philip Glass, the latter a major experimenter in his own right when it comes to combining the traditions of classical and popular music.[41] Eno combined these primarily classical interests with his own early work in Glam Rock via Roxy Music to create music that would be, as he put it, "as ignorable as it is interesting."[42] In ambient music, Eno helped to further the tradition of music as non-narrative. Not only does his music emphasize the spatial, but he composes by "tak[ing] sounds and chang[ing] them into words."[43] A process he says is "the exact opposite of the technique used in phonetic poetry where words are changed into pure sounds."[44] When Eno did include lyrics—used throughout his first four solo albums in the 1970s, only to vanish until the 1990s—his methodology was described by one reviewer of his second album, *Taking Tiger Mountain (By Strategy)* (1974), as "compos[ed] the same way William Burroughs writes: with a splicing scissor."[45]

As Simon Frith and Howard Horne note, "Musicians (using opportunities opened up by the development of magnetic tape recording and multi-tracking) began to make music as bricolage, quoting from other work, incorporating 'real' sounds, recontextualizing familiar sonic symbols."[46] While composers have always quoted from each other's work, the extreme *bricolage* effect of the Sex Pistols, like postmodernism itself, built upon pop art in an attempt to stitch together remnants of culture—popular and otherwise—to create something new. To take the detritus and construct a new kind of fake whole cloth that still, in its attitude and conceptualization, becomes something new. Repurposing culture in this way was part of what Eno himself accomplished. While all of Bowie's songs reverberate with references to the history of popular music, Eno created music from the found pieces of other times and places, reconfiguring not styles of music but sound. In Eno's hands, the sonic landscape is reduced to something other than recognizable quotes from other styles, and instead becomes atomized and reassembled as something fresh and new. These four albums had a great effect on Bowie, who claims to have enjoyed Eno's masterpiece, *Another Green World* (1975), especially. When Eno was brought in for the Berlin triptych, Bowie wanted to create, with the second album, *"Heroes,"* the only one actually recorded in Berlin, "an 'album for the future.'"[47] Bowie saw this futurity in the dance electronica that disco would later morph into (including his own *Earthling* [1997]). Eno provided the intellectual ballast. His *Music for Airports* (1978) perhaps suggesting more than any of his other explicitly ambient albums a "non-place" (Marc Augé), a version of the future that was totally spatial—the logical conclusion of Satie's experiments.

Eno's work with Talking Heads on *Fear of Music* (1979) owes as much to Krautrock as to Eno's own early ambient experiments.[48] It also contains an actual phonetic poem, Hugo Ball's Dadaist "I Zimbra," set to music.[49] Eno's best work with the band would be the magisterial *Remain in Light* (1980), which combined African polyrhythm percussion and layered, horizontal structures with the Heads' usual obsessions with everyday objects, environments, and social issues. Eno was to go on to help with Byrne's scoring of a Twyla Tharp ballet, the underpraised album *The Catherine Wheel* (1981), and the groundbreaking *My Life in the Bush of Ghosts* (1981). The latter was an apotheosis of sorts for Eno. Perhaps never was he able to experiment with the studio as an instrument as he was able to with Byrne on this project. The album's singing is made up entirely of voices, many taken from the radio in the San Francisco Bay area, that Eno captured on tape. They vary from an exorcism, to a sermon by a Pentecostal preacher, to an Algerian chanting from the "Qur'an" on a track by the same name that was deleted from the album after the first pressing. What Eno learned from this experience certainly helped to prepare him for *Remain in Light*, an album that not only forged first- and third-world musics, but also merged DJ-centric dance music with the call-and-response complexity of African drumming. As Sheppard explains:

> The mono-chordal backings meant melodies would have to be teased out and wound around the immutably modal frameworks. The only way a separation between verse and chorus could be achieved was by exploiting the "interlocking parts" . . . dropping a section of instruments for a set number of bars, then modifying the vocal line over the same segment, aping the way horn sections punctuated a Fela Kuti song, or the way guitars glided in and out in small formations on the records of another Nigerian musical eminence beloved of David Byrne, juju superstar King Sunny Adé.[50]

Byrne used the same method as Eno in his approach to writing the lyrics—sounding them out to match the music's beats.[51] Eno and the Heads achieved a huge success with the album, cementing Eno's reputation as a consummate artistic partner for other musicians, and building on his work with Bowie in Europe. Eno's success in the pop arena was only the shadow project of an arguably equally as important series of recordings that he made as the "Ambient" and "Fourth World" series with John Hassell and Daniel Lanois, among others. These works, almost unfailingly subtle and richly experimental, pushed at the boundary of avant-garde music, forging a link between popular and classical music every bit as impressively as Eno's work with Bowie and Byrne.[52]

What Eno creates, and Bowie builds upon, is for a time what Umberto Eco refers to as "open texts," works that are not complete without certain decisions being made by the performer or the listener. Eco uses as examples Karlheinz Stockhausen's *Kalvierstück XI* (1956), Luciano Berio's *Sequence for Solo Flute* (1958), Henri Pousseur's *Scambi* (1957), and Pierre Boulez's *Third Sonata for Piano* (1963)—pieces that are, as he says, left "incomplete" by the composers and that require the players to decide in what order something should be played, or in some other way, how they will sound. To some extent, this tradition points up the reality of all music. As he argues:

> A work of art, therefore, is a complete and *closed* form in its uniqueness as a balanced organic whole, while at the same time constituting an *open* product on account of its susceptibility to countless different interpretations which do not impinge on its unadulterable specificity. Hence every reception of a work of art is both an *interpretation* and a *performance* of it, because in every reception the work takes on a fresh perspective for itself.[53]

"Openness" might be the word we give to interpretability, or productive ambiguity, to use a more New Critical term. But Eco pushes on the line that blurs most art from art that requires closure to be constructed by the reader, viewer, or listener. Later in the essay, he focuses on serial music, to note that

> the multiple polarity of a serial composition in music, where the listener is not faced by an absolute conditioning center of reference, requires him to constitute his own center of reference, requires him to constitute his own system of auditory relationships. He must allow such a center to emerge from the sound continuum. Here are no privileged points of view, and all available perspectives are equally valid and rich in potential.[54]

As with Eno's work, music in this vein creates its own boundaries and is ever changing and new.

What Eco's musings look ahead to presciently, as does Bowie's work by the Ziggy period, is the notion that this musical tradition is actually the harbinger of a new approach to art itself, a realignment of the relationship between the artist and the artist's public. As Eco concludes:

> Certainly this new receptive mode vis-à-vis the work of art opens up a much vaster phase in culture and in this sense is not intellectually confined to the problem of aesthetics. The poetics of the *work in movement* . . . sets in motion a new cycle of relations between the artist and his audience, a new mechanics of aesthetic perception, a different status for the artistic product in contemporary society. It opens a new page in sociology and in pedagogy, as well as a new chapter in the history of art. It poses new practical problems by organizing new communicative situations. In short, it installs a new relationship between the *contemplation* and the *utilization* of a work of art.[55]

The song is never complete until the fan completes it. Bowie places the text in the public realm, but invites fans to interpret it, just as he does, via the videos for the singles, album cover, concert performances, dance remixes via other artists, covers of his old songs, etc. The fan and the artist are now locked in a mutual performance—"give me your hands"—that with Bowie is always already self-conscious and performative and calls attention not just to the intermixing of the star and the fan, their dependency upon each other for meaning, but also the way in which culture in general is changing to become one in which the fan must take the matrix of signifiers that Bowie produces and sort out the meanings in a field of their own defining. We are all artists now.

The concept album

For many, Bowie's *Ziggy Stardust* album might well seem like the apotheosis of the concept album. Looked at carefully, however, the album's overall concept does not really hold up. While the songwriting and performance are certainly singular, especially in terms of the sexual subject matter, which was and still is innovative, the album is not the coherent space opera that it promises in its title and in the content of many of its songs. It is important to keep in mind that Bowie is not Ziggy, but it is also important to understand, obviously, that the album is about a rock star sung by a rock star so it is also extremely self-referential. Bowie has said that he did not intend for there to be a lot of emphasis in the album on concept, but clearly there are at the very least scraps of various ideas at play and the album's musical allusions seem to deal directly with the history of rock in such a way that the album seems to make a sweeping, summative statement about the 1960s—to be a sort of 1970s version of *Sgt. Pepper* (1967), which is obvious in the repetition of the last chords of that album on Bowie's. Overall, the album is unconventional in structure and subject matter, but sounds conventional. If it is about anything, it is sexual ambiguity, yet that message is delivered in the form of very hard rock. The album is a paradox, and much more difficult to pin down than it might at first seem. The album is profound in its ability to link ideas about alienness—in terms of science fiction, sexual outsider, and rock—with the notion of rock star as god, alien being, and his acolytes, his fans. The rock star formula has never been so thoroughly constructed and deconstructed as on this album. But while the album contains many layers that fit well together and enhance the meaning, they tend to fall apart when seen as one coherent narrative. There are too many contradictions and question marks—the concept does not hold, though it is itself a convenient metaphor for the type of open-ended meaning making that are Bowie's and Ziggy's strengths as artists.

Most of the albums that Bowie was to go on to complete after *Ziggy Stardust* were nominally concept albums as well. Although he gave up that idea in the albums after the twentieth century, each of his albums has always been distinctly different from any other and the notion of an overarching concept has never been completely done away with. For the remainder of the seventies, in particular, Bowie seemed to attempt to perfect the idea of a concept album. A few examples would include *Aladdin Sane* (1973), which was written while on tour in the United States during the Ziggy concerts. The album is notable for Mike Garson's piano playing—from experimental jazz to the use of "stride" piano—and for its dislocation in time and space (especially the former). It is sort of a follow-up to *Ziggy*, but not really. The locales on the album include New York, the desert West, Detroit, New Orleans, London. In terms of places in time, the album includes the future ("Drive-In Saturday"); the here and now ("Panic in Detroit"); and during the first years of the two world wars ("Aladdin Sane"). While these displacements echo the effect of seeing America for the first time, the album perhaps follows the game plan of *Ziggy* too closely—from "Jean Genie" as "Suffragette" to "Lady Grinning Soul" as "Rock and Roll Suicide" and its own theme of decadence never completely gels.[56] Two years on, *Young Americans* would bring Bowie's long bout with glam rock to an abrupt end and suggest a strikingly different idea of what a concept could mean for Bowie. It contains two songs influenced by John Lennon; the first recording by Luther Vandross ("Fascination"); and the producers (Kenny Gamble and Leon Huff) at Sigma Sound. Bowie later termed the album "Plastic soul." "Fascination"/"Right"/"Somebody Up There Likes Me"/"Across the Universe"/"Can You Hear Me" follow: five slow songs in a row that begin to sound the same—aural wallpaper, or the feeling that we are getting a black nightclub performance done too seriously. This is not Bowie's most compelling music and seems to come close to becoming generic mood music. The album ends with "Fame," his first big hit in the United States. The song became a dance song; won a Grammy; and was a huge hit in black music groups. "Fame" contains a riff by Carlos Alomar, who used to play in James Brown's band. This song represents one of Bowie's most successful compositions. Everything comes together rhythmically with the syncopation between the drums, bass, guitar. It is by far the most original song on the album and ends up creating, along with the title track, a frame that is stronger than the work that it contains.

The fusion of a black rhythm section and his own brittle experimentation continues and deepens on *Station to Station*, which is, without any doubt a major change in Bowie's career and a sort of 'missing link' between the Philly Soul and the Berlin trilogy. In the first song, Bowie seems to be turning his back on the United States to announce a new "European canon." Yet the album is full of energy and, especially, confidence and sureness of touch. The album may ultimately be an odd blend of the occult and the religious in terms of subject matter, but it creates its own genre (much like "Fame") in terms of its musicality. The title seems to refer to Stations of the Cross, Kabbalah, radio, and TV. The album could be seen to retell the story of the Nicholas Roeg film that Bowie starred in the same year, *The Man Who Fell to Earth*.

One could go on to look at the intertwining effects on any one of Bowie's subsequent albums and how all of them contain effects that build upon the desire to create densely structured music that contains echoes and allusions to a wide range of music from the past—from British music hall to musical theater as represented on variety television shows to the history of rock, especially. By the 1990s Bowie's own success began to catch up with him and the allusions and connections were increasingly to his own music, especially as it seemed to crowd out more and more of other influences in popular music and to take up more and more space as the origin for music coming from younger musicians. By the time that Bowie got to *Earthling* in 1996, for example, he was referencing his own gender bending on "Hallo Spaceboy" ("do you like girls or boys? It's confusing these days"). At around this time, he even made a minimalist trip-hop version of his own "The Man Who Sold the World." Though probably in reaction to Nirvana's live version, Bowie's version might strike one as purposefully perverse. It is a cover that manages both to act as a homage to the original and to deconstruct it as well. Bowie completely rethinks the song and plays with our expectations of the original. The relationship between the words and the music are markedly different from the original version. Not surprisingly, as part of the lineup for his 1995 tour with Trent Reznor, it was performed on the MTV European video awards and reflects his experimental work on *Outside*. Likewise, "Seven Years in Tibet" on *Earthling* shows not only an interest in electronica, but perhaps how the style used to rethink "Sold the World" can also be made into something more fun. The Euro-minimalist form of the previous song—and album—are here transformed into something that attempts to be both more accessible and referential in a different way (in this case, to his album *Scary Monsters*). The song reflects both his political interests (he recorded a version in Mandarin) and his interest in technology as well.

To better understand Bowie's approach to songwriting we can look at one particularly successful and ambitious song, "Ashes to Ashes" from *Scary Monsters*. Conceptually the album holds together—when others, like *Ziggy*, which pretends to be a rewrite of Kurt Weil's *The Rise and Fall of the City of Mahagonny* (1930), do not. This does not mean that the album is linear with parts of an unfolding narrative about a character, which *Ziggy* purports to be, but that, like that album, *Scary Monsters* fits together thematically and imagistically, with all of the songs linked. In many ways this song epitomizes Bowie's attempt to stretch the medium of pop song writing as far as it can go and to bring his arsenal of effects to bear on the situation in such a way as to achieve an intended effect as opposed to replaying a successful formula. Although one might say that the song contains discrete sections (an intro-verse-prechorous-chorus), it is written as one continuous progression whose form represents Bowie's take on his own career and life. It develops, morphs, and has a climax ("hitting an all-time low," which comes at the highest melody notes—a counterintuitive rhetorical approach).[57] The song is layered, haunted, and mirrors the complexity of the album as a whole.

The song itself is like the echo of something you would tell a child, or a warning to yourself from the future, a going back in time. The song seems at times to stutter, as Bowie's characters do throughout the album, and to call attention to its own construction. It is a wind-up toy with a broken gear. The wheezy calliope-like mock-organ, created using a treated recording of a grand piano, has a chugging sound that makes the song seem both old-fashioned and futuristic at the same time, off-kilter and slightly ill. Asymmetry and elision are part of the introduction. A standard breakdown of the music (Am/G/Dm/Am/G/Dm//Em) suggests the song is a four-bar structure repeated five times, an unusual asymmetric structure. Key changes are at "Do you remember a guy that's been," "They got a message from the action man," "The shrieking of nothing is killing," "Ashes to ashes, funk to funky." The intro chords come back with "Hitting an all-time low" at the end. The chorus goes back to the first fundamental starting chord of the first pre-chorus. It is almost an anti-chorus in the sense that you get longer note values; the song's melodic structure stretches out and slows down. You have a sense of everything building to the chorus and then the chorus is laid back—strung out or numbed. The song creates a unique tension. You want the structure to propel you forward like a rock song, but it keeps going somewhere new. When you have gotten to the chorus you have completely forgotten about the unusual opening, and then the song sends you back to it. Each section changes—has some sort of subtle difference, especially in the background. As in all rock songs, there is sonic development, not thematic, but each section takes us further and further away from the opening only to return to it.

As Alexander Carpenter argues, Bowie's song comes out of a tradition of *commedia*. By 1884 the Pierrot figure had become, in Albert Geraud's last Pierrot poem, "the poet himself."[58] As Giraud writes: "I've dressed as Pierrot/To offer her whom I love/A ray of moonlight closed up."[59] The poet and Pierrot are the same speaker, as Bowie is in "Ashes to Ashes." As Carpenter goes on to note, Paul Verlaine, in his 1868 poem, "Pierrot," makes Pierrot into "a spectral, bloodless wraith, with eyes of burning phosphorous."[60] The moonlight of Giraud and the eyes in Verlaine also seem to look forward to the "eyes of green burning bright" of "Cat People" and the "serious moonlight" of "Let's Dance" on the next album of the same name. Schoenberg referred to art as "moon spots on our clothing" and "our power to sacrifice our lives to a moonbeam."[61] Carpenter's thesis is that Bowie's version of Pierrot shares many thematic and structural concerns of Schoenberg's *Pierrot Luniare*, Op. 21 (1912). The latter, like Bowie's song, speaks with multiple voices, but is arguably more unified (if also significantly shorter). At the heart of Schoenberg's melodrama, unifying these strands, is an autobiographical core: "Schoenberg's melodrama is a reflection upon both his musical and personal history, and it is not biographical fallacy to see Schoenberg assuming, contingently, the paradoxical guise of Pierrot himself."[62] Bowie's song similarly deals with multiple voices linked to autobiography. The back of the album cover shows the album covers for all of Bowie's Berlin period albums. *Scary Monsters*, this suggests, is a fusion of them as well, perhaps, as an escape from them. More pointedly, the song looks back to Bowie's original breakthrough hit, "Space Oddity," and resurrects Major Tom. This character is pointedly criticized. He is no longer the existential hero of the first song but has instead become a "junky strung-out on heaven's high seeking an all-time low." While the protagonist of the original song was hardly a hero in the usual sense—he gets into outer space but then seems trapped "in a tin can" and looks back to earth in a plaintively melancholy way—"planet Earth is blue and there's nothing I can do." The astronaut seems left in space, perhaps to end his life there ("tell my wife I love her very much"). In this aspect, the song seems to reflect its inspiration in Kubrick's *2001* (1968) more than in the possibility of space flight itself (it was written before the manned moon landing) and its rather sad, against-the-grain version of space travel echoes the strains of Aram Khachaturian's *Gayayne Ballet Suite* (*Adagio*) (1942) on Kubrick's soundtrack and his ambivalent prognosis of what space travel might really be like—lonely, technocratic, sterile, and dangerous.

Bowie's remake of "Space Oddity" nominally recasts Major Tom, but only to be able to use him as a stand-in for Bowie himself. As with Schoenberg, Bowie uses voices to express an essentially autobiographical story. Bowie is the junky, addicted to cocaine to a dangerous degree from 1974 to 1976 and at other times beyond those years. He replaced cocaine with alcohol in the later 1970s and clung to cigarettes until his heart attack in 2004. Always an addictive personality, Bowie was healthier in 1980, though far from completely free of the personal demons that he wrote about—the "little green wheels" that follow him still. At one level the song's lyrics are about his character, at another drug addiction, at another still a new character, a sci-fi Pierrot, who is lost in an inner if not an outer space. The multiple voices are echoed in the choric aspects of the song and in Bowie's schizophrenic doubling of his own voice—he sings the lyrics and then repeats them, one step behind, in a resigned spoken voice as though he is a shadow of his own self. As its cover suggests, Bowie appears on the album as a character and as a doppelganger, a dark twin, suggested by his brother Terry, perhaps, but also by Bowie's own dark and light halves. Indeed, on the cover, Bowie is shown not as Pierrot in full makeup, but as himself in partial makeup, smoking a cigarette. Bowie is, in other words, shown as Bowie playing Pierrot, perhaps taking a break from the performance. Pierrot is not as central to the album as the autobiographical story Bowie is trying to tell.

As Carpenter notes, the autobiographical aspect of *Pierrot Lunaire* focused on the representation of a love triangle that in real life consists of him, his unfaithful wife Mathilde, and "Richard Gerstl, the young painter who was Schoenberg's rival for his

Figure 3.1   Cover of *Scary Monsters (and Super Creeps)*, 1980.

wife's affections."[63] This threesome was a variation on the traditional Pierrot-Columbine-Harlequin triangle of the commedia tradition except this grouping existed to express Schoenberg's "psychological distress."[64] For Bowie, the reference to Pierrot actually predates "Space Oddity" and goes back to 1967 when he appeared in performances of a pantomime created by Lindsay Kemp, *Pierrot in Turquoise* (1967), which was filmed for Scottish television.[65] Bowie played the character of Cloud, who literally floats above the action and sings songs of Bowie's composition. Down on the ground, Kemp plays Pierrot who loses Columbine to Harlequin. This plotting follows the usual commedia formula, with Kemp giving himself the plum tragic role. While Bowie does not seem to have this sad love story in mind per se, the melodrama of lost love seems, to some extent, to get picked up by the array of characters that Bowie references—as though he has become, or played, all of the parts through the years and the result is always the same. Lurking beneath the lyrics is the even more subtle suggestion that the song is also about Bowie's loss of his marriage to Angela Barnett. While arguably an open marriage, it would have been one of the many scary monsters that Bowie was dealing with on the album—along with drug abuse, another large, difficult piece of personal psychological baggage from the late seventies. His final divorce came through the same year that the album debuted.

Carpenter points out that an alternative definition of Schoenberg's intentions in his piece is that it is essentially not about autobiography as it is art itself. Specifically, that it is about the distancing irony of fin-de-siècle Vienna, a reference that can be seen in the frequent use of waltzes in the piece.[66] If so, then further parallels with Bowie's song can be seen, as it is the most self-consciously artistic song on Bowie's most self-consciously artistic album—both of them being about Bowie's own artistic production over the course of the seventies. But if this train of thought is correct about Schoenberg, the Viennese parallels might bring us back to the Freudianism of late-nineteenth-century Vienna, the Dmitri Shostakovich *Suite for Variety Orchestra* (post-1956) that begins and ends Kubrick's *Eyes Wide Shut* (1999), which replays Viennese tropes in a contemporary American setting. Freudian psychology would still be present as the dominant way to interpret both Schoenberg's and Bowie's art. For Bowie, the Viennese connection could also reference Berlin between the world wars, which is the real subject of Bowie's Berlin albums. Carpenter ultimately concludes that *Pierrot Lunaire* deals not merely with irony and detachment, but "rather, a paradoxical blend of both detachment and unmediated self-examination and self-expression. For Schoenberg, Pierrot's is a momentary but necessary mask: it is the modern artists' mask of extravagance . . . to be sure, but behind the mask of Pierrot we find the artist irresolute."[67] For both Schoenberg and Bowie, Pierrot becomes "an archetypal hysteric-androgyne—a hybrid of sorts, without clearly defined gender, struggling to express himself."[68] While Bowie may not be living through a crisis of male hysteria, it is unwise to underestimate the character he has dawned, the final mask that references all his others in its heightened theatricality, yet by remaining the most mute, also seems the most expressive, personal, and poignant.

In the video for the song, which arguably remains to this day as the most influential and important music video ever created, Bowie further multiplies the characters on the album and the story that the album tells. The video begins with Bowie as Pierrot, looking directly at the audience and holding up a tiny mirror, which is also, perhaps, a sort of movie screen, on which "a guy in such another song" appears. We immediately understand from this gesture that the video will itself contain a story within a story, and that the video, like the song, will be a text about other texts—a self-conscious interpretation.

"Ashes to Ashes" is the most self-conscious song on an already extremely self-conscious album. Containing as it does the framing device of "It's No Game" parts one and two, the album features some of Bowie's most innovative work in terms of song structure, guitar playing, and suggestive lyrics that stitch together an extremely complex thematics that have to do with personal and political revolution. The album manages to keep the edginess of Bowie's work on the Berlin albums with a new forthright ideological anger—at politicians, cultural change, generational shifts—that is refreshing in its bluntness. An extremely effective album, it is the sine qua non of Bowie's attempts at a dense texture as well as at an album whose many elements reflect and refract each other. In the opening song, "It's No Game (No. 1)," Bowie sings, "to be insulted by these fascists is so degrading it's not game." His pronunciation on "fascists" drags the syllables out and blurs the "sts" at the end of the word with "is so" that it moves into. The effect is the same sort of stutter that shows up throughout the album but that also causes the listener to hear some of the sounds as separate and distinct from their context to add the sense that what we are listening to has an actual materiality—a fact called attention to by the album beginning and ending with the sound of the audio recording tape recorded winding through its spool (and Bowie's cuing the band: "One two, one two two. . ."). As in Ingmar Bergman's *Persona* (1966), which begins and ends with the camera film running through its shutter, Bowie is making an album about the process of making an album—a work of art that is about the limits of the medium, of the self-consciousness of art. As in Bergman's film, which also references the Vietnam war, Bowie's is an engaged work of art that sees the personae of the album frustrated by outside forces at work politically and culturally to attack or contain them. On "It's No Game" Bowie also sings, "I throw a rock against the road and it breaks into pieces." The last word, like the image it creates, breaks apart into another slowed down stuttering separating of syllables, echoing the one on "fascists." The image of rocks breaking—of heads being broken—shows up throughout the album.

The song that begins shortly thereafter, "Up the Hill Backwards," is a completely reworked version of a song originally written in 1973. In this incarnation Bowie sticks with the idea of political and literal violence—"a series of shocks sneakers fall apart." Later he intones, "we're legally crippled/it's the death of love." We next move into the title song, which is the darkest on the album. Sung in a mock-Cockney accent that Bowie has used at times since the 1960s and with occasional electronic treatment to thicken it added on, it deals with mental instability ("I looked in her eyes they were blue but nobody home"), paranoia ("she had an horror of rooms"), and "strange doors we'd never close again." This last reference could be anything from Aldous Huxley's doors of perception to, perhaps, Lovecraftian horror, but the landscape is the bleakest until Bowie's *Outside* fifteen years later and plays up the emphasis throughout the album on violence and something being at stake.

The first side continues with the magnificent "Ashes to Ashes," a song that itself, in its own structure, seems fragile and about to break apart. The side ends with the sardonic "Fashion," which turns going to a dance hall into a political statement with Bowie shouting "turn to the left, turn to the right" and, "We are the goon squad and we're coming to town." The song pushes its repetitive percussion to the forefront in a parody of a disco beat gone bad. His more pointed criticism of culture begins here on the album as he notes, "It's loud and tasteless and I've heard it before."[69] This sentiment is picked up on the first song of the second side, "Teenage Wildlife," which expands upon the imagery of the first side with longer, more sweeping tracks like this one. "Teenage Wildlife" contains the biting lyrics "A broken nosed mogul are you/one of the new wave boys//same old thing in brand new drag/comes sweeping into view, oh-ooh/as ugly as a teenage millionaire/pretending/it's a whizz kid world." In this affront to eighties youth, Bowie mentions the hunt for "pieces of gold" and, later, in the voice of said youth, "I'm not a piece of teenage wildlife." The image of pieces, and of being struck down ("you fall to the ground/like a leaf from the tree"), echoes the first side of the album. In terms of cultural influence, he obviously feels empowered to talk. The side continues with "Scream Like a Baby," Bowie's most explicitly protest-like of any of his songs with the possible exception of "Panic in Detroit." Another song that is a reboot of a much earlier but never used composition, Bowie creates a speaker who, like Sam, is caught up in a kind of dragnet in the future. The brutality used against Sam is painted in frightening pictures: "Well they came down hard on the faggots/and they came down hard on the street/they came down harder on Sam/and they all knew he was beat/he was thrown into the wagon/ blindfolded, chains,/and they stomped on us/and took away our clothes and things/ and pumped us full of strange drugs/and oh I saw Sam falling/spitting in their eyes." On the word "spitting" Bowie once again uses a staggered dissonance, drawing the word out and repeating the effect later in the song when the speaker says, apparently under the effects of the drugs, "Now I'm learning/to be a part of soc-society." The speaker has a great deal of trouble finishing the word "society," which is not only ironic but is another use of the "s" sibilant on the album that calls attention to the play of sounds and sense. The song ends with a brilliant deminundo reminiscent of the one on "Fame." It is clear that this side of the album lacks all humor, even the sardonic humor of the first side.

Bowie next does a cover of Tome Verlaine's "Kingdom Come," a song whose lyrics work perfectly in the context of the album. Nominally a song about a prison chain gang, the repeated lyric "I'll be breaking these rocks/what's my price to pay?" brings us back to the image of breaking to pieces, but in a wholly new context. From the standpoint of this side of the album, we have gone from teenage wildlife, to a political arrest, to prison—a sort of mini-arc that keeps the sympathetic listener attuned to the notion of the use of force on political dissenters. The final original song on the album, "Because You're Young," could almost be a coda to this arc. We take up the story of a "psychodelicate girl" and a "metal faced-boy" who are "so war-torn and resigned/

she can't talk anymore." As Bowie concludes, "these pieces are broken." In the second verse the song continues their story as a sort of love story in which "He punishes hard/ was loving her such a crime/she took back everything she said/left him nearly out of his mind/they're people I know—people I love/they seem so unhappy—dead or alive." The images of prisons, of punishment, come back, as does that of mental illness. Even love is not immune. Everyone has been left damaged. As on "Teenage Wildlife," Bowie comes in as an elder spokesman and seems to address the audience directly. His message is not a positive one, but he clearly has empathy ("people I love"). The song concludes, however, on a despairing note: "These pieces are broken/hope I'm wrong but I know."

And indeed, the album ends where it began, with a second version of "It's No Game" this time with Bowie singing alone and in a voice of narcotized flatness. Though the lyrics repeat, the effect is different. Anger has given over to resignation and, while all the more poignant for that, serves to underscore the point made over and over again on the album, that this is no game, this is real, this is life. Bowie seems to take his advice on "Ashes to Ashes" to "break the ice" and "come down" from the sky. The result is a blistering album that reflects the mood of punk rock but, at the same time, is also his most masterfully constructed album on which the banging percussion, guitar dissonance, consistently inventive writing, and experimental production all combine to create a total artistic statement in which no detail is lost and the album, as a whole, looks back and comments on Bowie's artistic accomplishments while also warning of the political dangers of the present—the new Thatcher government in Britain and the rise of Reganism in the United States. The future, Bowie, bemoans, is going to be ugly. And it was and is.

Bowie comes full circle as well away from the "European canon" of *Station to Station*, which marked a moving away from America back to Europe, and again on *Scary Monsters*, recorded in New York, back once again to the States. The difference is that this time Bowie is not full of naïve or romantic notions about American culture. On "Teenage Wildlife" he has the young mogul "shadow boxing" and on "Because You're Young" he sighs, "So I'll dance my life away." He would do both on his next album, *Let's Dance*, whose cover shows him shadow boxing and whose title says it all.

Notes

1   Williams talks about Adorno's social interest: "Adorno's topic is indeed the commercialization of life and the conditions in which culture is produced. He describes a closed system in which the production of predigested culture determines reception, in which, as he puts it, 'the composition listens for the listener.'" Alastair Williams, *Constructing Musicology* (Aldershot: Ashgate, 2001), 77.
2   Theodor W. Adorno, "On Popular Music," *Cultural Theory and Popular Culture: A Reader*, ed. and intrd. John Storey (New York: Harvester Wheatsheaf, 1994), 202.
3   According to Theodore Gracyk, Adorno does not locate the text of the music in the score or in the performance—the former, as a notational system, can get in the

way of meaning and only an artistically successful version of the latter can express the "truth" of the composer's intent, though the lack of knowledge of the audience can always be a problem as well. He seems to have gotten closer to accepting the notion of a recorded performance as a sort of unmediated text that is not dependent upon some extra layer of interpretation. Theodore Gracyk, *Rhythm and Noise: An Aesthetics of Rock* (Durham: Duke University Press, 1996), 169.

4   This is parallel to saying that Stanley Kubrick makes a horror film, with *The Shining* (1980), but does not follow the generic dictates so much as to use them to create something better, or more serious.

5   To continue the Kubrick comparison, one might ask how Kubrick uses "The Blue Danube" waltz in *2001*. Does this early sequence of the movie use the music to indicate the beauty of space flight? Or to parody the glibness of the future, where extraordinary technological achievements are viewed as routine and everyday? The real beauty lost on the technocrats that partake of it?

6   One could imagine here the cyclically recurring attacks on the "morals" of rock music—from Elvis to rap. The essence of the argument is summed up in Allan Bloom, "Music," *The Closing of the American Mind: How Higher Education Has Failed Democracy and Impoverished the Souls of Today's Students* (New York: Simon and Schuster, 1987), 68–81.

7   Adorno, *Cultural Theory and Popular Culture*, 212.

8   Ibid.

9   Adorno, *Cultural Theory and Popular Culture*, 213.

10   Bernard Gendron, "Theodor Adorno Meets the Cadillacs," *Studies in Entertainment: Critical Approaches to Mass Culture*, ed. Tania Modleski (Bloomington: Indiana University Press, 1986), 21.

11   The technical aspects of Bowie's earlier albums are explained in Ken Scott, *Abbey Road to Ziggy Stardust: Off the Record with the Beatles, Bowie, Elton, and So Much More* (Los Angeles: Alfred Music, 2012), 140–41. The rawness of the production of this period had its own pleasures.

12   Allan F. Moore, *Rock, The Primary Text: Developing a Musicology of Rock*, 2nd ed. (Aldershot: Ashgate, 2001), 37.

13   Moore, *Rock, The Primary Text*, 37–38.

14   Moore, *Rock, The Primary Text*, 202.

15   Ibid.

16   Ibid.

17   Moore, *Rock, The Primary Text*, 205.

18   Moore, *Rock, The Primary Text*, 204.

19   Moore, *Rock, The Primary Text*, 205.

20   Compare or contrast any of the following: the duo of Carlos Alomar (rhythm) and Earl Slick (lead) on *Station to Station*; Robert Fripp on *Scary Monsters*; Stevie Ray Vaughan on *Let's Dance*; Reeves Gabrels on *Earthling*; Mick Ronson on *Ziggy Stardust*; Gerry Leonard on *The Next Day* (2013). And, to a lesser extent, Bowie on *Diamond Dogs* (1974); Nile Rodgers on *Let's Dance*; and Adrian Belew on *Lodger*. This last is the distillation of Bowie's work in the seventies, often finding a way to reference classical work while also undermining it.

21   Moore, *Rock, The Primary Text*, 203.

22   Ibid.

23 One could argue that most music sounds mushy when you hear it live anyway. It sounds best at home. When Bowie performs live, especially his periodic reinterpretations of some of his classics on acoustic guitar, he pares things down: he is trying to get you to listen to the right things.

24 David Bowie, "Journal for Friday, January 7th 2000," January 8, 2000. http://. davidbowie.com/premium/bowie/journal/journal01-07-00.html.

25 Although Bowie has almost always made a point of being inauthentic, the essentially virtual nature of rock music can be taken to mean that all rock music is at base inauthentic already. As David R. Shumway argues:

> The authenticity of stars is also made problematic because film and sound recording seem particularly artificial. Compared to print, cinema and sound recoding entail more levels of mediation. These greater degrees of mediation mean that authenticity is more of an issue in the case of more recent forms of mechanical reproduction. Moreover, because these media almost always entail collaborative production, their authenticity is not as easily grounded in the Romantic idea of individual expression. . . . As a result, authenticity has been a particular problem because of the conditions under which rock is practiced.

He concludes: "The importance of authenticity to rock has meant that the gaps between persona and person and between original and copy have haunted rock (as they haunt modernism more generally) as a cultural practice." David R. Shumway, "Authenticity: Modernity, Stardom, and Rock and Roll," *Modernism/Modernity* 14, no. 2 (September 2007): 531.

26 Qtd. in Nicholas Pegg, *The Complete David Bowie*, 6th ed. (London: Titan Books, 2011), 348.

27 Carlos creates memorable versions of Henry Purcell's March from "Funeral Music of Queen Mary" (1695) and a portion of Beethoven's Ninth Symphony. Other classical music in the film, Giocchino Rossini's overtures to *The Thieving Magpie* (1817) and *William Tell* (1829), for example, or Edward Elgar's *Pomp and Circumstances Marches One and Four* (1901, 1904), are left unsynthesized, presumably because Carlos ran out of time. Her best work with Kubrick was yet to come with the soundtrack to *The Shining*, which combined Hector Berloiz's *Symphonie Fantastique* (1830) with found sounds on a Native-American motif. Though not electronic, it is arguably Kubrick's most influential soundtrack and certainly plays a big role in the film.

28 For more on how Bowie and Visconti created the unique sound of *Scary Monsters*, see Tony Visconti, *Tony Visconti: Bowie, Bolan and the Brooklyn Boy: The Autobiography* (London: Harper Collins, 2007), 278–79.

29 William Duckworth, *Virtual Music: How the Web Got Wired for Sound* (New York: Routledge, 2005), 2.

30 Duckworth, *Virtual Music*, 5.

31 Duckworth, *Virtual Music*, 6.

32 Duckworth, *Virtual Music*, 4.

33 Duckworth, *Virtual Music*, 3, 9.

34 Duckworth, *Virtual Music*, 10.

35 Duckworth, *Virtual Music*, 11.

36 Qtd. in Duckworth, *Virtual Music*, 12.

37 Duckworth, *Virtual Music*, 14.

38 Mark Prendergast, *The Ambient Century: From Mahler to Trance—The Evolution of Sound in the Electronic Age* (New York: Bloomsbury, 2000), xii

39 Duckworth, *Virtual Music*, 23.

40 See my comments on this in Aaron Jentzen, "The Renegade Who Had It Made: How Long Can Girl Talk Run?," *Pittsburgh City Paper*, September 4, 2008. http://www.pghcitypaper.com/pittsburgh/the-renegade-who-had-it-made/Content?oid=1340712.

41 *North Star* (1977) is typical work by the Philip Glass Ensemble. Glass' most famous opera, and perhaps his masterpiece, is *Einstein On the Beach* (1975–76) for Robert Wilson's avant-garde theater. Of special note here are, of course, Glass' *Symphony Number 1* (1992) and *Symphony Number 4* (1996), based on *Low* and *"Heroes,"* respectively.

42 Qtd. in Prendergast, *The Ambient Century*, 115.

43 Qtd. in David Sheppard, *On Some Faraway Beach: The Life and Times of Brian Eno* (Chicago: Chicago Review Press, 2009), 148.

44 Sheppard, *On Some Faraway Beach*, 148.

45 Qtd. in Sheppard, *On Some Faraway Beach*, 183.

46 Simon Frith and Howard Horne, *Art into Pop* (New York: Methuen, 1987), 107.

47 Qtd. in Shepphard, *On Some Faraway Beach*, 252.

48 Sheppard, *On Some Faraway Beach*, 319.

49 In this context, perhaps one should note Bowie's two attempts at faux-languages on the B-side of *Low*.

50 Sheppard, *On Some Faraway Beach*, 341.

51 Sheppard, *On Some Faraway Beach*, 341–42.

52 A list of these works would include, just to name a few, *Ensemble Pieces* (1978) by Christopher Hobbs, John Adams, and Gavin Bryars; *Possible Musics* (Fourth World Vol. 1) (1980) by Eno and Jon Hassell; and Jon Hassell's *Dream Theory in Malaya* (Fourth World Vol. Two) (1981).

53 Umberto Eco, *The Role of the Reader: Explorations in the Semiotics of Texts* (Bloomington: Indiana University Press, 1979), 49.

54 Eco, *The Role of the Reader*, 61.

55 Eco, *The Role of the Reader*, 65.

56 The last album of Bowie's glam period, *Diamond Dogs*, is his most successful in terms of concepts. I discuss it at some length in Chapter 6.

57 The chord changes can be seen here: http://tabs.ultimate-guitar.com/d/david_bowie/ashes_to_ashes_ver2_crd.htm.

58 Alexander Carpenter, "'Give a Man a Mask and He'll Tell the Truth': Arnold Schoenberg, David Bowie, and the Mask of Pierrot," *Intersections: Canadian Journal of Music/Intersections: revue canadienne de musique* 30, no. 2 (2010): 7.

59 Qtd. in Carpenter, *Intersections*, 7.

60 Carpenter, *Intersections*, 7; note no. 5.

61 Qtd. in Carpenter, *Intersections*, 12.

62 Carpenter, *Intersections*, 10.

63 Carpenter, *Intersections*, 11.

64 Ibid.

65 Before he met Bowie, Kemp was using Bowie's music during intermissions in a show entitled *Clowns Hour*. The notion of the clown tradition, especially the white clown

one, suffuses the training that Kemp provided Bowie. Peter Doggett, *The Man Who Sold the World: David Bowie in the 1970s* (New York: Harper Collins, 2012), 46.

66 Carpenter, *Intersections*, 11–12.

67 Carpenter, *Intersections*, 14.

68 Carpenter, *Intersections*, 17; note no. 22.

69 Buckley notes that in the video Bowie appears on the dance floor while

> Bowie the artist stands on stage, snarling dismissively at Bowie the fan, looking on. Bowie the icon is literally elevated on the stage, the camera, at stage level, looking up at the pop star and down at the fan. The scene encapsulates the icon-fan relationship, with its impersonality, detachment and inequality, and provides a visual statement of the quintessence of Bowie's 70s stage shows. (David Buckley, *Strange Fascination: David Bowie, The Definitive Story*, rev. ed. (London: Virgin, 2001), 372)

One might say this is an update to the whole *Ziggy* album and to other songs about, in part, the fan/star legend such as "Sweet Thing" on *Diamond Dogs*.

4

The Grain of the Voice:
Autobiography and Multiplicity

Having looked at the musical structure of David Bowie's songs, I would like to examine his voice in relationship to lyrics—especially the autobiographical elements—but also in terms of queerness and race, two areas that demonstrate the slippage between the voice and the song, the body and the text. Bowie's approach to vocal style is to combine the autobiographical with the other, the singular with the multiple, to create a uniquely self-conscious embodiment.

Sound Effects

Simon Frith's book *Sound Effects* provides an overview of the development of rock music—mainly in the United States—by a noted British cultural theorist and, arguably, the most important contemporary theorist of rock music. One of Frith's earliest books, it adapts a textbook he wrote for the study of rock music. The sections of the book cover those aspects of rock music culture that are essential to study. Early on in the book, Frith comments on the role of lyrics in rock music and their importance to the embodiment of voice: "The words, if they are noticed at all, are absorbed after the music has made its mark. The crucial variables are sound and rhythm."[1] Yet Frith gives primacy not to music but to the voice itself: "Because so much of rock music depends on the social effects of the voice, the questions about how rock's effects are produced are vocal, not musicological."[2] For Frith, rock is "primitive." The point of rock is not the music, but its physical effects, the physical effect versus the cultural meaning—the non-musical-like aspects of rock, in other words.

Frith proceeds to use black music as an example of the various forms of music "that lose their original force and meaning as they pass through the bland wringer of mass music but are rediscovered by each new generation of hip musicians and audiences."[3] Frith characterizes black music as performative, that it is about the human voice. He argues, "At the center of Afro-American music is the performance. Black music is performance music rather than composition music. . . ."[4] In this sense, it contrasts with white music: "Black music is based on the immediate effects of melody and rhythm rather than on the linear development of theme and harmony."[5] He goes on to add that "the value of black music derives not from its solutions to musical problems or from the performers' expertise in interpreting written pieces of music, but from its emotional impact, its account of the performers' own feelings."[6] And, finally, "this emphasis on the voice as the source of human expression has a number of musical consequences."[7] Jazz and Blues musicians were known for "vocal techniques such as melisma" as opposed to "the perfect pitch and enunciation of a classical singer."[8] This notion of voice moved into rock music—whether the vocal aspects of the electric guitar or the call-and-response of gospel music. Black singers continued, according to Frith, to privilege music as a builder of community while white rock stars were more interested in the notion of a one-to-one contact with the listener that you would get in something like the crooner.[9] Pop music signals a shift from performance to song, from sheet music to the record during the Depression.[10] The lyrics in pop music make the mundane into poetry, but refuse to write like poetry. Frith seems to come close to Adorno in thinking that the lyrics are an advertisement for the song. Overall, though, Frith still seems to want to subordinate the lyrics to the music, to pure sound.

In a later discussion of rock as art Frith notes that in the 1970s the definition of rock's worth shifted to art. Frith, however, thinks that art depends upon the *auteur*—a concept that enters into discourse in the 1970s, suggesting a different type of listener— and that some rock musicians attempted to respond to this idea by making their music more "difficult." Frith finds these positions contradictory because he claims that rock is based on stardom, not artistic "success." It is the product of the market. To Frith, rock is a mass medium or culture. One should examine its effects, social and otherwise, and how it functions, not in spite of its strictures but because of them. Analyzing rock in terms of "realist" versus "formalist" ideologies, Frith asks about the characteristics of each. Media distort reality by showing a false—yet convincingly real-like—image of society. The realists want the means to media production; the formalists want to decode the meanings of sign production (semiotics). Frith wants some sort of mixing of Theodor Adorno and Walter Benjamin: "The problem, then, is to determine the relationship between rock's commercial function and its cultural use."[11]

The problem for black musicians was that the recording industry compensated musicians for compositions, not performative texts or styles.[12] One effect of this fact was that the

> direct communication between artist and audience, in which the performance drew its meaning from the immediate experience, became the rehearsed distance between the star and the consumer, and a tension developed between the artists' concerns, the audiences' demands for reassurance, and the industry's assessments of consumer tastes. This tension emerged most clearly with respect to the third element of black music—its *rhythm*.[13]

Rhythm expresses itself most clearly in the physical form of dance music, which itself expresses sexuality: "Black musicians work . . . with a highly developed aesthetic of *public* sexuality."[14]

In Frith's overview of rock history and the tools we have for analyzing it, he comes back to the question of lyrics and voice. He notes that "a song is always a performance and song words are always spoken out—vehicles for the voice. The voice can also use nonverbal devices to make its points—accents, signs, emphases, hesitations, changes of tone. Song words, in short, work as *speech*, as structures of sound that are *direct* signs of emotion and marks of character."[15] Or, as he also says, "pop signs celebrate not the articulate but the inarticulate, the evaluation of pop singers depends not on words but on sounds—on the noises around the words."[16]

For Frith, black singers "struggle *against* words."[17] By contrast, "British rock has always used a peculiarly ironic performing style, a vocal approach in which the singers seem to watch and comment on their own acts. The classic British rock performers . . . present themselves as performers, acknowledge the fan's viewpoint *musically*."[18] The connection Frith makes between the complexity of the status of lyrics—needed, yet purposefully performative verbal utterances—and the racialized aspect of this part of rock music history is important to understanding Bowie and his own use of his voice in his music. Obviously his voice is itself a sort of fetish, a part of the complex sexualization that is part of his own display of public sexuality. Though, by Frith's standards, Bowie is the most British of British singers, he has done his part to remove the voice from a merely private conversation between him and the listener. While not communal in the racial sense that Frith means, it does help to build a unique fan base for Bowie of outsiders who identify as much through each other as through him.

Image-Music-Text

More than perhaps any other theorist of music, Roland Barthes talks about music in relation to the body, or its embodiment, in the Western music tradition. He begins the first of his two essays on music in his seminal *Image-Music-Text*, the chapter *Musica Practica*, by making the distinction between playing music as an amateur for oneself and enjoying the music as a performance one is creating versus listening to music (which he terms, perhaps incorrectly, as "passive"[19]) as a listener. He argues that our way of experiencing music has changed from the former to the latter. This shift, from one "as though the body were hearing" to one in which "the soul" is and can be seen in the movement from women playing the piano at home to men playing the guitar. We have moved from music in which mistakes can be made to one in which the technical perfection of the performance is assumed. The ultimate result of this movement is to "[abolish] in the sphere of music the very notion of *doing*."[20]

A pivotal figure for this change for Barthes is Beethoven—an artist blamed for so much in modern music. For Barthes, Beethoven was the technician par excellence, someone whose work was too difficult for an amateur to play.[21] He was the first mythic composer—someone who "was acknowledged the right of metamorphosis."[22] He could change what Barthes terms his "manners" or styles and have it be seen in a positive way. He could also "be dissatisfied with himself or, more profoundly, with his language, he could change his codes as he went through life."[23] As Barthes sums up, "Beethoven was the first man of music to be *free*."[24] The Romantic Beethoven thus developed a number of "structural features": "the paroxysmal development of contrasts in intensity"; "the shattering of the melody"; "the emphatic redundancy of moments of excitement and termination"; "the experience of limits"; and "the production of musical chimera."[25] With this mastery and creation of a myth to which Bowie is very much an heir also comes the destruction of the "song," which is replaced with the orchestra, "escaping from the fetishism of a single element (voice or rhythm)."[26] The unity of the body and its connection to a totalizing single instrument is replaced with the division of the performer into multiple selves, or more precisely, the transformation into the conductor.[27] Beethoven's music cannot be played so much as organized. What we want to do when we want to play Beethoven is to conduct.[28]

Barthes' formulation of a dichotomy between song and orchestra, voice and multiple instruments, foreshadows his famous distinction in the next musical essay, "The Grain of the Voice." Here Barthes moves from a discussion of music generally and Beethoven in particular to one about vocal music and song structure. He distinguishes between the "geno-song," the tension "where melody explores how the language works and identifies with that work," and the "pheno-text," a term he uses to cover all of the usual features associated with singing—"communication, representation, expression."[29] Focusing further, Barthes takes up *lied* and *mélodie* in order to locate "the very precise space . . . of *the encounter between a language and a voice*."[30] This frisson is what he terms the "*grain* of the voice."[31] Barthes uses the example of the famed German Bach specialist, Dietrich Fischer-Dieskau, who sings technically correctly, but like Barthes' earlier designation of professional music one listens to rather than plays, what one seems to be hearing is the soul, not the body. Specifically, what one is hearing is the lungs—breathing, the soul itself, mastered and made perfect. As Barthes writes, "His art is inordinately expressive (the diction is dramatic, the pauses, the checkings and releasings of breath, occur like shudders of passion) and hence never exceeds culture."[32] Barthes contrasts this singing with that of Panzera, a specialist in Jewish cantor music, who is outside the tradition of German music and brings none of the expectations. Yet in his singing we hear the glottis, the tongue, the lips, the throat and the movement of vowels and sounds against the melody. We hear the body. We are aware of language. This style contrasts Fischer-Dieskau's, whose "art—expressive, dramatic, *sentimentally clear*, borne by a voice lacking in any 'grain', in signifying weight."[33] What Panzera does, and Bowie as well, when he wants to, is to use the grain of the voice: "the very friction between the music and something else, which something else is the particular language (and nowise the message)."[34]

Ultimately Barthes bemoans the loss of the *mélodie* tradition, the amateur, body-based, single-instrument, pre-orchestra way of experiencing music as a practitioner of it rather than a listener: "Mass 'good' music (records, radio) has left it [*mélodie*] behind, preferring either the more pathetic orchestra (success after Mahler) or less bourgeois instruments than the piano (harpsichord, trumpet)."[35] Finally, Barthes agrees with Adorno that the rise of recorded music, of mass taste in music, has forever changed the musical landscape and our relationship to music, for the ill.[36] At the end of his essay, however, he does say that the grain "persists in instrumental music" and is present to him whenever the performer's body can be sensed or felt in a performance—the volume at which an instrument is played,[37] or the awareness of the body of a harpsichordist, or even "the clutch of the finger-tips" on a piano.[38] And the grain can range across any genre of music, any age, any culture. As he notes, "Were we to succeed in refining a certain 'aesthetics' of musical pleasure, then doubtless we would attach less importance to the formidable break in tonality accomplished by modernity."[39]

One might say that this is an example of the "formalist" analysis of which Frith speaks. Barthes is also acting, to some extent, as a cultural critic as well. He begins with the problem we have often run up against: how does one talk about music—more specifically, how does one use language to describe something that is, sometimes, partially composed of language? Barthes raises this point, but then veers away from satisfying it. Instead, he discusses something else: the point at which language and music brush up against each other: the concept of the grain of the voice. Barthes deals, therefore, with singing, and with language that is neither music nor language: an effect, perhaps, of a certain type of singer and/or singing.[40] Barthes wants an erotics of music.

The embodied voice

As Alyster Williams notes, all Western music contains the tradition of composers referencing the work of other composers in their work: "Schumann's Op. 17 Fantasy for piano . . . includes a quotation from Beethoven's song cycle *An die ferne Geliebte* (*To the Distant Beloved*), a gesture that cannot be attributed entirely to an internal logic."[41] Likewise, Haydn and Mozart were always in dialogue with each other.[42] Whether it is Brahms' variations on a theme by Haydn, or any of the hundreds of other contributions to that tradition, composers consciously and unconsciously echo each other. This fact is one among many reasons that there is no definitive musical text. Classical composers create pastiches of each other's work, but likewise, the presumed absoluteness of the notational text is undermined by the fact that different composers have vastly different definitions of what a complete text is. Beethoven left much interpretation of how his music was to be played to the conductor or performers, while Mahler went out of his way to leave intricate instructions on the musical notation itself.[43] Where the text lies, therefore, is contextual, cultural, traditional, and always open to interpretation. That it is also always a performance is made abundantly clear by rock music. Again, as Williams argues, this "intertextual" tradition in classical music is specifically tied to an anxiety of influence within the male canon.[44] This canon itself has emphasized structural aspects of music and tended to avoid others—"its timbre and intensity; its affect on the body and its ability to give pleasure."[45] One might argue that these are the same characteristics that separate rock from classical music. Women are an absent presence in classical music, becoming either feminized into a certain type of melody, or even transformed into certain types of instruments such as the flute or the piano. Male composers express their feminine side in their music, but only with the anxiety of feeling that music itself always already contains "feminine and sometimes queer connotations."[46]

Music, in other words, often lacks embodiment. Rock music in general and David Bowie in particular counter this absence. Opera represents perhaps one counter tradition in that a male opera composer might splinter his authorial voice into multiple voices on a stage, including some female ones, disrupting the usual attempt on the part of the composer to control the performance of self and to remain the subject, not the object, of contemplation.[47] Bowie's own operatic approach to rock music, clear from *Ziggy Stardust* (1972) onwards, is to similarly splinter his personality, multiplying or doubling the effect of multiple genders, especially. The many instances of Bowie double-tracking his voice on his albums points to the multiple personalities that emerge, the literally numerous voices or shadows of voices that he creates in any one song—from "Bewlay Brothers" to "Ashes to Ashes."[48] As Williams says:

> An instrumental doubling of a vocal line is a particular device for creating an imaginary, or fantasy, object, and relates this mechanism to a stage in infancy where the baby hears a vocal mirror in its mother's voice. By listening to and imitating its mother's voice, the child experiences a sense of abundance, and it is a recollection of this imaginary fulfillment that the voice mirroring of an instrumental vocal doubling attempts to capture.[49]

Or, put more bluntly:

> Music is encountered as the discourse of the other when we experience ourselves being addressed by it: that is, when we feel personal memories are being organized and relocated by something outside of ourselves, inserting us in a domain of intersubjectivity. Musical experience is shot through with a desire for reconciliation, but is also continually frustrated because . . . desire is constantly deferred by its own desire for itself. Put another way, what desire desires is desire.[50]

Giles Deleuze similarly talks about music's importance as a haptic form. As he writes, "Musical art has . . . two aspects: the one like a dance of sonorous molecules . . . acting upon the whole body that it deploys as its stage, and the other like the creation of human relations in this sonorous matter, which directly produces the affects that are ordinarily explained by psychology."[51] For Deleuze, these two aspects come together in opera, especially in the work of Giuseppe Verdi. The real focus of Deleuze's thoughts on music here, however, is François Châtelet, a contemporary and fellow philosopher, whose work he quotes at some length:

> The metaphors that I have just used all share a common defect: they situate the musical effect in the domain of representation. But music neither presents nor represents anything, not even apparently. It has this privilege: to render sensible by means of its artifices the impact of sonorous qualities and their combinations on the entire surface of the body including its so-called profound parts.[52]

Music is able to make an audience experience emotions better than drama by giving "reality and strength to . . . elemental psychology. . . ."[53] As he concludes, "The fear, the carnal passion, the hate which reflexive or scientific psychology laboriously deduces or induces, music makes exist in their singular situations."[54]

One might say that Bowie's voice is unique and that what gives it its startling quality is the fact that no one else sounds like him. His voice is always recognizable on a song, and he calls a lot of attention to it by the many ways he manipulates it. But even if it were not the case that he often changes his voice from song to song, much as he has done with his musical style from album to album or multiple personae, the fact remains that his voice would remain distinct and always recognizable. Of course, one could say the same for any number of popular performers such as Ella Fitzgerald or Peter Gabriel. Likewise, anyone can sing well. What Bowie has is a vocal quality that remains consistent and recognizable across songs, even if he changes his voice. Like Tom Waits (on *The Black Rider* [1993] and *Blood Money* [2002], for example), Bowie's voice is thickly textured. He frequently uses his voice counterintuitively. He has great inflection and range. His highest recorded note is G#5 on the closing line of "Lady Grinning Soul" on *Aladdin Sane* (1973); the lowest is a C2 in the opening line of "Sweet Thing" on *Diamond Dogs* (1974). This is not to say that his vocals are perfect. His vibrato can be a bit uncontrolled with leaps to low notes often out of tune. His voice does not always get from one harmony to another—all the steps are not there. This result is probably in part because of all of the factors involved in recording the vocal parts—improvisation, lyrics, etc. If one accepts Simon Frith's claim that what matters in vocal performances is not clarity and enunciation but feelings and imperfections, then often on Bowie's recordings lyrics can be easily misunderstood—at least on the seventies albums—with unusual pronunciations or intonation contours being used in many of his songs. Many of his fans, casual and otherwise, probably have been unable to make out what Bowie is singing and have naturally made up their own words— or what they think he is saying—only to read the lyrics at a later date to discover, for better or worse, the actual words being used. The lyrics on his songs often seem subsumed by the music, fitting the melody, not vice versa. Often written quickly, they have a stream of consciousness effect. In many cases his live vocal performances are better than his recorded ones—probably due to the need to rehearse, cleanup, etc., for live performances.

Allan F. Moore notes that "throughout the early 1970s 'rock' phase he [Bowie] frequently used a 'strained' voice. The later 1970s saw him develop a rich, full-throated style which has since remained a mainstream of his technique."[55] This phase probably reached a peak on the song "Young Americans," where Bowie calls attention to his own singing, panting in a nearly breathless patter.[56] In this instance, Bowie perhaps best illustrates Barthes' "grain of the voice." In another context, Barthes writes about the intricacies of the voice in terms of the Japanese performance of *Bunraku* dolls. This puppet theater utilizes three people: "the puppet, the manipulator, the vociferant: the effect gesture, the effective gesture, and the vocal gesture."[57] About the last, Barthes notes:

> *Bunraku* has a *limited* notion of the voice; it does not suppress the voice, but assigns it a very clearly defined, essentially trivial function. In the speaker's voice are gathered together: exaggerated declamation, tremolos, a falsetto tonality, broken intonations, tears, paroxysms of rage, of supplication, of astonishment,

indecent pathos, the whole cuisine of emotion, openly elaborated on the level of that internal, visceral body of which the larynx is the mediating muscle. Yet this excess is given only within the very code of excess.[58]

As he does when he talks about the geno-voice, Barthes assigns to this type of vocal performance the act of writing. Similarly, Bowie writes with his voice, externalizing the internal and creating no difference between the two, creating a magnification of the body in song.[59]

Song as autobiography

David Bowie's long career and many accomplishments have often been discussed in terms of his chameleon-like changes of style and substance and his extremely British approach to the rock star formula, one that seemingly pits theatricality against sincerity to act as a counter-model to American "authenticity." Bowie's own emphasis on his emergence in the early 1970s as an alternative to the 1960s flower-power model of rock has actually obscured some of the ways in which Bowie's music has acted as a series of autobiographical entries that both reflect and shape his interactions with fame and fans.[60] The emphasis on the interactivity of Bowie's performances—concerts, music videos, film roles, etc.—has further deflected attention from the music itself. In the numerous, sometimes competing multimedia fronts on which Bowie assaults the public whenever he unveils a new album, the text of the album can get lost—just one more persona or reference, one that might be almost immediately subsumed in its reinterpretation as music video or concert performance. Yet underneath the songs' layers of irony and surface, Bowie often encodes fairly straightforward narratives about his life and struggles with a very public fame. Read over the course of several years, his albums tell various stories—establish multiple narrative strands—in which he often analyzes the vicissitudes of stardom and offers up a rich, though often dark, emotional landscape. That is, we spend much time reading Bowie's songs in terms of his personae, and they open themselves up to so many different levels of interpretation, but we need to make sure not to ignore the autobiographical level as well.

Beginning with the justly famous music of the *Ziggy Stardust* album, Bowie instructs the listener on how to interpret his songs as complex individual performances. The album contains songs in which different voices speak, the same event appears from several perspectives, and a productive ambiguity emerges at the literal level of the album as a whole. While some of the tracks are sung by the title character himself—the famous polysexual alien who comes to earth as a prophet only to be torn apart by his overly ardent fans—others are apparently performed by different people: someone listening to Ziggy on the radio, a member of his band, a fan in the audience at a concert, and other characters who are never clearly identified. This complex, even disembodied approach to songwriting continues throughout the decade of the seventies, which still constitutes Bowie's most exciting work. By the time of the outwardly experimental albums of the "Berlin period" (1977–79), Bowie has applied the approach on the *Ziggy* album to music that is outside of the rock genre. By this point Bowie's fame was global, with multiple versions of Bowie and his career existing distinctly but simultaneously in different parts of the world. No longer merely an Anglo-American phenomenon, Bowie's late-seventies albums reflect both his peripatetic nature and the ways in which his gender and genre-bending work of the early seventies has morphed into a proto-world music that nevertheless functions to tell a coherent story about a particular person. Bowie balances the concretely human with the postmodern to redefine the notion of the self as a simple equation. His ability to render this complexity on his albums contributes to the multiple cultures to which his albums appeal, but also to the numerous subcultural formations that are associated with him. By constructing himself through his songs, Bowie is able to render himself as both self and other—familiar and alien, local and global—by defining music as both the estrangement and reconciliation of multiple identities.

Taken as a whole, the Berlin trilogy can be read on two general levels. On perhaps the more familiar level, it seems to reflect Bowie's rejection of the US version of stardom that began with the Ziggy period and eventually landed him in Los Angeles with the cocaine habit that reaches its peak on the album *Young Americans* (1975), which also contains Bowie's biggest American hit, the ironically named "Fame." The next album, *Station to Station* (1976), turns the searing indictment of the American way of life inward and marks the beginning of the movement away from the United States while also painting a portrait of someone in desperate spiritual and mental pain. The destination of the long trip that the title song "Station to Station" seems to refer to is Berlin, a state of mind, perhaps, more than an actual place, which becomes the signifier for the next three albums—*Low* (1977), *"Heroes"* (1978), and *Lodger* (1979). While actually recorded in France, Berlin, and Switzerland, respectively, the albums are also associated with Brian Eno, who is a collaborator on the albums, though not a producer, and with the German band Kraftwerk, whose aural experiments with synthesized sound were an immediate influence on late-seventies Bowie. The album *Low*, especially, has kept its associations with the psychic collapse that Bowie is supposed to have had at that time and that becomes the other dimension that the albums explore.

In 1977 Bowie was living above an auto-supply shop in Berlin, a city divided between East and West, but really comprising an island in the middle of Eastern Europe. The sparse lyrics on the album seem to suggest the singer's state of mind, perhaps most especially on the album's most famous song, "Sound and Vision." Bowie sings, "Pale blinds drawn on day/nothing to do/nothing to say/I will sit right down/waiting for the gift/of sound and vision." The almost textbook-perfect notion of depression that the album seems to record here and elsewhere is not just a role or a device, but also an accurate reflection of the singer-songwriter's recent experiences.[61] Likewise, the notion of sound and vision—of Bowie's emphasis on both singing and visuals, in his music and in his various types of live and recorded media—can also be read as personal.[62] While taking nothing away from the many other levels at which the album functions— the overall tone or mood could perhaps be described as melancholy, haunting, and ultimately oddly comforting—many of the songs are themselves raw and moving. While the Berlin period is often associated with dissonance, experimentation, and the invention of a new kind of blurry line between pop and art, the mainstream and the avant-garde as they might be defined by rock music, far from distancing himself through these effects, Bowie actually pulls the listener closer to him.

A further step in this process can be seen in Bowie's next album, *"Heroes,"* whose album title and song have been taken straight by many people even though the use of quotation marks around the titles are supposed to suggest that the word *heroes* is meant to be taken contingently and ironically. Though this song is about a couple that Bowie and his producer friends used to see meeting by the Berlin wall and for whom Bowie imagined a very anti-glamorous, Fassbinder-like backstory, the album contains other lyric-based songs that seem, once again, quite autobiographical.[63] While this album contains a slightly jauntier feel than *Low*, with the lyrics given more emphasis, if anything *"Heroes"* pushes more at the notion of noise as art, replacing the surreal desert landscape of the American West of *Low* with a more hard-edged sound that is based stylistically and emotionally on the German Expressionist painters of the early twentieth century. Depression is replaced with schizophrenia, or at least paranoia, best seen, perhaps, in the song "Blackout."

This song literalizes the abrupt mixing of styles that can be found throughout the album, which shifts between self-loathing and anger, romance and realism. On this song, Bowie seems to address a "beauty in a cage," perhaps the person he later says he will "kiss . . . in the rain." These stanzas, however, alternate with stanzas about an actual blackout that Bowie once had, here triggered by the section that begins "someone's back in town/the chips are down/I just cut and blackout/I'm under Japanese influence/and my honour's at stake." Bowie tradition has it that the "someone" is Angela Bowie, with whom Bowie was going through a messy divorce. In any case, the song suggests extreme fragility, as though it were about a person who is trying to be whole, but cannot quite get there yet. The album begins with the song "Beauty and the Beast," a reference to, among other things, the notion of the shadow figure or dual nature that frequently crops up in Bowie's music and comes across most famously in the song "Ashes to Ashes." Like the album *Low*, *"Heroes"* moves into primarily instrumental music on the album's second side, which contains not only a specific reference to Berlin's Turkish section, the song "Neuköln," but also to what Edward Said might call the "Oriental" in "Moss Garden" and "The Secret Life of Arabia." The East comes to signify here a postmodern fragmentation of self, or perhaps more accurately, a superficial pastiche of notions about the East (and the self) that mirror the romantic verses of "Blackout" and the last three lines of "The Secret Life of Arabia," which end the album: "you must see the movie, the sand in my eyes/I walk through a desert song/when the heroine dies." A difficult song to decipher, its strange, shard-like structure seems calculated more to suggest an emotional effect than a coherent commentary on "Arabia," which in this context can never be anything more than a cultural cliché anyway.[64]

Bowie's interest in the cultural clichés of travel carries over into his last album of his trilogy. *Lodger* returns Bowie to seemingly more conventional songwriting in that it is an album that consists entirely of three-to-five minute pop songs. The songs themselves, however, are rife with Eno-esque experimentation. The content of the songs split almost evenly into two parts: songs about political topics (nuclear war, wifebeating, male privilege) and world travel (Africa, Turkey, Japan). Bowie seems to be entering a new phase. While the stories about journeys to faraway places continue the multicultural aspects of *"Heroes,"* the overt political lyrics on some of the songs suggest a politically engaged Bowie, one that would peak on the next album, *Scary Monsters* (1980), an ominously prescient look at the age of Reagan and Thatcher. The first song on *Lodger*, "Fantastic Voyage," sets the album's tone and attempts to bridge the two motifs. The long-sought sense of place that is missing on the first two albums by Bowie and Eno seems to emerge in the string section here, which is lush with mandolins. Bowie finally seems to be at peace. He sings in a calm voice—almost like that of someone who was once agitated and is now medicated. It is unclear how seriously we are supposed to take the lyrics, which mix references to "missiles" and genocide and implicitly criticize world leaders ("And the wrong words make you listen in this criminal world.") with lyrics that seem to refer directly to himself as a singer, poet, or artist—that is, as someone who also bears some sort of responsibility ("I've got to write it down"). The lyrics also clash with the string music as it quickly becomes clear that the mock-serious voice in which Bowie sings ("We'll get by, I suppose") is meant to underscore the difference between the weighty subject matter and the gentle manner in which it is sung. Bowie weaves together personal depression with the more dangerous depression of people who have their finger on the nuclear button, as when Bowie sings: "We're learning to live with somebody's depression/and I don't want to live with somebody's depression." The "somebody" of "Blackout" returns here as a pointed reference to politics, one that arguably outweighs the personal. The "fantastic voyage" of the title refers existentially to life itself, but also to the individual lives of everyone on the planet. Moving from this song into the songs about travel on the first side, Bowie attempts to unite disparate cultures and, along the way, almost incidentally creates world music. The figure of the artist returns on other cuts on the album such as "DJ" and "Look Back in Anger," but what is perhaps most notable is that despite these dark moments the album seems to suggest that Bowie has successfully come out of his depression. Bowie transforms the isolation of Berlin into a view of the world that is the opposite of the inner-directed or solipsistic and that begins to combine American directness with European stylistics. Significantly, Bowie sings on "Fantastic Voyage" that "Our lives are valuable too," signaling that he is once again a citizen of the world, not just of his room.

Bowie's music from the end of his great decade is a movement from the self toward not only the outer world but also toward a new definition of the foreign as the East, the Oriental, the other as real, not imagined. This trajectory culminates in the early 1980s with Bowie's performances in *The Elephant Man* and Oshima's *Merry Christmas, Mr. Lawrence* (1983), the evocation of the Far East during the Serious Moonlight concert tour, and in the music videos for "China Girl" and "Loving the Alien." Bowie transformed his personal crisis into one that informed the outer world of politics and ideas. Bowie matures, but also fragments himself and completes his disassociation. Since the early 1980s, Bowie has entered a kind of postmodern existence as a rock star in which he has only been able to replay his 1970s selves (for example, in the elaborate characters created for the album *Outside* [1995]). The few performances Bowie has made since his heart attack and subsequent bypass operation in 2004 have consisted of an extremely stripped-down version of a few of his more classic tunes in which he pushes his sincerity as far as possible—singing without inflection or the studied gestures of his performative style. Susanne Vega, for one, has said that this approach to singing makes his music even more moving. Bowie has said that he is no longer even performing the persona "David Bowie," but is now only "David Jones." If so, the process that began in 1977 has finally come to an end.

Queer Blues

One could argue that with the rise of queer culture that subcultures based upon alternative sexualities began to merge with alternative culture generally. Postmodernist effects, perhaps tracing their origins back to William S. Burroughs and the Beat movement, became more and more common. For example, "Sex Fantasy #68: Yo Ho Ho" by Daniel Babcock, included in a compilation of gay 'zines from the 1990s, *Discontents*, edited by Dennis Cooper, is a pornographic fantasy about being captured by a group of pirates (really the band Mötley Crüe) and becoming a sex slave. It contains many of the characteristics of postmodern culture given an underground or gay inflection, including references to pop culture as the very material the story is based upon and turning "straight" stars and genres into something attractive to a gay-identified man (Matt Dillon, tattoos, Mötley Crüe, etc.).[65] The story embodies a boyish delight in "punk" attitude that is anti-new wave and anti-hippie and is written with tongue-in-cheek irony and a surreal melodramatic writing style that is common to much of queer postmodern writing. Pirates are themselves already a form of drag, a trope that gets played on here. Likewise, the story also turns the fantasies of Metal music on their head while also enjoying them, very much like a fantasy a teen might write (compare to the fake novel being written by the teen protagonist of Burroughs' *Place of Dead Roads* [1983]), except that it is not so much a literalization of the homoerotic content of Metal videos and songs made real as a queer version of *This Is Spinal Tap* (1984). At one point Babcock writes, "The Catholic church and U.S. government had merged into one governing murder corporation."[66] This paranoia about control and the government is similar to Burroughs'.

The story's best joke is that the pirates are into sadomasochism that expresses itself in a mixture of tenderness and brutality (such as a poem left carved on the protagonist's ass). Words and phrases used throughout the story, like "piss" and "'Bad-Ass Captain,'" work in several ways to connote adolescence, music culture, and queerness.[67] The porn aspect is, however, very different from what one would have in an actual porn film. Sex here is not based upon the penis or upon sexuality being tied to an act or to a way of looking at life. The protagonist Dave is simply queer. The story assumes this, although it does eroticize or show how something straight is also really queer (like a Lesley Gore song, for example).

Bowie's own demonstration of the playing with self and other and the fracturing of self in his work from the late seventies and beyond builds upon the notion of the double-mindedness of racial or gender identity but also presages the complex or contradictory multiplicity of queer identity. While the notion of *queer* seems to unite and unify various political and identificatory positions across a large spectrum, including back through time, people who self-identify as queer might come from very different subject positions—female, black, Asian, Jewish, etc.—and deal with different problems they have with reconciling their queerness with their other identities. The notion of queer risks eliding some distinctions for which people fought—gay, lesbian, etc.—and other subject positions as well. Compounding this problem is the question of how to analyze the notion of queer when it is allied with the notion of performance. Further complicating this issue is the limited nature of the tools we have available to analyze queer performances. Many of the same problems with vocabulary or methodological approach that we might find in performance studies generally can be said to show up when working on theories of queer performance.

One such problem involves what I term the phenomenology of queer performance. That is, what happens when we use a term like *camp*, seemingly so popular a choice of terminology, when talking about performances that we might label as queer? As suggested by queer theorists such as Kate Davy and Michael Moon, it is as profoundly important not to depoliticize gay practices by discussing them as a "sensibility" or "aesthetics." In other words, "camp" as a concept is both more than envisioned by a theorizer of it like Susan Sontag and less than adequate when used as an umbrella term to explain or even designate the many and varied queer performances that might erupt in and around this definitional site. Though perhaps *camp* is useful when applied in a new way—lesbian camp, for instance—it has lost much of its ability to do work as a term for gay male or queer performance. Andrew Ross is correct in identifying Mark Booth's work on camp as the most helpful, yet Ross himself in his "Uses of Camp" does not so much explain the phenomenon as use it as a vague term with which to stitch together some genuinely interesting observations about popular culture. A better approach to analyzing queer performative practices may well be to follow in the footsteps of Esther Newton to investigate the phenomenology of actual queer spaces. In other words, the problem with camp is the problem with generalization and a lack of specification. Camp is difficult to imagine now either as a term of opprobrium or of liberation beyond the very specific practices to which it might refer. As with other areas of performance study, queer theorists must attempt to establish links between phenomena rather than attempt simply to summarize a dense nexus of subcultural practice in one word or concept.

Performance as an approach or model for scholarly critique has been embraced by scholars of queer production and culture. Some of this embracing has come about because of the usual idea that queer culture or identity involves some type of performance on the quotidian level that, not surprisingly, has become part of the queer identificatory matrix or sensibility. On the other hand, many people working in queer studies are also working in cultural studies. I want to end my discussion of musical performance by raising questions about the vocabulary we have for discussing performance generally. With the possible exception of the ongoing theorizing in queer studies over the use of the performative—J. L. Austin's term for a performative utterance—as it was picked up by Eve Kosofsky Sedgwick, Judith Butler, and Cindy Patton as a way to discuss the various fields and enclosures that have to do with shame, the closet, and political activism connected to HIV disease, we tend not to theorize performance so much as describe it. That is, performance studies, more than, say, literary theory, seems to be based upon inductive processes rather than deductive ones. We theorize from the artist's actual performance to the theory we can infer from it—or develop for it as a part of our own analysis. Though I certainly do not wish to suggest that performance theory does not exist, it does seem that performance studies—as opposed to more traditional theater and drama—is still in the process of formulating its own methodologies and approaches.

One key difference between performance studies and theater studies—or, really, most any other traditionally defined discipline—is its necessarily interdisciplinary nature. That is, performance studies, like performance art of the 1960s, say, resists definition, commodification, reproducibility. This interdisciplinarity can probably be connected to the breakdown of the barriers separating "high" art and "low" art, which, though they became, after the advent of cultural studies, in some respects, simply cultural production, still retained enough of a problematic division to make the discussion of certain kinds of performance a difficult task for many critics. That is, though we know that we should—indeed, often must—discuss works that combine elements of mass culture and elite art forms, we often do not have a handy vocabulary for doing so. This situation is compounded by the fact that different disciplines approach the study of performance—including avant-garde and popular performance—in vastly different ways. Art history, which has charted the rise of performance from the Futurists' cabaret-like events to the work of the Black Mountain school and Allan Kaprow to the body art and conceptual performances of the seventies to the technology-drenched work of Laurie Anderson and David Byrne in the eighties has remained connected to the idea of performance as high art. Anthropology, in the hands of someone like Victor Turner, takes a more global and ethnographic approach and explores performance's connection to myth and ritual to expose the mystical aspects of the everyday. Similarly, sociology, in the work of Erving Goffman and others, shows us how the performance of self—or of everyday life—legitimizes the paradigm of performance as a method for understanding human communication. Theater studies, in the work of Richard Schechner, for example, sees performance as tied to various outgrowths to—though distinct from—theater in the Northeast and in California in the sixties and seventies. No matter how you cut it, performance is now an historically complicated field that encompasses so many different types of cultural production, performers, venues, and spaces, that we who study it need some markers to show us what it is exactly that we are doing when we say "performance studies" or even what we mean when we say "performance." Performance is also difficult to define, perhaps, because it is ever changing. The very excitement that we feel about the general field of work is in proportion to its continued newness—in fact, now more than ever. Technology, to take but one possible example, has opened up the area of virtual performance. CD-ROM technology and the Internet allow artists and ordinary people to mix media and develop their own characters, narratives, and special effects to create performances of themselves that embody the characteristics of subcultures.

The relationship of pop performance to performance theory is a complex one that we have only really begun to understand and Bowie's highly ironic and self-conscious casting of his performances as performances of self makes an analysis of his work particularly instructive. With that in mind, I would like to return to the question of how we decode performances and the tools we have for doing this and look briefly at Jennie Livingston's 1991 documentary *Paris Is Burning*. The film attempts to chronicle and explain drag balls held in Harlem in the late 1980s usually attended by African-American and Hispanic gay men. At the beginning of the film, the grand entrance of Pepper Labeija in full drag-glamour regalia seems to mark the occasion of the balls as one of high camp. Turning aside for the moment from the extremely important question of whether or not Livingston, as a white lesbian, is representing an African-American subculture in her film as a subjectivity or whether she is objectifying it, I want to ask how the obvious exaggeration of camp markers that Labeija promotes in the design of her costume and gestures relates to the other categories in the contest that are defined by the term "realness" such as "Upcoming Pretty Girl," "Town and Country," and "Executive Realness." What is being represented in these categories is certainly related to both class and whiteness, but they are lifted from media representations of fantasies about both. In other words, in what way are these elaborate performances about anything "real"?

One way to explain what might be meant by "realness" is to think of it as an update of the concept of passing. Just as the film's participants explain and illustrate that "to read" is an earlier version of "to shade," which ultimately becomes the art form "to vogue," so, too, does passing seem to transmute, within the space of Paris, into "realness." For the critic, then, one major question that seems to remain—other than the ethnographic one—is whether or not the drag stars want to pass when outside of this particular performance space. The film provides only a few possible answers. In the case of Venus Xtravaganza, who was in the process of changing biologically into a woman but is murdered in the course of the film, passing as female was, indeed, her ultimate goal. However, what is the point of passing when the category is one like military realness? Though soldiers are certainly a mainstay of gay erotic objectification, what exactly would you be passing as? The military already contains men who are both African-American and gay—a point made extremely obvious after the film's release with the advent of the "don't ask, don't tell" policy. In a sense, this policy required that all military personnel "pass" as straight at all times.

When he published his controversial *Black Book* (1986), Robert Mapplethorpe placed photos of his deceased lover dressed in a military uniform in the middle of his artistically posed images of nude black men. Though the photos of his lover seem quite ordinary, within the context of the book, they raised troubling concerns about the objectification of black male sexuality. In the context of the balls, the performance of everyday life—even when it is the military—calls into question the limits of transgression. Though critics have speculated about which of the film's performers are subversive and which have been duped into buying into images that illustrate—in sometimes highly complex forms—their own oppression, this approach underestimates the participants as authors of themselves as texts. The younger performers of the "realness" categories transform camp by pushing at the limits of what we can call queer performance practices to redefine camp's relationship both to fantasy and to the supposedly opposite realm of the real. The complexity of the lines of identification within the scenes of the performances in the film are already hopelessly complicated enough by the questions of the film's generic identity as documentary, the filmmaker's intentional or unintentional effect on the performances she witnessed, the court suits that have followed the film, the controversy over the family-like hierarchy of the "houses" in the film, etc. Is Paris burning? asks bell hooks. Yes and no, of course.

The drag stars in a film such as *Paris Is Burning* reverse the expectations of drag from something that signifies high fashion or the *bricolage* of a certain feminine type to one that calls into question our ideas about the authenticity of characters who can pass on the street. Oscar Wilde's famous dictum that life always mirrors art seems illustrated in the destablizing relationship between fantasy and realness that the new realness categories represent. In *Paris Is Burning*, the complexity of the lines of identification and disidentification within the scenes of the performances in the film present a complicated task for anyone hoping to map the exigencies of its use of camp and drag into an originary subculture. In each of these instances, we must ask ourselves how we theorize the performances we are seeing. Luckily, the individual performers seem always to demand that we do nothing less.

Notes

1   Simon Frith, *Sound Effects: Youth, Leisure, and the Politics of Rock 'n' Roll* (New York: Pantheon, 1981), 14–15.
2   Frith, *Sound Effects*, 14.
3   Frith, *Sound Effects*, 16.
4   Ibid.
5   Ibid.
6   Ibid.
7   Frith, *Sound Effects*, 18.
8   Ibid.
9   As Alastair Williams notes, "the Austro-German canon," with "Bach and Beethoven at the centre of its orbit," privileges "art rooted in text" and works "to exclude musics" "more firmly rooted in performance than in text." Alastair Williams, *Constructing Musicology* (Aldershot: Ashgate, 2001), 4.
10 This earlier version of pop music as sheet music can be seen in the film *Pennies From Heaven* (1981).
11 Frith, *Sound Effects*, 57.
12 Frith, *Sound Effects*, 17.
13 Frith, *Sound Effects*, 18.

14 Frith, *Sound Effects*, 19.
15 Frith, *Sound Effects*, 35.
16 Ibid.
17 Frith, *Sound Effects*, 36.
18 Frith, *Sound Effects*, 80.
19 Roland Barthes, *Image-Music-Text*, trans. Stephen Heath (New York: Hill and Wang, 1977), 149.
20 Barthes, *Image-Music-Text*, 150.
21 Barthes, *Image-Music-Text*, 152.
22 Barthes, *Image-Music-Text*, 150.
23 Barthes, *Image-Music-Text*, 151.
24 Barthes, *Image-Music-Text*, 150.
25 Barthes, *Image-Music-Text*, 151.
26 Barthes, *Image-Music-Text*, 152.
27 Ibid.
28 Ibid.
29 Barthes, *Image-Music-Text*, 182.
30 Barthes, *Image-Music-Text*, 181.
31 Ibid.
32 Barthes, *Image-Music-Text*, 183.
33 Barthes, *Image-Music-Text*, 185.
34 Ibid.
35 Barthes, *Image-Music-Text*, 187.
36 As Barthes argues:

> Such a culture, defined by the growth of the number of listeners and the disappearance of practitioners (no more amateurs), wants art, wants music, provided they be clear, that they "translate" an emotion and represent a signified . . . an art that inoculates pleasure (by reducing it to a known, coded emotion) and reconciles the subject to what in music . . . is said about it, predicatively, by Institution, Criticism, Opinion. (Barthes, *Image-Music-Text*, 185)

37 Barthes, *Image-Music-Text*, 188.
38 Ibid.
39 Ibid.
40 It may be worth noting that though quarter notes can be achieved on the violin, voice has the greatest range.
41 Williams, *Constructing Musicology*, 36.
42 Ibid.
43 Williams, *Constructing Musicology*, 36–37.
44 Williams, *Constructing Musicology*, 50.
45 Williams, *Constructing Musicology*, 54.
46 Williams, *Constructing Musicology*, 55.
47 Williams, *Constructing Musicology*, 65.
48 As Alf Björnberg notes, the use of multiple voices, of various sorts, is a trope throughout music:

> A basic feature of Western music since the Renaissance, and particularly of popular music, is the structural dualism of melody and accompaniment.

As [P.] Tagg indicates, this dualism is generally conceived in terms of a relationship between figure and background, or between individual/character and environment/setting. These are frequently consistently identifiable with separate musical "voices"; however, the structural specificities and polysemic nature of music also allow for the same "voice" to alternate between various functions, such as a guitar first playing a riff as part of the background, then switching to fill in the vocal line as a "secondary character," and subsequently becoming the "main character" in a guitar solo. As for the quality of "eventhood," musical structure may appropriately be described as a succession (and/or simultaneity) of events, ranging from instantaneous changes to long-term processes. From this point of view, "musical form" is defined by the particular nature of each musical event, by the temporal density of events and by their distribution throughout the duration of the piece in question. (Alf Björnberg, "Structural Relationship of Music and Images in Music Video," *Reading Pop: Approaches to Textual Analysis in Popular Music*, ed. Richard Middleton (New York: Oxford University Press, 2000), 353)

49 Williams, *Constructing Musicology*, 72.
50 Williams, *Constructing Musicology*, 74.
51 Gilles Deleuze and Claire Parnet, *Dialogues II*, rev. ed, trans. Hugh Tomlinson and Barbara Habberjam (New York: Columbia University Press, 2007), 164.
52 Qtd. in Deleuze and Parnet, *Dialogues II*, 165.
53 Ibid.
54 Ibid.
55 Allan F. Moore, *Rock, The Primary Text: Developing a Musicology of Rock*, 2nd ed. (Aldershot: Ashgate, 2001), 49.
56 Moore, *Rock, The Primary Text*, 206.
57 Roland Barthes, *Empire of Signs*, trans. Richard Howard (New York: Hill and Wang, 1982), 49.
58 Barthes, *Empire*, 49.
59 Barthes continues: "The vocal substance remains written, discontinuous, coded, subject to an irony (if we may strip this word of any caustic meaning); hence, what the voice ultimately externalizes is not what it carries (the 'sentiments') but itself its own prostitution; the signifier cunningly does nothing but turn itself inside out, like a glove." Barthes, *Empire*, 49.
60 Allan F. Moore provides the interesting notion of the "'third-person' authenticity, or *authenticity of execution*." He gives as an example Eric Clapton performing Robert Johnson's "Crossroads" in such a way that he seems to double the pain or the authenticity and to be himself, Johnson, and himself playing Johnson. "Within the blues rock movement of the 1960s, it became a matter of ideology that to employ the 'blues' within a thoroughly different social context, by venerating its originators, thereby enabled the appropriation of their very authenticity." Moore, *Rock, The Primary Text*, 200.
61 One can compare Bowie's lyrics on "Sound and Vision" to those written by German composer Karlheinz Stockhausen when he was similarly recovering from depression: "Play a sound,/Play it for so long,/Until you feel that you should stop." They are similarly Haiku-like, but also self-conscious about the composition process—or lack thereof. Mark Prendergast, *The Ambient Century: From Mahler to Trance—The Evolution of Sound in the Electronic Age* (New York: Bloomsbury, 2000), 114.

62   Bowie has said that on *Low*

> I kept them [lyrics] very precise. Little imagery in the lyrics, the imagery came
> in the music. I focused more attention onto the complexities and the textures
> of the music and let that do the talking more. . . . The most interesting thing
> about it [*Lodger*] is that it still used the textures of *Low* and *"Heroes"* but it
> applied more to a more conservative kind of melodic line which is something
> I hadn't used on those two albums and only fifty percent of *Station to Station*
> as well so it was a return to a strong melody form which then, of course,
> evolved into *Scary Monsters*. (David Bowie Countdown Interview 1980 part
> 2; accessed on YouTube.com, November 20, 2006)

63   The famous reference to "dolphins" on the song is a reference to the story "A Grave
      for a Dolphin," by Alberto Denti di Pirajno, which not only inspires the song but, in
      containing a Somali character, prefigures his second marriage as well. David Bowie,
      foreword, *I Am Iman*, by Iman (New York: Universe, 2001).

64   Note that I explore the Orientalizing effects on this album in more detail in Chapter 5.

65   While the number of subcultures or styles, musical and otherwise, that Bowie has
      influenced directly are too numerous to discuss here, some particular attention
      should be paid to the heavy metal genre. From Twisted Sister, Poison, and Guns and
      Roses in the 1980s to Marilyn Manson and KMFDM in the 1990s to The Darkness
      and Mercury Rev in the next century, the glam movement has always had a direct
      impact on heavy metal, which has, in turn, kept glam fresh and relevant. In some
      ways, the Mötley Crüe epitomized the Ziggy aesthetic ten years after it appeared—
      skinny bodies, dyed hair, and a vague rebelliousness tied to the anti-social aspect of
      homosexuality. On a song like "Girls, Girls, Girls" (1987) they reproduce the same
      homoerotic economy that one sees in the songs of the girl groups of the 1960s. Many
      of the girl-group songs, though often about boys, seem in retrospect to be about
      girls talking to each other ("It's My Party") and using the subject of boys as a way to
      communicate. The boys themselves often seem unimportant, or to never actually
      appear in the song as anything other than a reference point. If so, then Leslie Gore's
      song "You Don't Own Me" seems the rare moment of a direct address to a boy,
      but only as a way for the girl to proclaim her independence from him. Likewise,
      the exaggerated heterosexuality of the Crüe's song was really an excuse for boys to
      communicate with each other, and more pointedly, the descriptions of the girls in
      the song, while erstwhile strippers, could easily describe the band's members: "Girls,
      Girls, Girls/Long legs and burgundy lips/Girls/Dancin' down on Sunset Strip/Girls/
      Red lips, fingertips." See Rebecca Randall, "The Subcultures of 1970s Glam Rock and
      How They Influenced 1980s Glam Metal," unpublished essay, 2003.

66   Daniel Babcock, "Sex Fantasy #68: Yo Ho Ho," Dennis Cooper, *Discontents: New
      Queer Writers* (New York: Amethyst Press, 1992), 51.

67   Babcock, *Discontents*, 52.

5

The Lost Decade: Reconsidering the 1980s

Reassessing David Bowie's cultural production in the 1980s has always been a scarily difficult task. From the commercialization of his work in children's films and nostalgia projects to the disastrous self-absorption in some of his late-eighties albums, the decade is one that Bowie fans tend to avoid because of the seemingly weak work he produced after a string of artistic successes in the 1970s. Yet there are significant accomplishments, such as the short mini-movie, *Jazzin' for Blue Jean* (1984), some of his work with Iggy Pop, and a few memorable songs of his own, such as the nuclear horror show, "Time Will Crawl."[1] Most problematic, however, is the question of how to approach *Let's Dance*, the album from 1983 that did the most to redefine Bowie's career, for better or worse.[2] Either it is a cliff that Bowie walks off never to return (scrambling desperately to, in the 1990s, perhaps, or maybe even as late as *Heathen* in 2002), or it is the embarkation point for a great adventure that allowed him to change his audience and finally become the larger-than-life superman about which he had always dreamed. In either case, it is difficult not to see the album as connected to the 1970s and Bowie's now-central role in the music of that decade, especially as he defined its rejection of the 1960s. For Bowie seemingly to turn against the 1970s seems unconscionable, especially if it resulted in his defining the 1980s as something new and, ultimately, so very different from the art-rock ambience and general experimentation of his work in the 1970s, especially as the direction he went in was steadily away from the high-water mark of the Berlin period. In either case, this chapter will attempt to rectify the realities of the 1980s work with Bowie's artistic desires for it, looking not only at the music on his albums at that time but also at his exploration of what Edward Said calls "the Oriental" during his Serious Moonlight tour and his starring role in Nagisa Oshima's film of the same year, *Merry Christmas, Mr. Lawrence* (1983). I hope to show that in the 1980s Bowie's artistic production frequently references his great work of the 1970s, by throwing an interestingly complex light on it and frequently contains subtleties that are lost under the bombast and economies of scale that swept him toward a future he later claimed to abhor.[3]

At the time of the release of *Let's Dance*, however, it was difficult to see any grand plan on Bowie's part or to imagine the album as a blueprint for anything. The only context for it was the immediate one of *Scary Monsters*, which, though from 1980, was clearly a seventies album, one that self-consciously brought that decade to a satisfying close. While some would see it as Bowie's first eighties album, its signature single, "Ashes to Ashes," revisits Major Tom from "Space Oddity" (1969) and hence casts a backward glance from the vantage point of 1980 over the length of his entire seventies output. The album, also, is determinedly aestheticist in its construction, echoing the early glam and later avant-garde styles of his most productive decade. While much about *Let's Dance* sounded strikingly different, that difference could at first be taken for its own kind of experimentation—the bold, clean sound; a blues guitar put with dance numbers; spare, frequently opaque lyrics; songs seemingly lacking intros and outros, simply appearing then disappearing, all middle ground. Almost everything we had grown to expect of Bowie seemed to be missing. The startling changes seemed connected to his move from the record label RCA to EMI, another attempt to reinvent himself. The new sound of the album was difficult to process precisely because it was so different. In some ways, this very change was very Bowie-like, yet the new sound was diametrically opposed to *Scary Monsters* and was definitely one that Bowie fans would not have expected. Even now, it is difficult to know if Bowie was consciously selling out to the mainstream or trying to connect to his seventies output, especially *Scary Monsters,* by attempting to extend it into a wholly new direction. While Bowie seems to have been placing many of his themes from the seventies into a new sonic landscape, the fit was often awkward, and he was to find, in his magnificent concert tour to promote the album, that his back catalog of songs often represented a body of work that simply did not fit the new hits. The HBO television special that was based on the tour features a few songs from the album plus carefully chosen hits from the past but does not include the work from *Low* (1977) and elsewhere that would pad out the full concert. Once past "'Heroes,'" "Young Americans," and a few songs from *Ziggy Stardust* (1972), Bowie would soon tread into territory that would undercut the seeming 1980s-ness of *Let's Dance*. The full concert video shows the concert as much less audience-friendly than one might suppose. Likewise, songs like "'Heroes,'" "Young Americans," and "Station to Station" have often been misinterpreted by audiences as being less dark than they actually are, and Bowie certainly let audiences think what they would about those songs and others, though he avoided the cloying tendency he showed in the 1987 tour, where he purposefully misrepresented "'Heroes'" as a love song and "Let's Dance" as just a song about a party.

In 1983, *Let's Dance* seemed as though it reached back to the interconnected thematics of his seventies albums, almost all of which were, to varying degrees, concept albums. The opening song, "Modern Love," was the most experimental, with producer Nile Rodgers' scrapping guitar riff opening the track with a jarring feel followed by Bowie's spoken-word semi-intro. The ambiguity of the lyric, "It's not really words, it's just the power to charm," seemed like both a reference to his former aesthetic self— rock music as a theater of effects—as well as the romantic theme of the album, the abandonment (perhaps) to surface beauty and "sway." Slowly the album seems to give itself over to the latter instead of the former, though perhaps not on purpose. The straightforward politics of *Lodger* (1979) and *Scary Monsters* reappear on "Ricochet." Gender bending comes into play in the cover of Metro's "Criminal World." Those former elements do not work as well as before, in part because they fail to jive with the sound, are not reducible to the spare sonics of Rodgers' production[4], and seem, for the first time in Bowie's oeuvre, not to be genuine. Still, his old nature haunts the title song,

"Let's Dance," especially in the snarled, directionless singing that seems to undercut the romantic potential of the song, which is neither a luscious ballad nor a deconstruction of romance or false ideology the accompanying music video suggests.[5] His own cerebral thinking, in other words, screws up "Let's Dance," which is anything but a dance song. The title, however, is not quite ironic enough (à la "'Heroes'"). What wins out is a new heterosexual point of view that is tied to a nominal narrative that straight young people could relate to, especially males: falling in love while being suspicious of it ("Modern Love"); wooing the girl ("Let's Dance," "China Girl," "Without You"); growing bored, suspicious, or distracted by the girl ("Putting Out Fire," "Shake It," even "Criminal World"). Only "Ricochet" does not fit this pattern of teen love and angst over love.

Yet the lyrics of the album overall, while remaining distractingly obscure or noncommittal, give the surface illusion of connectedness. "Modern love" links to the "serious moonlight" of "Let's Dance" to the "love that never bends" of "Cat People." "I duck and I sway" of "Shake It" connects to the album cover, of Bowie boxing, and to the "sway through the dance floor" of "Let's Dance." "Color lights up your face" on "Let's Dance" and on "Criminal World" "the girls are like baby-faced boys." The red shoes of "Let's Dance" seem to reappear as the "eyes of red" in "Cat People." The serious moonlight comes in again in the "colder than the moon" of "Cat People" and the "full moon" of "Shake It." The "white of my eyes" of "China Girl" seems to get referenced again when Bowie sings "I look into my eyes" in "Without You" where there is "no smoke without fire," though in "Cat People" "I've been putting out fire with gasoline." Depending upon how you look at it, the album seems to contain either very few images (eyes, the moon, fire, dancing/boxing, women/girls, and love), or an elliptical structure that attempts to replay these bits toward some kind of end, some sort of productive ambiguity. But what exactly that story is, other than the eternal one of falling in love, is never clear. The real key seems to be the "serious moonlight": the attempt to make the theme of love and romance something more, to connect it to some sort of political agenda. The pivot for this issue is not the political posturing of "Ricochet" but the postcolonial complexity of his remake of "China Girl," which continues the theme of the Orient on *Lodger* ("spent some nights in old Kyoto sleeping on the matted ground") and *Scary Monsters* ("I'm under Japanese influence and my honor's at stake"; "Jap girls in synthesis") and carries over into his work in the 1980s with Oshima Nagisa on *Merry Christmas, Mr. Lawrence* and in the Serious Moonlight tour itself, which visited parts of Asia (Singapore, Thailand, and Hong Kong) for the first time for a tour of this size. Bowie's relationship with Asia, while that of a fan, is problematic on his remake of the song, however. Penned with Pop, the original song was far more personal, as Iggy sang about his relationship with his Vietnamese girlfriend, Kuelan Nguyen.[6] At the point where she supposedly croons to him to "just you shut your mouth," she prefaces it with "Oh, Jimmy," a reference to Pop's real name, James Osterberg. In this original version, recorded for Pop's album *The Idiot* (1977), Pop's dialogue with the "China girl" seems real and even touching—as though the listener has access to an intimacy shared between two lovers.[7] The song is built up of layers of guitars that shimmer and flush with the same depth of feeling that the song seems to try to convey. Bowie's version, by contrast, seems to emphasize the notion of the stereotype or cliché of the Chinese woman by emphasizing its artificiality, its fiction. Bowie's video for the song, therefore, contains numerous references to classic movies—from the make-out session on the beach lifted from the film *From Here to Eternity* (1953) to Bowie's running into town to reunite with the China girl while melodramatically pulling at his collar. Bowie is supposed to signify the man with the blue eyes, the Westerner who "wants to rule the world," but Bowie reduces the male character in the song to a cinematic type. Despite the exaggeration of the roles that the two characters represent, the video suggests that the relationship itself is supposed to be taken as genuine; that is, the China girl is supposed to be the object of his love—an early instance of the sort of interracial couple that Bowie would eventually inhabit as more than just a cliché.

When the video was originally made, in 1983, Bowie said it was a sincere attempt on his part to counter racism and was, like his video for "Let's Dance," filmed in Sydney, Australia, as a pointed rebuke to that country's then racist practices. Bowie purposefully went down under to create two videos with pithy antiracist messages and he spoke in interviews of what he saw as the "separate but equal" conditions much akin to the American South prior to Civil Rights legislation when black-and-white people would not be served together in the same bar or restaurant.[8] The video for "Let's Dance" purposefully films Aboriginal and white Australians dancing together and has, as its titular plot, an allegory about the dangers of globalization that stars young Aboriginal actors.[9] Bowie was attempting something similar with "China Girl," where he and director David Mallet cast New Zealand model Geeling Ng, whom Bowie met as a waitress, in the female lead. Filmed in Sydney's Chinatown during February and

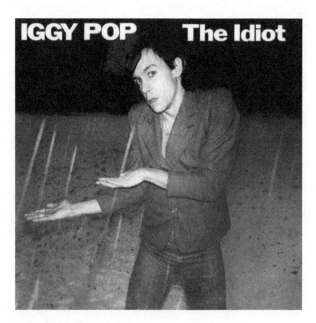

Figure 5.1 Cover of *The Idiot*, 1977.

Figure 5.2   Cover of *Let's Dance*, 1983.

March of 1983, the video's message was supposed to be fairly straightforward and won Bowie the MTV Best Male Video of the year. Even though Bowie's video seems to emphasize the line in the song "I feel a-tragic like I'm Marlon Brando" to call the falsity of the whole racial construct into question—that they are clearly and self-consciously playing two roles as actors—the video, by playing so close to clichés about Asian women, creates its own group of potentially racist issues. Though Bowie may mean to parody what people say about "China girls," the video seems, by so clearly representing the stereotypes, to be in danger of supporting them by not critiquing them enough—or by making the critique too subtle. The stereotype of the "China girl" itself is a dangerous one to play with, one that has numerous potential pitfalls that include, but are not limited to, the reduction of women from numerous separate races to one pan-Asian identity (hence, Pop's Vietnamese girlfriend and Bowie's Vietnamese actress are both called "Chinese"); the reduction of Asian women to the hyper-feminine, as though they are doubly marked as female (hence, Bowie and Pop's use of "girl"); the further objectification of the Asian woman as something to be protected, a fragile sub-First-World colonial subject to be given "television," though it may "ruin everything you are." Criticism of the song's lyrics, in other words, points up the song's—and the video's—potential datedness. The Orientalized subject of the song seems to reference conflicting historical notions of Asia. China was not, at the time of the song's composition, the world power that it is today, and Japan, the apex of the technology of "television," was hardly in need of colonial protection. By shifting the song's intention from personal romance to something like politics or ideological critique, Bowie opened the text to multiple interpretations, but also destabilized meaning in the song's text, creating possibilities that he was perhaps not fully able to anticipate or control. In the video, however, the actress becomes a character while Bowie, well known to his Western audience, does not. He remains David Bowie acting a part. The genders—and the races—are not equal, and Bowie's attempt to deflect attention away from himself (he is frequently the only real character in his videos for *Lodger* and *Scary Monsters*—his first important forays into the art form that would become the music video) just emphasizes the enormous gulf between him and other people, other artists or performers. Likewise, in the video to the song "Let's Dance" Bowie himself is clearly separate from other people—a god-like face in the sky, or a performer in a bar who is, with his white gloves and perfect tan, as aloof from the paunchy white Australians or Aboriginal stars of the video as he was as Ziggy Stardust on the stage or TV ten years earlier. His attempt to co-star, then, does not work. What the two videos share is an attempt to ladle essentially extraneous meaning onto romantic songs—or songs that appear that way to most listeners. The album's motto, "serious moonlight," suggests that the romantic situations and ideals in most of its marquee songs are balanced by a seriousness of message. But nowhere on the album is this seriousness present except perhaps on "Ricochet," one of the album's least successful tracks, and, maybe, the opening song, "Modern Love," which, in its faux-Victorian title, seems to suggest the possibility of taking something seriously: "want to stay in/get things done." This gesture toward the outside world is supposed to be present in the concert tour of the same name, "The Serious Moonlight Tour," which Bowie took literally.

The best-known critique of Bowie's video comes from Ellie M. Hisama's essay "Postcolonialism on the Make: The Music of John Mellencamp, David Bowie, and John Zorn." Hisama places Bowie's video in relation to the schlock–pop of Mellencamp and the more avant-garde stylings of Zorn who has also penned songs about the objectification of Asian women that emphasize them as demure fetishized objects, effectively eliding sexual desire with race. Hisama understands that Bowie attempts to do something different here, that he does not want to reduce the putative China girl to a sex object, but, though Bowie's song could be read "as a brilliant piece of irony,"[10] she also thinks that the song fails convincingly to represent the China girl as having any agency. As Hisama notes, "despite the narrator's claim that she has the power to get him to shut up, the chinagirl is never permitted to speak in her own voice—the first and only time she gets the opportunity to say anything, she mouths her line while Bowie delivers it in a monotone."[11] Ultimately, Hisama includes Bowie's version of the song in a long list of "Asiophilia" in which men enter into relationships with Asian women precisely because they seem more like "real" women, the essence of heterosexuality, finally somehow purer and less adulterated than women of other cultures.[12] In this sense, Bowie's video shows the Asian woman transgressing simply by being seen as equal to Bowie, a subject within a romantic pairing. Finally the bar is set low for Asian women because they are presumed to be preternaturally female to begin with. Bowie seems to be replaying an effect he used on the album *Scary Monsters* where he had poet Michi Hirota belt out the lyrics of "It's No Game" like a drunken Samurai soldier. The "little China girl" does not have the same kick, despite the video's attempt to suggest it should. Hisami's critique of Bowie finally rests on what she sees as his homogenization of the China Girl, refusing to give her specificity or individuality. The point of the song, however, may well be that she is a type—just as the speaker of the song is—though one could argue that this distinction is not enough since they are not equals to begin with. Bowie's version of the song de-individualizes the China Girl in order to play up the political and cultural meaning of the song, but again, strays into such dangerous territory that Bowie risks easily being misunderstood. Still, the music video goes further than the song does to make the China Girl tougher, more complex, and less of a cliché. As Hisama also notes, to the close-knit community of female Asians living in the West taking a white male lover is a kind of transgression—at one time an illegal one.[13] Bowie's video makes clear that this aspect of the attraction between the lovers is central to their relationship.

"China Girl" was not, however, Bowie's only engagement with the Orient in 1983. Asia became a general motif for the Serious Moonlight tour of the same year as the album. The tour, which sold over two and a half million tickets in almost one hundred separate venues, placed Bowie and his backing band and singers in an unspecified Asian port (possibly Singapore), a setting that comes through most clearly when Bowie performs "China Girl," the second biggest single of the album, which gets an elaborate treatment on stage. The song begins with Bowie's band sporting a mélange of Asian styles—a dashiki here, a pith helmet there—while his backup singers casually play cards and pass the time.[14] The "colonial fantasia" clothes were developed by opera designer Peter J. Hall with definite military touches.[15] Bowie saunters out with the coat of his pastel zoot suit flung over his shoulder. His song to his China girl seems low-key and romantic and a part of a narrative that suggests the song is both sentimental and seductive, possibly part of a bigger story to which we are not privy. Bowie appears suave and captivating, essentially himself rather than the character in the video, though he gives one of his most elaborate physical performances, at one point miming a couple in the middle of an embrace much like Sean Connery does as James Bond at the beginning of *From Russia with Love* (1963). Bowie again attempts to suggest the filmic or mythic origins of the song—that it is a song about simulacra, if you will, at least in his version. The setting at a port on a wharf also connotes the song's implicit implications of some sort of liminal space—a zone, like the wharves of London in Oscar Wilde's *The Picture of Dorian Gray* (1891), where cultures can come into contact and interact. Meaning becomes unstable in the watery atmosphere of racial and sexual blurring. Ports are the means to get to other places and the points where other places can get to you. The British Empire spread through naval power, but coasts are also vulnerable to "reverse empire," to the people who have been conquered coming back to the heart of empire to intermingle and affect the body politic. Bowie's stage performance suggests such a meeting, a moment when a white man and an Asian woman connect in some sort of British colonial port city bathed in the light of romance, a serious moonlight. Bowie drives this point home in the introduction and filler he filmed for HBO when the network aired a truncated version of the concert later released in its entirety in 1984 (and on DVD in 2006) in which Bowie and his band wander around an Asian port city

Figure 5.3　David Bowie, the Serious Moonlight tour, 1983.

like tourists from afar, wearing sunglasses, shopping. Bowie buys a grasshopper in a tiny cage, a Chinese symbol for good luck.

When Bowie's video for "China Girl" first aired, what was perhaps most surprising about it was the starkly heterosexual nature of the persona that Bowie had created. Not only was it romantic and seemingly, at first glance, mainstream, but the video presented Bowie as unabashedly straight, a shocking image from someone who had made a career in the 1970s creating a series of proto-queer personae. Even if Bowie's visual performance emphasized its very performativity, the character for the song seemed to go against type—a decision that angered many in his very loyal fan base. The new straight personality as seen on the album and in the video and concert versions of the song contrasted with his role in Oshima's *Merry Christmas, Mr. Lawrence*, in which Bowie played Jack Celliers, a British officer and man's man who is captured by the Japanese Imperial Army and interred in a prisoner of war camp in Java in 1942. As the focus of the camp commander's sexual interest, Bowie himself becomes a figure in a foreign environment—feminized, if you will, and made into an object of desire.

The very signifiers of white Westernness that Bowie sports for the concert—blond hair, blue eyes, sparkling tan—transform him in the film into everything that the camp commander, Yanoi (Ryuichi Sakamoto), wants. That is, Bowie becomes the Other. This transformation is emphasized at the end of the film, when Bowie is killed in a ritual suicide by being buried up to his neck in the sand, his beautiful head all that is left sticking out, defiant and sculptural to the end—a metonym for the West and a cherished token to Yanoi, who cuts some of Bowie's hair off to save.

In the context of Bowie's other Asian-inspired creations from the same year, one has to wonder whether or not Oshima's film offers another perspective on "China Girl": does it reverse the polarity of those performances to have Bowie taking the place of the "China girl" in Oshima's film? Does the movement into a same-sex environment place the work in "China Girl" into another perspective? Does it alter Hisami's damning critique of Bowie's racial and gender politics? Does it offer any insight into Bowie's antiracist and anti-imperialist intentions in his music videos? It is perhaps difficult to say, though Bowie's work from that year should be seen as all of a piece. He does not represent one but four China girls to the public, each one different but connected in some way. The problem for Bowie, and it was the problem for him throughout the 1980s, was that though he had more at his disposal than ever, he was not always able to convey the complexity of his choices to the public. The Asian port motif of the Serious Moonlight tour was surely lost on most of the many people who saw it; the viewers of "China Girl" the video and Oshima's film were from two very different fan bases. The "China Girl" phenomenon, then, was a sort of hologram of the 1980s in which each part contained the pattern for the whole, but the meaning was lost on most of his critics and his fans.

The interests and obsessions that Bowie had during the 1970s were carried over into the 1980s, though often in forms that were hard to see. The hand-swipe gesture that became a part of his gestural vocabulary at the end of the video for "Boys Keep Swinging" in 1979 reappears again at the end of the "China Girl" video when Geeling Ng smears her makeup—a gesture Bowie stole from the transgendered Berlin performer Romy Hagg, Bowie's erstwhile girlfriend[16]—to break the audience's illusion and make clear that what one is seeing is merely an act, a performance of gender.[17] Likewise, the barbed wire that appears at the beginning and the end of "China Girl" suggests the prison that Bowie is in in *Merry Christmas* and perhaps other imprisoning structures—like gender, race, class, and sexuality—as well. As film critic Adam Bingham has argued, "Playing at times like a riposte to David Lean's bloated *The Bridge Over the River Kwai* (1957), Oshima's film . . . plays out in a hermetic, enclosed milieu in which notions, indeed clichés, of national character and identity become performative, almost ritualistic, rites of passage."[18] In terms of the film's specific dynamics the connection between gender and nationality references how the West has often feminized and objectified Asian men as somehow less than real men, sexualized as passive objects. As Hisami notes, this tradition is at least as old as Giacomo Puccini's *Madame Butterfly* (1898) or as recent as David Henry Hwang's *M. Butterfly* (1998).[19] The notion of the Asian man as passing for female is tied to the notion of duplicity, of misreading the surface for the symbol, or applying Western standards to an identity that is not formed within a Western context. Oshima's film, however, and possibly Bowie's performances of "China Girl" as well, work the space between identification and objectification. As Takayuki Tatsumi writes about J. G. Ballard's childhood obsession with Japanese fighter pilots and their planes (outlined in *Empire of the Sun* [1984] and *A User's Guide to the Millennium* [1996], among other places), Ballard's "homosexually binational romance with brave Japanese kamikazes turns out to be intricately tangled with man's cybersexually fetishistic romance with sophisticated machines."[20] In *Empire of the Sun*, Ballard, as a young "Jim," is attracted both to the kamikaze pilots and to the ultimately superior technology of the Americans' B-29s. Tatsumi concludes, "It is through a looking glass called Japan that Ballard feels more comfortable effacing himself and creating an interzone where his British body melds with his American fantasy technosexually and multinationally."[21] Through the medium of film and video Bowie does the same, giving representation to a desire of escaping gender and nation, space and time, to become the sort of international presence that he had been since his album *Lodger* in 1979, which celebrates his peripatetic nature, his ability to be a citizen of the world.

The violence of sexual attraction does not seem to be lost on Bowie, who includes in the "China Girl" video a disturbing scene in which Bowie, as a sort of European financier in top hat and tails, first sees the China Girl working in a field (in some sort of Maoist retraining program?) and chooses her for a job in his factory. Bowie and a Chinese military officer approach her as she lies on the ground. Bowie makes his fingers into a gun and mimes shooting her. She rises toward him and Bowie pats her head in a demeaning way. By running the actual encounter between Bowie and the China Girl in reverse, some of the shock of the scene is muted, but when pictured in linear time, it is clear that Bowie is actually touching her hair and then miming shooting her. Captured in Bowie's usual miniature gestural form is a mimed reference to one of the iconic photographs of the Vietnam War, the brutal point-blank killing of Nguyễn Văn Lém by Nguyễn Ngọc Loan taken in Saigon in February 1968 (*General Nguyen Ngoc Loan executing a Viet Cong prisoner in Saigon*). As if to underline this reference, the image of Bowie and Ng momentarily loses its color saturation and becomes almost black and white. The sudden transition from color to black and white suggests the brightness of a gunshot as well as the iconicity of the black-and-white photo on which the scene is based. Bowie seems to make reference to the history of brutality of Asians by Westerners by depicting the brutality of war. In that sense, Vietnam becomes a generational stand-in for the Second World War as Bowie translates from one era to another.

What changes about Bowie with *Let's Dance* is that while previously videos and live concert performances had enabled him to expand and layer meanings onto songs that already had a large number of meanings—were indeed, elliptical or circular machines for producing nearly endless numbers of productively ambiguous meanings (from *Ziggy Stardust* through *Scary Monsters*)—his music in the 1980s depended upon the music videos and the Serious Moonlight tour to explain the music, or at least to provide it with a palatable political and/or cultural backstory to make it clear to some of Bowie's fans (or to Bowie himself) that he was still doing something artistic, if not avant-garde. The 1980s were a decade on which subtlety in general was lost or never took hold. And while Bowie may have been reaching, he was to plumb lower depths to come. For better or worse, throughout the 1980s Bowie was to say that he was doing things that were not clear to his audience: that, for example, the over-the-top theatrics of the Glass Spider tour of 1987 and 1988 were an attempt to do Pina Bausch in its combination of dancing and theatrics, as if Bowie had created his own attempt at "tanztheater."[22] The 1980s, or Bowie himself, would never let him have it both ways.

Music video

"China Girl" also came out, as did all of his 1980s work, at the moment of Bowie's MTV saturation, and indeed at the moment that the music video probably reached its peak. As J. Hoberman has noted, the music video form is an odd one in that it is putatively an advertisement for the music and/or the musicians, but it has also been stretched, via such venues as MTV, into an art form. The standard music video must cram the narrative or other meaning of the song into roughly three minutes. This extreme concision means that music videos have to eschew the dictates of most visual narratives. Though there is one tradition of music videos consisting of essentially filmed concerts, the more common is to offer some kind of illustration or interpretation of the song's lyrics. Working in such a concentrated time frame, directors of videos must often use the techniques of avant-garde filmmakers rather than classical Hollywood directors.[23] Music videos are, therefore, often a smorgasbord of effects often not used in typical linear television or film: rapid editing, including jump cuts; little character development; a self-conscious calling of attention to the materiality and conventions of the medium itself; effects borrowed from other art forms, visual and literary; and a blissful disdain for anything we might refer to as "realism." Music videos, in other words, tend to allow, even require, that the performers make clear to the audience that what they are seeing is not, cannot be, conventional according to the usual dictates of visual narrative. Music videos reverse the hierarchy of sound and image seen in film.[24]

In an overview of the scholarship on the structure of music videos, Alf Björnberg notes that B. Allan argues that music videos are held together by the songs themselves, which act as a ground or structuring device that glues the different effects or strands of the video together.[25] He also notes that critics fail to agree on the relationship between sound and imagery, some taking a specifically "Adornian" approach, others a more metaphorical one.[26] He takes Simon Frith's analyses to task, while acknowledging that the notion that the visual imagery of music videos is subordinated to the music has been influential.[27] Ten years later, Frith emphasizes the visual freedom of the music video form, agreeing with Hoberman, but arguing for the structural experimentation of music video, not from the standpoint of film, Hoberman's context, but where videos are shown: television (or, now, the Internet). That is, Frith argues "[that] videos are ideologically important . . . because they enable musicians . . . to translate their performing ideal into televisual terms directly, without having to be mediated by the established norms of TV entertainment."[28] Two aspects of this are especially important to Frith: "First, video performance isn't restricted to the usual performing settings." And stars can be

> move[d] . . . out of a musical context—into the everyday (the street, the home). . . . And what makes such movement coherent is not the song . . . but the performer (whose ability to impose herself on all visual circumstances parallels the ability of the live performer to impose herself on all musical circumstances, to register the continuity between sad and happy song, rocker and ballad).[29]

The aptness of music video for Bowie's skills resides not only in his own interest in the visual and film or in his photogenic qualities, but also in the very sketch-like quality of the medium itself. Performers in music videos appear somewhere between a role and a persona they play on an everyday basis. They are something like a personality, a news anchor, say, who is neither himself/herself nor someone else.[30] In terms of overall structure, the fragmentation of music videos parallels the rise of hip-hop music and its basis in sampling in the late 1970s. As Tony Mitchell argues:

> Scratching and sampling, the activity of "putting the needle on the record" . . . has become a focal point of pop performance in a decentered process of instant pastiche and recycling. It is a process remarkably similar to William Burroughs's notion of cut-ups in literature, in which the work of randomly selected writers can be cut up, juxtaposed, and "sampled" in a form of collage writing.[31]

As Mitchell goes on to note, this process has had a profound effect on Bowie's writing. It is not surprising that music videos, in their profoundly postmodern effects, would seem to be mastered so seamlessly, so early on by Bowie. Though his greatest videos may have been for *Lodger* and *Scary Monsters* in the seventies, his work in the eighties was seen by far more people and was associated with him during the advent of the first wave of MTV. Like David Byrne and Laurie Anderson, Bowie understood the essentially semiotic structure of music videos, the fact that they did not so much create originary content as quote from it. Like most of Bowie's style, it was always already ironic.

One can see Bowie's desire to place these avant-garde effects into his video work signaled by his showing Luis Buñuel and Salvador Dalí's short film *Un Chien Andalou* (1929) before concerts during the 1976 Isolar tour. A catalog of surrealist effects, the movie recreates in filmic terms effects from surrealist paintings. Some of these references are obvious, such as a mound of ants appearing on a character's hand—a private symbol used by Dalí in his paintings to suggest reality being eaten away by time—but some were seemingly unique to the film, such as sudden juxtapositions of different planes of reality—an actor suddenly finds himself dragging a grand piano behind which two priests are harnessed or a woman's underarm hair suddenly becoming a sea urchin and then reappearing on her face. Surrealism often tries to create a link between the conscious and subconscious mind through juxtapositions of objects appearing where they are not supposed to be. For this effect to work, the surrealist painters believed (at least some of them, like Dalí) that the image must be rendered as realistically as possible. Hence Dalí mastered the oil technique of seventeenth-century Spanish masters. The brilliance of the surrealists was in emphasizing the morphological similarities of objects and how they would substitute for each other in a dream, bringing a sort of dream logic into everyday reality. In this sense, then, music videos, or at least those that experiment with the structure of the song they illustrate, are mini-movies of surreality.

In going against the dictates of classic Hollywood film, music videos are also naturally avant-garde. They represent effects that film theorist Peter Wollen associates with the notion of "counter-cinema." That is, an alternative tradition to Hollywood film is to offer the idea that cinema can be about anti-mystification: a transformation in cinema that demands that we expose or show the way that Hollywood narrative mystifies or obscures the real relations of production of cinematic representations. Counter-cinema argues for a change not only in the content of film, but also in the modes of cinematic representation. If we were to list the characteristics of these two traditions and juxtapose them, they might look like the following: Classic Cinema is characterized by narrative transitivity, identification, transparency, single diegesis, closure, pleasure, and fiction. In contrast, Counter-Cinema utilizes narrative intransitivity, estrangement, foregrounding, multiple diegesis, aperture, unpleasure, and reality.[32] The avant-garde cinema that develops from the second list can be seen especially in the films of Jean-Luc Godard or in the work of such directors as Marie Straub and Daniele Huillet. The effect on the audience of avoiding linear narrative and character development can be called Brechtian—that is, estrangement of the audience, often for political effects. Many different kinds of directors, however, follow these techniques to varying degrees and effects and are just not as pure in their implementation of them as are some of the directors that we have been discussing here.

Orientalisms

The thread of the Oriental that runs through so much of Bowie's career, from the interest in Buddhism as a young man, to the Japanese-inspired costumes of Ziggy, to the Kabuki theater of the Diamond Dogs tour, to the references to "Arabia" and Japan on *"Heroes"* (1978), and to Turkey, Africa, and Japan on *Lodger*, to the use of Japanese lyrics on *Scary Monster*, to Bali and Palestine on *Tonight* (1984), Bowie made consistent use of the East as a mirror for Western thought, following in a tradition that goes back now for centuries. It is difficult to underestimate the importance of Asian culture throughout Bowie's career. Some of his sixties songs deal with Buddhism ("Silly Boy Blue," for example). He recorded a version of "Seven Years in Tibet" in Mandarin during the *Earthling* (1997) period. He also wrote pieces based upon Japanese music such as "Weeping Wall" and "Moss Garden" on *Low* and *"Heroes,"* respectively. Most importantly, perhaps, is the centrality of various Asian identities that he saw as androgynous and that affected his creation of the Ziggy Stardust persona. The Japanese designer Kansai Yamomoto, whom Bowie worked with on some of the most spectacular Ziggy costumes, has said he likes to make clothes for Bowie because he is "neither man nor woman."[33] It is important to investigate as thoroughly as possible, then, the relationship between Bowie and Orientalism that is opened up by his version of "China Girl" as well as by its presence throughout his long career. While many scholars have contributed to the study of postcolonialism, such as Homi Bhabha and Gayatri Spivak, it is Edward Said's *Orientalism*, first published in 1978, that gives us many of the essential concepts of the notion of the Oriental, especially as the antithesis or mirror to the West. Much of Said's book deals with the institutional history of the study of the Orient and he makes clear that the concept of the Orient is impossible to separate from the study of it—that the East becomes for the West an object, not a subject, that mirrors its "feminine" nature as a place acted upon but never acting. That is, as a region frequently colonized by Western nations, those same nations feel free to construct an idea or mythos of the East that reflects the West's preoccupations and projections onto it. The "Oriental," therefore, is the complement to the occidental—the exotic East that is really just a reflection of the West, however, at times subconsciously.

This argument, as Said cautions, does not mean that "Orientalism is . . . an airy European fantasy about the Orient" but is instead "a created body of theory and practice in which, for many generations, there has been a considerable material investment."[34] For Said, Orientalism is "particularly valuable as a sign of European-Atlantic power over the Orient" and is important because "continued investment made Orientalism, as a system of knowledge about the Orient, an accepted grid for filtering through the Orient into Western consciousness, just as that same investment multiplied—indeed, made truly productive—the statements proliferating out from Orientalism into the general culture."[35] Orientalism would not have its staying power if it were not hegemonic, itself never far from seeming inevitable and supported by the very people whom the concept burdens the most. It is not surprising that Orientalism is a European invention in that the notion of Europeanness is itself "a collective notion identifying 'us' Europeans as against all 'those' non-Europeans and indeed it can be argued that the major component in European culture is precisely what makes that culture hegemonic both in and outside Europe: the idea of European identity as a superior one in comparison with all the non-European peoples and cultures."[36] In its construction, however, the Orient is depicted as "irrational, depraved (fallen), childlike, 'different'; thus the European is rational, virtuous, mature, 'normal.'"[37] Therefore, Said explains, "knowledge of the Orient, because generated out of strength, in a sense *creates* the Orient, the Oriental and his world."[38] The give and take between the China Girl and Pop/Bowie seems to comment on this complex dynamic. On the one hand, there is some truth in the construction of the Orient via the West; on the other hand, Bowie never really allows the Orientalized subject to speak, perhaps inadvertently commenting on the power dynamics that the romantic relationship replicates, including offering the illusion of symmetry in a situation that is far from equal.

The history of the creation of the East as a distinct other runs as far back, for Said, as Aeschylus' *The Persians* (472 BC) and Euripides' *The Bacchae* (405 BC). As Said argues: "The two aspects of the Orient that set it off from the West in this pair of plays will remain essential motifs of European imaginative geography. A line is drawn between two continents. Europe is powerful and articulate; Asia is defeated and different."[39] Therefore: "It is Europe that articulates the Orient; this articulation is the prerogative, not of a puppet master, but of a genuine creator, whose life-giving power represents, animates, constitutes the otherwise silent and dangerous space beyond familiar boundaries."[40] And it is the danger that is the other defining characteristic of the Orient: "The motif of the Orient as insinuating danger. Rationality is undermined by Eastern excesses, those mysteriously attractive opposites to what seem to be normal values."[41] Bowie's version of the song could be said to match Said's claim that "hereafter Oriental mysteries will be taken seriously, not least because they challenge the rational Western mind to new exercise of its enduring ambition and power."[42] Bowie's song, and much of Bowie's work on the Orient, whether he is discussing Japan or Palestine, confirms and even makes self-conscious Said's point that "the Orient at large . . . vacillates between the West's contempt for what is familiar and its shivers of delight in—or fear of—novelty."[43] The novelty of the China girl is everywhere present in the song. In the winking parody of the pentatonic scale that opens and closes Bowie's remake, especially, Bowie calls attention to the novelty of an Asian-European romance.[44] Said is talking here, however, about the representation of the Middle East by Westerners, one in which "the European representation of the Muslim, Ottoman, or Arab was always a way of controlling the redoubtable Orient, and to a certain extent the same is true of the methods of contemporary learned Orientalists, whose subject is not so much the East itself as the East made known, and therefore less fearsome, to the Western reading public."[45] Bowie seems to go out of his way to make this point as well on "Loving the Alien" (1984). In the song, he talks about the campaigns against the Middle East ("Saracens") by the British ("Coeur de Lion"). In the second verse, he switches to the present ("Thinking about a different time"). The point, of course, is that nothing has changed, and the same religiosity is fueling the battles even today. The song's central message, the pathetic act of "loving the alien," could be read as a self-conscious homage, the alien being Bowie, but is more clearly about religion, which is literally a love of the alien, of that which is not human. The chorus drives this point home by noting that "prayers, they hide the saddest view," one in which "all your hopes are pinned upon a star." The anti-religious sentiment, however, is given an historical context—the war over Palestine—though it expands out from that specific context to embrace other aspects of the dangers of religiosity as well.

The Orient, as used by Bowie, is a form of Orientalism, which is not the real place, but what Said calls "a closed field, a theatrical stage affixed to Europe."[46] Bowie is tapping into a rich history of representation of the East as the exotic other. As Said notes, "The Orientalist stage . . . becomes a system of moral and epistemological rigor. As a discipline representing institutionalized Western knowledge of the Orient, Orientalism thus comes to exert a three-way force, on the Orient, on the Orientalist, and on the Western 'consumer' of Orientalism."[47] The Orient "is corrected, even penalized, for lying outside the boundaries of European society"; it becomes "the province of the Orientalist"; and it and the Westerner, likewise, must accept "Orientalist codifications . . . as the *true* Orient."[48] What was meant by the "Orient" also changed. From the Middle Ages until the eighteenth century it referred to "the Islamic Orient"[49] not the "Asiatic East."[50] "It is not surprising, then," notes Said, "that the first major work of Oriental scholarship after [Barthélemy] d'Herbelot's *Bibliothèque* [*orientale*] was Simon Ockley's *History of the Saracens* whose first volume appeared in 1708."[51] In the video accompanying the song, Bowie appears to animate a slightly surreal set that seems to be a town that looks vaguely Spanish or Middle Eastern. He runs from semi-abstracted painterly knights, who seem to represent the Europeans during the Crusades, and ultimately has a Middle Eastern bride. In an echo of the "Let's Dance" video, Bowie appears in a top hat and formal wedding regalia while his bride is in a dress made of money.[52] Later in the video, we see her tearing the money from the dress and throwing it at her chagrined groom. An Orientalist atmosphere pervades the video. A major motif is the stained glass window that is on the cover of the album. While in reality a tribute to performance artists Gilbert and George and their large photo collages, which sometimes maintain the sharp lines around separate panels thus giving them a stained-glass look, here it is also clearly a reference to the church wedding and to Middle Eastern art that is semiabstract and purposefully lacking in perspectival depth. In live album promotions that Bowie did at the time he wore highly patterned jackets, further echoing the intricate tile-like patterns. The bride wearing a veil ultimately morphs into an attendant at what looks like a hospital. Bowie, now with blue skin, like his portrait on the album cover, appears to be an inmate. At the end of the video, he takes off a pair of earphones, which we realize is the source of the song we have been hearing, and that the music in the video is diegetic. Bowie's former bride, now dressed in Western clothes, enters to give him a glass of water and bends down to kiss him. Suddenly, the video fast-forwards and Bowie appears to be falling through space, apparently becoming the person we see at the very beginning—his eyes folded in devout Christian prayer. At the beginning and the end of the video he chants the "ha–ha–ha" of the song with a light emanating from his mouth in obvious tribute to Laurie Anderson's similar intonations on her song "O Superman (for Massenet)" (1981).

In this song and, especially, in "China Girl," Bowie literally and figuratively acts out many of the precepts of Said's text. At the beginning of the "Alien" video, Bowie's seemingly Muslim bride turns his head toward a mirror, as if to make him see or confront himself. This act, a motif throughout the video, reverses a notion that Said says is typical in the construction of the Orient: "The Orient is *watched*, since its almost (but never quite) offensive behavior issues out of a reservoir of infinite peculiarity; the European, whose sensibility tours the Orient, is a watcher, never involved, always detached, always ready for new examples. . . . The Orient becomes a living tableau of queerness."[53] In this video, to some extent, the Orient watches the West—or, at least, looks back. If in "China Girl," the "girl" does not really talk back, in this video, made the next year, she does. But the point is that this is a deconstruction of the usual situation. The Orient is watched, commanded, lorded over. While making this point clear, Bowie also risks himself becoming the Orientalist, one who displays knowledge of the Orient, and intervenes in this discourse, but who also risks reproducing it. As Said notes, "The limitations of Orientalism are . . . the limitations that follow upon disregarding, essentializing, denuding the humanity of another culture, people, or geographical region. But Orientalism has taken a further step than that: it views the Orient as something whose existence is not only displayed but has remained fixed in time and place for the West."[54] This freezing of the Orient into an object was made possible by Orientalism as a field of study, which presumed, like Bowie in the "China Girl" video, to "put into cultural circulation a form of discursive currency by whose presence the Orient henceforth would be *spoken for.*"[55] Bowie, like other Orientalists historically, "is required to *present* the Orient by a series of representative fragments."[56] Indeed, Orientalism no longer refers to the "body" but to an "abstract realm ruled over by such hothouse formulations as race, mind, culture, and nation."[57] One denies the right of "Oriental culture the right to be generated, except artificially . . . in the laboratory."[58] Linked to this phenomenon is the overriding association of the Orient with sexuality. Said argues that no other aspect of Oriental identity is more important in a Western concept than this association. It is not surprising, then, that Bowie's China girl is in a romantic relationship with him or that he is married (seemingly) in "Loving the Alien." Sex was supposed to be given freely in the Orient because it was so eagerly desired by its citizenry. From Flaubert to other chroniclers of the Orient such as Richard Burton, the chief distinction between the West and the East was supposed to be the availability of sex, in a variety of forms, and a clearly unending supply and need for it.[59]

In the end, for Said, "Orientalism is fundamentally a political doctrine willed over the Orient because the Orient was weaker than the West, which elided the Orient's difference with its weakness."[60] The result of this doctrine was that "Orientals were rarely seen or looked at; they were seen through, analyzed not as citizens, or even people, but as problems to be solved or confined or . . . taken over."[61] In his more explicit engagement with the Orient in the 1980s, Bowie played the part of the Orientalist, which meant, paradoxically, a distancing from the Orient itself. As Said notes, "The Orientalist remained outside the Orient, which, however much it was made to appear intelligible, remained beyond the Occident. This cultural, temporal, and geographical distance was expressed . . . with such cultural metaphors as the veiled bride or the 'inscrutable Orient.'"[62] Both of these clichés show up in Bowie's videos, "Loving the Alien" and "China Girl," respectively. Bowie exemplified the nineteenth-century tendency to "[deploy] large generalizations by which reality is divided into various collectives: languages, races, types, colors, mentalities, each category being not so much a neutral designation as an evaluative interpretation."[63] This meant that seemingly Oriental decadence was "perceivable," in part because "a vocabulary of sweeping generalities (the Semites, the Aryans, the Orientals) referred not to a set of fictions but rather to a whole array of seemingly objective and agreed-upon distinctions."[64] This does not mean, however, that Bowie was completely wrong in these Orientalist gestures. The reality is much more complex. As Said notes toward the end of his magisterial study:

> My whole point about this system is not that it is a misrepresentation of some Oriental essence . . . but that it operates as representations usually do, for a purpose, according to a tendency, in a specific historical, intellectual, and even economic setting. In other words, representations have purposes, they are effective much of the time, they accomplish one of many tasks.[65]

The late eighties

"Loving the Alien," arguably a strong song weighed down by poor production, is one of many examples of good songwriting trapped within the dysfunctional album concepts of *Tonight* and *Never Let Me Down* (1987) and, like the handful of good songs on both albums, looks ahead to the politics and snarl of Tin Machine, though Bowie was unable to make the transition completely at this early date. In addition to "Loving the Alien" there is the short, pithy hit, "Blue Jean," which spawned one of Bowie's best videos, and the underrated remakes of Iggy Pop's "Neighborhood Threat" and "Dancing with the Big Boys." The big-band feel of the last two numbers is undercut by the unfortunate use of a reggae style on other tracks ("Tumble and Twirl," "Tonight") and the large number of covers on the album, which ultimately give it a tired sense of filler. Whereas *Tonight* was an obvious attempt at a sort of *Let's Dance*, part two, *Never Let Me Down* seemed to be an attempt at something different. Many of the songs are infused with a fifties or sixties rock sound and the songs that work the best—"Time Will Crawl," "Beat of Your Drum"—are fairly stripped down and minimal. The themes that lurk within the album are strangely disconcerting, however, and the album can perhaps be considered, at best, schizophrenic. While almost every song has something interesting going on in its arrangements or lyrics, the big-band sound of *Tonight* continues on some of the more overproduced numbers, which fits uneasily not only with the minimal songs but also with the seemingly political content of some of the album.[66] "Day-In, Day-Out" is a critique of poverty as told from a mother's point of view, which seems to continue a theme in the album's prelude, "Glass Spider," which is supposedly based upon a documentary Bowie saw on black widow spiders.[67] The song " '87 and Cry" is somewhat similarly about the political agonies of Thatcherism while "Time Will Crawl" critiques Chernobyl. This string of topically political songs is placed with two that are about older men preying on younger women: "Beat of Your Drum" and the Iggy Pop cover "Bang, Bang." The personae of these songs and others, while arguably political as well, certainly confuse the album's point of view. The political side seems to reference the first and best song of *Tonight*.

The video to "Day-In, Day-Out" opens promisingly with two angels filming the proceedings with oversized retro film cameras, one painted black and one white. Bowie proceeds to sing with the equally promising line, "born in a handbag," which references Oscar Wilde's brilliant comedy, *The Importance of Being Earnest* (1895), where the title character is accidentally left in a handbag by his distracted nanny who thinks he is a novel that she has written. The proto-surreal mixing of a baby with a novel adds a touch of self-conscious humor to Bowie's tale of economic plight and one woman's attempt to escape from it. Bowie seems to place himself in a Wilde-like position commenting on the reality of the scene, but framing it with several different layers: race (the woman is Latina); morality (the two angels); gender (Bowie is male, the woman is a victim of men); and sexuality (she ultimately takes recourse in prostitution). The video, in other words, tries to bring in other meanings than just the (fairly) realistic one of the story that it tells. This mixing of realism with stylization or surreality can be seen even better in the elaborate concert tour for the album in which Bowie attempts to add avant-garde touches to themes that are often overly simple or unsubtle, bringing to a point the problems he had in the eighties, especially the latter part of the decade, when he tried to expand upon his avant-garde credibility while simultaneously pandering to the masses.

While Bowie's Serious Moonlight tour was of a scale and perhaps an aesthetic unlike any that Bowie had produced before, his Glass Spider and subsequent Sound and Vision tours were both clearly modeled on formulae that had worked for him in the seventies. Specifically, Sound and Vision was a stripped down tour of his back catalog that looked back, in 1990, to his Isolar tour of 1976. Bowie even dressed similarly in white shirt and black pants commanding a stage not of bright white lights but of a scrim that played prerecorded video of him dancing with La La La Human Steps' Louise Lecavalier. Though co-conceived with Human Steps choreographer Édouard Lock, the tour combined touches of the Gothic—the gargoyles flanking the stage, the ruffles on Bowie's sleeves—with the minimalist Expressionistic style of the mid-seventies tour to support the Thin White Duke and his "sure white stains." While much more artistically effective than the earlier Glass Spider tour, the Sound and Vision tour was perhaps a sign that Bowie was trying to put his past behind him and ultimately rejuvenate himself artistically, something he would really not do until later in the 1990s. It was also a less ambitious tour than the one in 1987, which for all about it that failed, nevertheless attempted to mirror an even earlier seventies tour, the Diamond Dogs tour of 1974.

In returning to such large-scale grandiosity with the Glass Spider tour, Bowie was clearly referencing his mid-seventies experiment, combining the artistic ambition of that show with the stadium-scale success of his Serious Moonlight tour. Unfortunately for Bowie the show was not well received critically, though one can see within it glimmers of Bowie's attempts to reference other artists and to renew his seventies ambitions. The use of four dancers who were almost always on stage allowed for some elaborate choreography that was sometimes effective, especially on "Time Will Crawl," a performance that was captured on film and used as a music video. Bowie's collaboration with Toni Basil paid off in this number and one sees in others as well the blending of street moves and high-concept artistic influences that mark her work with Bowie, Talking Heads, and other rock acts.[68] The various platforms underneath the giant spider also allowed for multiple layers of effects, turning the space into a kind of circus, an image referenced on the covers of the album. The seventies are here most especially in the spoken prologue of "Glass Spider," which clearly references "Future Legend" on *Diamond Dogs* (1974), though the narrative, on the new album, is unclear. Other themes and connections are as well, especially the use of Pop's pedophilic "Bang, Bang" as the opening for the concert's most striking bit of spectacle when a young woman is seemingly randomly chosen from the audience (in reality, Melissa Hurley) appearing later in the number in a wedding gown that itself becomes a scrim over part of the stage. Video images, solos by Peter Frampton, some pantomiming by Bowie ensue, but the result is a sort of sticky soup of effects that cohere neither as narrative nor as performance art. While Bowie deserves credit for trying to find a way to recreate his aborted attempts with the Diamond Dog tour, he stumbles badly and fails to move beyond his work in the seventies, though he is obviously attempting to, at least on one level.

The concert begins strongly with a mélange of guitar licks by Carlos Alomar before the dancers begin to sing "Up the Hill Backwards." Bowie finally comes onto the stage suspended in a chair while talking on a corded phone just as he did during the Diamond Dogs tour, only here he is not singing "Space Oddity" but a song from *Never Let Me Down*. It is at this point that the audience realizes, in retrospect, that the concert will not really contain the hard-edged artistry of *Scary Monsters* or have Bowie's musical canon of the seventies to back up the theatrical effects. The material from the new album simply does not work well and does not in and of itself contain a narrative thread the way that *Diamond Dogs* does. The one entirely transcendent moment in the concert is the performance of "Time" that opens the concert's second half. Bowie ascends to a precarious platform above the mother spider's head to intone the song while gold wings unfold behind him. Bowie's vocal performance is spot on but the spectacle itself is touchingly effective, maybe because it is one of the few times he is on stage alone, without the dancers and the variously competing musicians wandering around. One focuses on the music, his voice, and despairs at the performance art that Bowie might have made in the show but failed to so very spectacularly.

As we attempt to take stock of Bowie's influence and the enormous amount of material that he produced in a career spanning more than four decades, we must keep in mind that it may be only now that we can begin to understand what was happening in his output in the 1980s—and perhaps, by extension, the early 1990s. The "Let's Dance" phenomenon represented not only the high-water mark of his fame, but also the point of highest saturation of his ability to make any one album into a multi-performative model in which the meaning of the individual songs are merely the Ur-text on which to drape other possible interpretations and performances—visual and otherwise—in the form of live concerts, music videos, interviews, photo shoots, etc. The album, tour, and subsequent publicity placed Bowie into the pantheon of highly paid stars and allowed him for the first time to hold his own with the likes of the Beatles or Michael

Jackson. The fact that Bowie would not stray near the top ever again was probably to his benefit as an artist, but the early 1980s emphasize the extent to which we have to examine not just Bowie's music but other concomitant performances as well. Bowie's work needs to be seen in the terms outlined by Raymond Williams, as "the whole way of life."[69] This cultural materialist approach, which I try to illustrate here, is the only way to understand what Bowie has achieved. We have to recreate as fully as possible the texture of each performative moment he created. Now that it seems increasingly clear that Bowie's career may indeed be coming to an end and we begin to access and archive it like the show at the Victoria and Albert Museum, we need to put emphasis on those areas of Bowie's career that we have not fully reckoned with: the late albums *Hours* (1999), *Heathen* (2002), *Reality* (2003); the leaked material from *Toy* and *Contamination*; the new material on *The Next Day* (2013); and to return to the periods previously found fallow, like the sixties and the eighties, when Bowie was constantly retooling, trying to overcome himself, and attempting to find his own place within history and to come out of a dark time alive and well.

Notes

1 Other highlights of the decade would include another remake with Pop, "Dancing with the Big Boys," which has great lyrics and is underestimated as a political song, and Bowie's greatest creation of the decade, his production and writing on Pop's album *Blah Blah Blah* (1986).

2 *Let's Dance* was a huge commercial success for Bowie, especially in terms of the tour that supported the album. The album went platinum in the United States, France, and the United Kingdom. The song "Let's Dance" reached the number-one spot on the Billboard Hot 100 for the United States. "Modern Love" and "China Girl" were in the top fifteen. The album received a mostly positive critical reception.

3 See, for example, Bowie's claim in Alan Yentob's documentary, *Changes: Bowie at Fifty*, that in the period 1983–84, "Commercially I sold . . . an awful lot of albums with work that I now feel was very inferior . . . artistically and aesthetically it was probably my lowest point" (Yentob, "Changes").

4 Though Bowie is given the sole songwriting credit for "Let's Dance," Rodgers has described in detail the process he went through to rearrange the chords of this song and "China Girl." See, for example, Nile Rodgers, *Le Freak: An Upside Down Story of Family, Disco, and Destiny* (New York, Spiegel and Grau, 2011), 190, 195–96.

5 "Let's Dance" is itself an unusual song. Just as the album of the same title is the black hole of Bowie's 1980s production, so the song is on the album, receiving by far the most ornate attention and production. Rodgers spatializes the song—much as Bowie does on his song "Win" from *Young Americans* (1975)—and brings his signature breakouts to the song—each instrument getting isolated and disconnected from the rest of the song while being forced to carry the rhythm or melody.

6 Pop was later to marry Suchi Asano, a young woman he met at a concert in Japan, in 1985. They divorced in 1999. Some of the songs on Pop's third and final album with Bowie, *Blah Blah Blah*, are probably addressed to her. According to biographer Wendy Leigh, Bowie had his own interests in Asian lovers. In 1977, he is purported

to have said, "I only like black women and Asian men." Wendy Leigh, *Bowie: The Biography* (New York: Gallery Books, 2014), 18. He dated Geeling Ng of the "China Girl" video while filming it in Sydney. Leigh, *Bowie*, 219.

7   Nile Rodgers speculates that the lyrics to "China Girl" might refer to "one of the nicknames for heroin among users . . . 'China White.'" Rodgers, *Le Freak*, 195. Iggy Pop was definitely known to have used heroin and at the time of the making of *The Idiot* he and Bowie were in Europe's heroin capital, Berlin. If Rodgers is correct, then the song's violent imagery takes on another level of meaning and the paranoid underpinnings of some of its lyrics might be explained as partly an explanation of the effects of drug use.

8   Among other places he spoke about this topic, see Ed Gibbs, "Dancing to Bowie's Tune Still Resonates 30 Years On," *Brisbane Times*, May 6, 2013 to May 13, 2013. http://www.brisbanetimes.com.au/action/printArticle?id=4247082. Here Bowie notes, "'As much as I love this country,' Bowie told the magazine, 'it's probably one of the most racially intolerant in the world, well in line with South Africa.'" Bowie had explored the area of the Outback in a Range Rover in 1978. "Bowie Don Laine Show 10.11.83". http://www.youtube.com/watch?v=p_88AR98z4Y.

9   As Buckley notes, the way Bowie places himself within the video he "visually and narratively becomes the 'bridge' between the dominant and oppressed cultures, partly with the capitalists, partly with the oppressed. He reveals the multi-layered complexities of keeping one's culture while participating with another, and the essential problem of the Aborigines being able to participate *at all* in a white dominated world." David Buckley, *Strange Fascination: David Bowie, The Definitive Story*, rev. ed. (London: Virgin, 2001), 397.

10   Ellie M. Hisama, "Postcolonialism on the Make: The Music of John Mellencamp, David Bowie, and John Zorn," in *Reading Pop: Approaches to Textual Analysis in Popular Music*, ed. Richard Middleton (New York: Oxford University Press, 2000), 335.

11   Hisama, *Reading Pop*, 335.

12   Hisama, *Reading Pop*, 341.

13   Ibid.

14   For more on the concert and Bowie's use of Asian motifs, please see chapter 5 of my book *The Aesthetics of Self-Invention: Oscar Wilde to David Bowie* (Minneapolis: University of Minnesota Press, 2004).

15   David Bowie Is, Art Gallery of Ontario, Toronto, November 20, 2013.

16   Buckley, *Strange Fascination*, 311.

17   Bowie repeats this gesture in his video "Jump They Say" (1993; dir. Mark Romanek), which is also about the violence done to the body by the imposition of allocentric identity systems.

18   Adam Bingham, "Merry Christmas, Mr. Lawrence," *Cineaste* 36, no. 2 (Spring 2011): 63.

19   Hisama, *Reading Pop*, 331; note no. 5. As Williams notes about Madame Butterfly: "Butterfly loses out twice, once as a woman and once as an Oriental, in two interwoven strands that constitute her status as other." Alastair Williams, *Constructing Musicology* (Aldershot: Ashgate, 2001), 62. Roland Barthes says that in Japanese theater the concept of "Woman is an idea, not a nature; as such, she is restored to the classifying function and to the truth of her pure difference: the

Western transvestite wants to be a (particular) woman, the Oriental actor seeks nothing more than to combine the signs of Woman." Roland Barthes, *Empire of Signs*, trans. Richard Howard (New York: Hill and Wang, 1982), 91.

20 Takayuki Tatsumi, *Full Metal Apache: Transactions Between Cyberpunk Japan and Avant-Pop America* (Durham: Duke University Press, 2006), 90.

21 Tatsumi, *Full Metal Apache*, 91.

22 See, for example, Bausch's signature fall, which Bowie seemed to incorporate into the dance steps of the concert and to use as early as his video for "Fashion" from *Scary Monsters*. Bowie's choreographer for the tour was Toni Basil, whom he had used before. Bowie's interest in calling attention to dance continued in his next tour, 1990's the Sound and Vision tour, which featured La La La Human Steps dancer Louise Lecavalier and was much more artistically successful.

23 J. Hoberman, *Vulgar Modernism: Writing on Movies and Other Media* (Philadelphia: Temple University Press, 1991), 154.

24 Hoberman, *Vulgar Modernism*, 150.

25 Alf Björnberg, "Structural Relationship of Music and Images in Music Video," in *Reading Pop: Approaches to Textual Analysis in Popular Music*, ed. Richard Middleton (New York: Oxford University Press, 2000), 350.

26 Björnberg, *Reading Pop*, 350.

27 Björnberg, *Reading Pop*, 351.

28 Simon Frith, *Performing Rites: On the Value of Popular Music* (Cambridge, MA: Harvard University Press, 1996), 225.

29 Frith, *Performing Rites*, 225.

30 Tony Mitchell, "Performance and the Postmodern in Pop Music," *Theatre Journal* 41 (October 1989): 275.

31 Mitchell, *Theatre Journal*, 287.

32 Peter Wollen, *Readings and Writings: Semiotic Counter-Strategies* (London: Verso, 1982), 79–91.

33 "Japanese culture, he once said, attracted him as 'the alien culture because I couldn't conceive a Martian culture.'" Qtd. in Ian Buruma, "The Invention of David Bowie" [review of David Bowie Is and of *The Next Day*], *New York Review of Books*, May 23, 2013. http://www.nybooks.com/articles/archives/2013/may/23/invention-david-bowie/?pagination=false&printpage=true.

34 Edward W. Said, *Orientalism* (New York: Vintage Books, 1979), 6.

35 Said, *Orientalism*, 6.

36 Said, *Orientalism*, 7.

37 Said, *Orientalism*, 40.

38 Ibid.

39 Said, *Orientalism*, 57.

40 Ibid.

41 Ibid.

42 Ibid.

43 Said, *Orientalism*, 59.

44 A pentatonic or gapped scale has five as opposed to the usual eight notes in a diatonic (major or minor) scale. The particular melodic pattern set up by notes with uneven intervals (spaces between notes) is often perceived as representing older musical scales from more ancient music cultures. In the case of China, the

pentatonic-scaled melodies, played on Chinese instruments, become a sonic shorthand, to Western ears, for the "East" (also part of the Orientalizing project).

45 Said, *Orientalism*, 60.
46 Said, *Orientalism*, 63.
47 Said, *Orientalism*, 67.
48 Ibid.
49 Said, *Orientalism*, 74–75.
50 Said, *Orientalism*, 74.
51 Said, *Orientalism*, 75.
52 An image that comes back in his video for "Black Tie, White Noise" almost ten years later.
53 Said, *Orientalism*, 103.
54 Said, *Orientalism*, 108. Later, Said notes, "Sensuality, promise, terror, sublimity, idyllic pleasure, intense energy: the Orient as a figure in the pre-Romantic, pretechnical Orientalist imagination of late-eighteenth-century Europe was really a chameleonlike quality called (adjectively) 'Oriental.'" Said, *Orientalism*, 118–19.
55 Said, *Orientalism*, 122.
56 Said, *Orientalism*, 128.
57 Said, *Orientalism*, 148.
58 Ibid.
59 For more on Burton and Western constructions of a sexualized Orient, see chapter 2 of my *The Aesthetics of Self-Invention: Oscar Wilde to David Bowie* (Minneapolis: University of Minnesota Press, 2004), 23–47.
60 Said, *Orientalism*, 204.
61 Said, *Orientalism*, 207.
62 Said, *Orientalism*, 222.
63 Said, *Orientalism*, 227.
64 Said, *Orientalism*, 233.
65 Said, *Orientalism*, 273.
66 Bowie has often bemoaned the production on both of these albums, though, in an interview I conducted via email with Bob Ludwig, who mastered *Let's Dance*, *Never Let Me Down*, *Black Tie, White Noise* (1993), and *Earthling*, the tapes that Bowie delivered were always in excellent shape. Bowie did not attend the mastering sessions and Ludwig worked directly with Nile Rodgers (on *Let's Dance* and *Black Tie, White Noise*). Like many other people, Ludwig was taken by the astonishing sound of *Let's Dance*—especially Stevie Ray Vaughan's guitar playing. While Ludwig gives a lot of credit to Rodgers for his arrangement of the songs and rhythm guitar playing, he also singles out the mix engineer on *Let's Dance*, Bob Clearmountain, for providing much of the album's successful sound:

> Bob was one of the first engineers in the USA to use the SSL (Solid State Logic) consoles which had specific EQs and buss compression that helped Bob to create his sound. Of course it is ultimately Bob's ears. It was Bob's use of reverb and the way the mix glued together, it was a very "hot" sound, even before the mastering. I once asked Bob how he did it and he said "I don't know, I keep patching things in until it sounds right to me!" (Bob Ludwig, personal interview, June 26–27, 2013)

67 "Glass Spider," *Pushing Ahead of the Dame*, March 30, 2012 to March 31, 2012. http://bowiesongs.wordpress.com/.

68 The dancing takes up a lot of the spectacle and represents a real emphasis on it for two concerts—this and the Sound and Vision tour of 1990. Here Bowie utilizes the troupe ISO Dance Theatre in a performance that was supposed to represent the "Chaos of Life." One of the performers, Spazz Attack, was the boyfriend of Toni Basil. And the choreography clearly references that of modernist and postmodernist choreographers who merged everyday movements onto the stage—whether Merce Cunningham or Twyla Tharp. Formed in 1986, the company performed a dance entitled "Psycho Killer," based on the Talking Heads song, in 1990. The company had connections to Pilobolus, whose athleticism is similar.

69 Raymond Williams, "The Analysis of Culture," in *Cultural Theory and Popular Culture: A Reader*, ed. John Storey (New York: Harvester Wheatsheaf, 1994), 60.

6

Music for Cyborgs: Fictions of Disability

After the surprise release of his new album *The Next Day* in 2013, David Bowie was in the news again a few months later, this time for releasing a list of his 100 essential novels.[1] While a wide-ranging list that shows the extent to which seminal novels of the fifties and sixties seem to have formed the core of his intellectual influences, there were other patterns as well, such as a penchant for postmodern novels written in the eighties and nineties. Not surprisingly, there were a number of books related to science fiction and fantasy, such as Anthony Burgess' *A Clockwork Orange* (1962), and to underground culture, especially sexual culture, such as John Rechy's *City of Night* (1963). Some of the literary influences by writers who did not make his list—J. G. Ballard and William S. Burroughs—have been mentioned by Bowie before in songs or in interviews and have a great deal in common with Bowie's own worldview. Both writers represent the outer limits of the science fiction genre itself, with neither writer really identifying with its mainstream. Both writers also provided alternative definitions of identity that centered on the body and sexuality. For Burroughs this meant the rejection of what he saw as the normative definition of male homosexuality, which he explored realistically in his early novels *Queer* (1951–53; 1985) and *Junky* (1953) and more surreally in later novels like *Naked Lunch* (1959) or *The Wild Boys* (1971). In Ballard, it was the fusion of the body with machines to create a kind of technosexuality, reframing the body for new urban landscapes as he does most famously in *Crash* (1973) but also in such novels as *High-Rise* (1975) and *Concrete Island* (1974). Bowie's music, concerts, and personae were affected by the multiple selves theorized by Ballard and Burroughs as can be seen in his own parahuman creations, which carried on their traditions of queer, alienated, postapocalyptic alternatives to mainstream culture generally and have recurred throughout his work.

Bowie's indebtedness to Burroughs is mainly during the time of his glam period, which encompasses *Ziggy Stardust* (1972), *Aladdin Sane* (1973), and *Diamond Dogs* (1974). The last often gets lost in the shuffle though it is better than *Aladdin Sane*, darker than all three, and brings the literary allusions that permeate the trilogy to a head. Based originally on George Orwell's *1984* (1949), Orwell's widow would not allow Bowie permission to do the full-scale rock opera version of the novel that he had envisioned. Instead, Bowie created his own characters, keeping some of the plotting from the novel in some of his songs, but overall inventing his own version of a postapocalyptic world. This alternate version of the future, one in which people have exhausted the landscape and live with a sense of ending, of telos and eschatology, is a theme on all three albums. Beginning with the cracked waltz-like cadences of "Five Years" on *Ziggy Stardust*, the theme of a world in which life itself is imperiled or hemmed in announced a new seventies version of the future. While not exactly a retro future of later steampunk invention, it was an antitechnological future, one that rejected the pop modernism of films, television, and theme parks that projected a gleaming, seamless world of man and machine, the apogee of which is perhaps Stanley Kubrick's *2001: A Space Odyssey* (1968). While hardly a simple utopian film, it could be read symbolically as a hopeful one by some. Bowie, who had been impressed by *2001*, bases "Space Oddity" (1969) on Kubrick's film. Written a year before the moon landing, the song is filled with the same kind of melancholy that suffuses all of Kubrick's late films. But overall Bowie's worldview is based much more on Kubrick's next film, *A Clockwork Orange* (1971), which offers a distinctly different version of the future.

Bowie borrows liberally from Kubrick for both his emphasis on a proto-punk aesthetic, an anti-hero who expresses nihilism and violent epicureanism as his personal philosophies, and for his emphasis on youth—that it is the kids who will prematurely dominate the earth, inherit a decrepit landscape, and be rewired by the sped-up consumption of sex and violence in music and film that they will act out with abandon. The prescience of Anthony Burgess' original novel is not lost on either Kubrick or Bowie. Yet *A Clockwork Orange* is the most Bowie-like of all of Kubrick's films because it ultimately approaches a science fiction future as an intensification of the present. Kubrick begins with the year 1971 and exaggerates everything—from the baroque design of interiors and clothes to the music video imagination with which the film's protagonist, Alex DeLarge, experiences sex and violence set to Wendy Carlos' synthesizer-treated classical music.

In Bowie's famous Ziggy Stardust album tour the pre-show music was the same version of Beethoven's Ninth Symphony. Bowie's costume in part owed something to the booted Englishness of Kubrick's version of Alex and his Droogs, with their immaculate, dandified codpieces and artificial eyelashes.[2] Bowie's reworking of these cinematic sources was central to the aesthetic he was to develop over the course of his career. Bowie always attempted to combine the effects of as many art forms as possible. As he notes in a famous interview with William S. Burroughs for *Rolling Stone*, "I must have the total image of a stage show. It has to be total with me. I'm not just content writing songs. I want to make it three-dimensional. Songwriting as an art is a bit archaic now. Just writing a song is not good enough."[3] As he later notes, "A song has to take on character, shape, body and influence people to an extent that they use it for their own devices. It must affect them not just as a song, but as a lifestyle."[4] In his use of theatrical props, elaborate costuming and makeup, and eventually sets and lighting, Bowie combined his own influences from mime, theater, fiction, philosophy, and a hyper-fan's intimate knowledge of the history of rock and roll to create not only a striking stage presence but extend it to life off the stage, where Bowie would stay in Ziggy costume, attending parties and concerts in the same clothing and appear, for all intents and purposes, to be Ziggy all the time. Bowie himself enacted the idea of taking a song and making it a lifestyle. Ziggy inaugurated the first of Bowie's great personae, which, while influential and defining for Bowie, also became, by the end of the seventies, a paradigm that he wanted to move on from as his own personality could be engulfed by those of his alter egos.

In the conversation with Burroughs for *Rolling Stone* Bowie also praised Burroughs' cut-up method, developed with Brion Gysin as a way to alter text randomly by cutting it up and rearranging it. Burroughs used this method to alter the syntax and meaning of sentences and words so that he could decenter the thought processes that are literally encoded by the brain as it learns to process language and other elaborate systems of thought. Bowie saw this technique in Burroughs' novel *Nova Express* (1964) and says in the interview that he was drawn to it because it reminded him of what he was trying to do with Ziggy Stardust. Burroughs remarks that Bowie is talking about "visual cut-up," "a very good idea."[5] Bowie was to go on to use the cut-up method literally to compose music, most obviously on the albums *Diamond Dogs* and, almost twenty years later, his second-darkest Goth creation, *Outside* (1995). Burroughs and Bowie were right, however, that Bowie's stage creations were already like cut-ups, even though it is possible that reading *Nova Express* in preparation for this interview was the first time Bowie had ever read Burroughs' writing.[6] At the time of the interview, in 1974, Bowie was working on a musical theater version of the Ziggy album, a project he mentioned periodically throughout his career. Some of what excites him about Burroughs' technique is the fact that it meshes with his dreams for this project, especially a Dadaist approach in which scenes would change randomly every night.[7] While this drama or opera has never come to pass, the tour that accompanied Bowie's release of the *Diamond Dogs* album is famous in the annals of rock history for its elaborate sets and scenery. Bowie hired Broadway set designer Jules Fisher to create a cityscape, Hunger City, as the backdrop for the show. The set consisted of a skyscraper, a bridge that could swing apart, and a giant cherry picker to elevate Bowie above the audience. The set was based in part upon the catwalks and cantilevered stage used by The Living Theatre and first used by Bowie in the 1972 *Ziggy Stardust Show* that Bowie produced with his mentor Lindsay Kemp.[8] At the time, the Diamond Dogs show was the most elaborate rock show ever created. All numbers were highly choreographed by Toni Basil, with Bowie often appearing with backup dancers and his band tucked discretely off the stage to emphasize the theatrical nature of the event, its role as something other than a rock concert.[9] Bowie's tour took further than anyone had at the time, and perhaps ever will, the idea of a rock concert as theater or performance art. While some of the numbers echoed the album—Bowie singing "Sweet Thing" from atop the bridge, for example—other numbers also had their own bit of theatricality. Bowie was a boxer in a ring ("Panic in Detroit"), an actor shouting Shakespeare ("Cracked Actor"), a performer in a Kabuki play ("Aladdin Sane"). The concert was an attempt by Bowie to combine the various arts that he practised into one multimedia show. It was ahead of its time, maybe literally from a technical standpoint as many of the props and parts of the set malfunctioned on a regular basis. Bowie scrapped the concept mid-tour and replaced it with the stripped-down Philly/Dogs tour, which showcased some of his new songs for Young Americans.

Like Bowie, Burroughs likewise worked with visual art, often parallel to his writing, but toward the end of his life, Burroughs devoted more and more time to it. Beginning as early as 1961 in Tangier, Burroughs experimented with a "fold-in" technique to create photographic collages. A visual equivalent to his cut-up technique for writing, Burroughs similarly borrowed the idea from the surrealists.[10] Burroughs' visual art, in the form of scrapbooks and limited editions, eventually led to his famous shotgun paintings, which brought to the fore the element of randomness that was central to the cut-up method. Shooting a shotgun at a can of spray paint near a canvas produced what he called a "randomizing technique."[11] Though never a part of a school of painting, Burroughs' art shares some similarities with the Nouveau Réalisme of Niki de Saint Phalle and Yves Klein. Burroughs knew Marcel Duchamp and once noted that "Duchamp shot at his paintings."[12] Burroughs also mentioned Klein in relation to his writing. The combination of Duchamp, the master conceptualist, and Klein, known as an important forerunner of both performance art and pop art, places Burroughs squarely in line with Bowie's aesthetic choices and points up the intermedial aspects of his novels, in which so much time and energy is put into specifically visual description rather than unfolding narrative.[13]

Bowie, similarly, worked seriously in other artistic media. Based upon research done on Bowie's work for the "David Bowie Is" exhibit at London's Victoria and Albert Museum, we now know that Bowie also planned to film the show. As early as 1973 Bowie produced storyboards that included videos. Most interestingly, the plans for the film project mention that the main character for the album, Halloween Jack, controls a gang of boys on roller skates. While obviously a reference to Charles Dickens' *Oliver Twist* (1838), the neo-Victorian setting seems also very close to, if not based upon, Burroughs' *Wild Boys: A Book of the Dead*, which was published in 1971 and details the near future of 1988. Typical of Bowie's work since 1970, there is a complex mesh of times, places, and other works of art to which he makes reference. The set for the concert also recalls Robert Wiene's *Caligari* (1920), Fritz Lang's *Metropolis* (1927), George Grosz's paintings of twenties Berlin, and Eric Hechel's *Self-Portrait* of 1917. There was even supposed to be a building with the name "Bowies." The set is, in other words, a palimpsest of Bowie's interests, a sort of Rorschach test of his mind at that time. The dark dystopianism seems both to reprocess the past, most specifically Berlin between the wars, and to provide a glimpse into a future that has become the past again, only in a different physical setting. As in Victorian London, packs of feral boys overrun the city, disorder reigns, and hunger and savagery are the name of the game. While the album's plot is a mixture of Orwell and Bowie's various interests, references to politicians and a secret love affair seem to be retained, as does the notion of Big Brother.

The soft machines

Bowie's invocation of the wild boys is mostly made in the album's opening title song, which explains the life of Halloween Jack, "a real cool cat" who lives on top of "Manhattan Chase." He swings down from his burned-out apartment block on a rope, since the elevator is gone, and lives among amputees who drag themselves along the street. The "peoploids" who inhabit this world are indeed "diamond dogs," parahumans who have evolved in an environment of ruin. In the album's opening prologue, "Future Legend," either the peoploids or wild boys can be heard in the background as a sort of choric accompaniment to Bowie.[14] As the title suggests, the album will combine a vision of the future via a form of the past—that is, a legend. Here and in the title song, Bowie uses distortion, feedback, and invented diction to create the futuristic edge that permeates much of the album and that is combined with purposefully primitive sound effects such as the repeated striking of a cowbell or the baying of dogs to create a contrasting noise that mimics something closer to the seediness of country or blues music.[15] Bowie's voice is frequently distorted and/or multitracked throughout the album to give it a theatrical effect that previews his use of distorted voice on *Outside* and that makes the album, in its use of vocal textures, sound at the time much like Brian Eno's *Taking Tiger Mountain (By Strategy)* (1974) or, later, Laurie Andersen's *Big Science* (1982).

It is difficult to imagine that Bowie did not have Burroughs' wild boys in mind for this environment, especially in terms of the planned-for filmed version of the concert. George Tremlatt quotes Bowie as saying in 1974:

> I had in mind this kind of half *Wild Boys, Nineteen Eighty-Four* world . . . and there were these ragamuffins, they were a bit more violent than ragamuffins. I guess they staggered through from *Clockwork Orange* too. They'd taken over this barren city, this city that was falling apart. They'd been able to break into windows of jewelers and things, so they'd dressed themselves up in furs and diamonds, but they had snaggle teeth—really filthy, kind of like violent Oliver Twists. It was a take on, what if those guys had gone malicious? If Fagin's gang had gone absolutely ape-shit?[16]

As he further elaborates:

> So I had the Diamond Dogs as living on the streets. They were all little Johnny Rottens and Sid Viciouses really. And, in my mind, there was no means of transport, so they were all rolling around in these roller-skates with huge wheels on them, and they squeaked because they hadn't been oiled properly. So there were these gangs of squeaking roller-skating, vicious hoods, with Bowie knives and furs on and they were all skinny because they hadn't eaten enough, and they all had funny-coloured hair. In a way it was a precursor to the punk thing.[17]

The image of starving children comes as well from stories that Bowie's father told him about destitute children who lived on the rooftops of buildings in London's late-Victorian slums, a detail perhaps echoed in the song "We Are the Dead" in a reference to the "Urchin one." In a way, the melding of Kubrick and Burroughs that Bowie makes here is a chance for him finally to use an image that had struck him as a child. *Diamond Dogs*, the album and the song, replays a Victorian trope as a sign of the future, a reality that will come to pass again only with different details and in an even more virulent form. Children have divided into gangs and filled the vacuum of the postapocalyptic urban landscape otherwise populated with corpses, disease, and vermin. It is not surprising that the album ends bleakly and ambiguously with the sinister song entitled "Chant of the Ever Circling Skeletal Family."

In a chapter of *The Wild Boys* entitled the same, Burroughs describes the wild boys thusly:

> Groups scattered over a wide area from the outskirts of Tangier to the Blue Desert of Silence . . . glider boys with bows and laser guns, roller-skate boys—blue jockstraps and steel helmets, eighteen-inch bowie knives—naked blowgun boys long hair down their backs a kris at the thigh, slingshot boys, knife throwers, bowmen, bare-hand fighters, shaman boys who ride the wind and those who have control over snakes and dogs, boys skilled in bone-pointing and Juju magic who can stab the enemy reflected in a gourd of water, boys who call the locusts and the fleas, desert boys shy as little sand foxes, dream boys who see each other's dreams. . . . Each group developed special skins and knowledge until it evolved into humanoid subspecies. One of the more spectacular units is the dreaded Warrior Ants made up of boys who have lost both hands in battle. They wear aluminum bikinis and sundials and light steel helmets. They are attended by musicians and dancing boys, medical and electronic attendants who carry the weapons that are screwed into their stumps, buckle them into their bikinis, lace their sandals, wash and anoint their bodies with a musk of genitals, roses, carbolic soap, gardenias, jasmine, oil of cloves, ambergris and rectal mucus.[18]

Though his description of the wild boys emphasizes their violence, their role as a sort of plague sweeping across the desert and into the suburbs to bring pestilence and danger, Burroughs also sympathizes with them. They are the apotheosis of a certain kind of adolescent sexuality containing not only his fantasies for the destruction of "dogmatic thinking," whether in the form of language or government, but also for the possibility of a pure gender. In the sometimes uneasy mixture of science and science fiction that is typical of Burroughs, the chapter goes on to explain the genesis of the wild boys, who find a way to reproduce themselves without the aid of female biology:

> A baby- and semen black market flourished in the corrupt border cites, and we recruited male infants from birth. You could take your boy friend's sperm to market, contact a broker who would arrange to inseminate medically inspected females. Nine months later the male crop was taken to one of the remote peaceful communes behind the front lines. A whole generation arose that had never seen a woman's face nor heard a woman's voice. In clandestine clinics fugitive technicians experimented with test tube babies and [anal] cuttings.[19]

While prescient in his imagining test tube babies, Burroughs is also guilty of a misogyny that makes itself explicit in some of the interviews that he participated in at the time he was writing the novel that were collected by Daniel Odier as *The Job: Interviews with William S. Burroughs* (1969). Burroughs' fantasy of a woman-less future is made explicit when he writes: "Little boy with out a navel . . . places an apple on the teacher's desk. 'I am giving you back your apple teacher.' He walks over to the blackboard and rubs out the word MOTHER."[20] The wild boys move on from here to find another way to regenerate themselves, finally not needing science at all, but reproducing during a ceremony that seems to be based upon Native American and other types of "primal" cultures. Burroughs' narrator ("a snippy Fulbright queen") describes the creation of the wild boys from a Zimbu:

> Another boy stepped onto the rug. He stood in the center of the rug and leaned forward hands on knees his eyes following the lines and patterns. His penis stiffened. He stood upright and walked to the four directions lifting his hands each time and saying one word I did not catch. A little wind sprang up that stirred the boy's pubic hairs and played over his body. He began to dance to the flutes and drums and as he danced a blue will-o'-the-wisp took shape in front of him shifting from one side of the rug to the other. The boy spread out his hands. The will-o'-the-wisp tried to dodge past but he caught it and brought his arms together pulling the blue shape against him. The color shifted from blue to pearly grey streaked with brown. His hands were stroking a naked flank and caressing a penis out of the air buttocks flattened against his body as he moved in fluid gyrations lips parted teeth bared. A brown body solid now ejaculated in shuddering gasps sperm hitting the rug left white streaks and spots that soaked into the crisscross of white lines. The boy held the Zimbu up pressing his chest in and out with his own breathing quivering to the blue tattoo. The Zimbu shuttered and ejaculated again. He hung limp in the other's arms. The attendants stepped forward with another litter. The Zimbu was carried away to the blue tent.[21]

Burroughs' unique mixture of pornography and poetic technique adds an emotional edge to this writing that makes it seem more a celebration of homoeroticism than a comment on gender politics.[22] The wild boys are a central feature of Bowie's dystopian world, and the homoerotic aspect shows up in his album as well. The chorus to the most ambitious song on *Diamond Dogs*, the suite entitled "Sweet Thing/Candidate/Sweet Thing," is, "boys, boys, get it here thing." While this song seems to have an especially complicated interweaving of subject matter, linking sex and drugs to politics and the French Revolution, it is clearly a song about come-ons, in whatever form, set against a background of doom.[23]

Burroughs' subject matter, however risible, emphasizes the positive view that he takes of his own postapocalyptic future. Rather than seeing the boys as beyond the female, in some sort of Peter Pan-like state of a return to nature that turns out better than the *Lord of the Flies* (1963), one can also see the wild boys as striking in their gayness. That is, Burroughs' utopian vision influences Bowie because of its queerness, not its gender phobia. The sensuous and sensual celebration of the bodies of the boys is Burroughs' way to emphasize that the physical bond between the boys is also an emotional, even spiritual one.[24] The celebration of their postmodern paraphernalia, their blue jock straps and metal helmets, emphasizes their bodies, the *bricolage* of their invention.[25] In that sense, Burroughs' utopianism is not dissimilar from that of Monique Wittig's in *Les Guérillères* (1969), where she reminds the reader of the materiality of the lesbian body, poeticizing it by detailing it lovingly but without the conventions of traditional feminine beauty.[26] As in the *Wild Boys*, the lesbians rewrite history, removing patriarchy and filling in the fragments of Western culture where women have been erased. After this book and its companion volumes, *The Lesbian Body* (1973) and *Lesbian Peoples—Materials for a Dictionary* (1976), Wittig was to go on and literally rewrite key texts of the Western canon—the Quixote in *The Constant Journey* (1985) and Dante in *Across the Acheron* (1985), for example. To some extent, Burroughs is doing the same. He would go on from the *Wild Boys* to write a trilogy of books—*Cities of the Red Night* (1981), *The Place of Dead Roads* (1983), and *The Western Lands* (1987)—told from the point of view of an adolescent boy, Kim Carsons, who weaves his tales with a mixture of fantasy and reality. Characters morph and change shape, become lovers and foes, monsters and angels, recalling the changeableness of Burroughs at the height of his surreal drug-induced masterpiece, *Naked Lunch* (1959).

As Scott Bukatman argues, "By engaging with the received, and authorless, structures of science fiction, Burroughs is able to excavate a new mythology, in which the avant-garde potentials of the genre are finally realized."[27] What Bukatman claims for Burroughs could also be said to be true of Bowie:

> Burroughs . . . utilizes . . . the discourses of popular culture, to reject the notion of an original or pure self. Like Warhol, Burroughs replaces *self* with *culture* as the source for the expressive and communicative forms of language. From the Nova Trilogy, with its emphasis on the discourse of science fiction, *Cities of the Red Night*, with its evocation of boys' adventure stories, Burroughs has spoken, as we all do, through other voices.[28]

As he later says in comparing Burroughs to David Cronenberg, Burroughs chronicles "the transformation of self into Other."[29] Central to Burroughs and Bowie's ability to do this is the cut-up method, a technique "metaphorically linking the textual and corporeal bodies . . . the cut-up demolishes the linear coherence that produces the identity of the text."[30]

Novelist Kathy Acker similarly wrote about Burroughs' prescience. He is clearly an influence on her, maybe most obviously in her one woman-centered work, *Pussy, King of the Pirates* (1996), where the punk pirate girls often seem like a parallel to Burroughs' lost boys. Acker argues that Burroughs' great topic is time: "the books' temporal structures are fractured; time juts into and becomes space; humans melt into cartoonlike characteristics and parts of bodies gone haywire; the quality of humanity seems to be green mush or resolves into unheard-of mutations. . . . Burroughs was able to portray futures which are now our present."[31] Acker's description is especially apt for Burroughs' later science-fictional work. His first two novels, *Junky* and *Queer*, introduce his two great topics but do so in a much more realistic mode. While all of Burroughs' fiction has a fair amount of autobiography in it, often via a character that is a clear stand-in for the author himself, *Junky* and *Queer* are fairly thinly veiled chunks of his life and travels rendered almost as memoir. The protagonist of both books is named William Lee, and given the extent to which his later work celebrates homosexuality, especially *The Wild Boys*, it is stunning how complex the topic is for Burroughs in these first two books. The books chronicle a time when Burroughs was himself coming to terms with his own homosexuality, with a marriage that turns out tragically wrong when Burroughs accidentally kills his wife during a "William Tell" routine at a party, and is dealing with his own version of repression. Years before it was fashionable, Burroughs prefers the word *queer*—at the time, a word of opprobrium. It is used in contrast to *fag*, then, as now, a word with negative connotations, especially, perhaps, the supposed taint of effeminacy. Although both novels represent same-sex sex and desire throughout, there is a studied way in which the protagonist/author separates himself from what he sees as the wrong kind of queer. This difference is perhaps expressed with the most detail in *Junky* in a scene set at a gay bar in New Orleans:

> In the French Quarter there are several queer bars so full every night the fags spill out on the sidewalk. A room full of fags gives me the horrors. They jerk around like puppets on invisible strings, galvanized into hideous activity that is the negation of everything living and spontaneous. The live human being has moved out of these bodies long ago. But something moved in when the original tenant moved out. Fags are ventriloquists' dummies who have moved in and taken over the ventriloquist. The dummy sits in a queer bar nursing his beer, and uncontrollably yapping out of a rigid doll face.[32]

This revulsion does not, however, keep Lee from visiting queer bars or from propositioning guys who "didn't come on faggish."[33] Later in the novel, when Lee is interviewed by a psychiatrist, Lee remarks, "He was not effeminate. He simply had none of whatever it is that makes a man a man."[34] Lee's, or Burroughs', definition of queer seems distinctly tied up with the notion of masculinity, or rather, maleness. While in this context, that might seem to be a form of self-loathing about his own sexuality, it is a theme that will ultimately become antifemale. The cultural and the biological are frequently blended in Burroughs' writing, and his obsession with types throughout the book—straight men who look queer, young men who seem queer but are actually asexual—is a strange interest in the surface of the body, the outside as an indicator of what is going on in the inside. In his later fiction, this barrier breaks down as the interior world literally becomes the exterior reality of the novels. For now, the one surface that is clear is that of the "fags." They have none of the inscrutability of straight men or straight-seeming gay men: in the Chimu Bar "three Mexican fags were posturing in front of the jukebox."[35] Junkies, as Burroughs remarks, also stand out in a crowd, because they, as Burroughs did his whole life, wear hats, a part of the junky costume. They also, like "fags," hang together in a group. The one group with which Burroughs identifies slowly takes on the identity that he refuses. Drug use takes the place of sexual identity for him and becomes, in some ways, just a metaphor and allegory for it.

Burroughs' companion novel, *Queer*, was published thirty years after it was written and contains many of the same distinctions between "fags" and "queers" that one sees in the earlier novel. In some cases, Burroughs repeats lines almost verbatim, especially descriptions of the former. The book chronicles the frustrating courtship of a fictional young man, Gene Allerton, by Lee. In real life, Allerton is a stand-in for Lewis Marker, a college student in Mexico with whom Burroughs was infatuated.[36] Throughout the novel, it is clear that Lee eventually realizes that Allerton is not gay, but pushes himself on him, as much for intimacy and attention as anything else. Lee knows that the relationship is doomed to be limited in scope, but Allerton's very straightness is part of his attraction to him. In a sense, the book is a love story, though Burroughs does not make clear that the book is also autobiographical. Lee and Allerton become friends, the latter an extremely reluctant lover, only because he does not initially suspect that Lee is gay: "It did not occur to him that Lee was queer, as he associated queerness with at least some degree of overt effeminacy. He decided finally that Lee valued him as an audience."[37] Burroughs claims it took him so long to publish the book because the shift from New Orleans to Mexico City, from junky to queer, reminded him of the death of his wife, Joan, and the guilt of her death that he spent the rest of his life trying to write his way out of. The frustration in his relationship with Allerton, demeaning and hopeless, "extremely painful and unpleasant and lacerating memories,"[38] was not one to which he wanted to return.

In the same introduction to *Queer*, Burroughs acknowledges his debt to English writer Denton Welch. Burroughs writes, "While I was writing *The Place of Dead Roads*, I felt in spiritual contact with the late English writer Denton Welch, and modeled the novel's hero, Kim Carson, directly on him."[39] What Burroughs likes about him in particular is that a "portentous second sight permeates Welch's writing: a scene, a cup of tea, an inkwell purchased for a few shillings, become charged with a special and often sinister significance."[40] As Barry Miles notes, "Welch's influence on Burroughs is seen in two ways: first, in Welch's 'No Art for Art's sake, but Art for my sake'; second, in his manner of construction. Welch eliminated scenic description in favor of presenting the narrative as a series of vivid anecdotes and experiences."[41]

Welch was born in Shanghai on March 29, 1915, to an English father and American mother. He was educated for two years in Repton and then entered Goldsmith School of Art in New Cross in 1933 to become a painter. On June 7, 1935, he suffered a horrible accident when he was knocked off a bicycle and cracked his spine. He was a partial invalid until his early death at thirty-three. As a somewhat bedridden person, he turned from painting to writing. He published a number of works: *The Journals of Denton Welch*, which he kept from 1942 to 1948 (1952); two novels: *Maiden Voyage* (1943) and *In Youth Is Pleasure* (1945); *A Voice Through a Cloud* (unfinished and posthumous; 1950); two collections of short stories: *Brave and Cruel* (1948) and the posthumous *A Last Sheaf* (1951; also with drawings and poems).

Welch endured a homophobic reaction to his work in the United Kingdom and in the United States. Some of the underground slang was even edited out and some passages censored. A frequent theme in his writing is the physicality of bodies—perhaps because he lost so much of his ability to be physical when he was hurt. His work was popular with Edith Sitwell—a famous eccentric writer—and was part of the modernist movement in art of the earlier part of the century. He wrote during the wars when society changed dramatically due to industrialization and modernization. Now we can say that his work seems both a part of the writing of this age but also unique in many ways.

It is possible that his work is autobiographical in places. It is also dangerous, however, to assume that he based everything on himself. This quandary within his writing is heightened by the fact that it is easy to assume that gay writing is in some way more autobiographical than straight writing. That is, that gay writing is about letting one in on a secret; that it incorporates the notion of gossip that is a part of gay culture; and, if you feel your life has been a tragedy, that you automatically look to your own life for material. While some of these assumptions may have been true for Welch and for Burroughs, Welch seems to take pains to write about events that are distant in time.

A classic Welch short story is "When I was Thirteen." The title invites an autobiographical reading, and perhaps erodes the boundary between fiction and memoir completely. At the very least, the story seems to be based upon a memory because it is set in a foreign land, comes from a child's point of view, obviously contains another point of view in the form of an adult narrator, and has as its theme what is and is not understood by adults and children—and children who eventually become adults. The story takes place at a hotel in Switzerland where the thirteen-year-old boy of the story is put in the care of his older brother while their parents are away. The boy, who is narrating from the vantage point of adulthood, tells the story of his first crush, on an older boy named Archer also staying at the hotel. The story itself is similar to much of the homoerotic feeling that gets expressed in writing between the wars: often physical (related to sports or roughhousing) and, for English youths, set in a faraway place—perhaps because one can do some things more easily in countries other than one's own. The characters seem to be the products of all-male private schools—a theme to appear in the work of a number of twentieth-century British writers such as Christopher Isherwood.

The reader first knows that something is different about Archer from the older brother's comment that he was not well liked. His brother's disapproval makes the boy more interested in Archer—evil attracts, but maybe he already sensed a kinship. But the boy explains his brother's dislike as being because they must have disagreed about something. This explanation is one of many subtle clues that demonstrate the innocence of the narrator as a young man—what he did not know then and does know now. Early in the story we learn that the narrator does not know much about sex. He is reading Tolstoy and does not understand the phrase "illegitimate child."

Abandoned by his parents and ignored by his brother, Archer is the only one at the hotel who pays attention to him. They soon form a bond and begin to do things together. They go skiing, and the narrator indulges in great physical details about Archer and his body. We learn, for example, that he wears as little as possible and even likes to ski shirtless. Descriptions of his body are surrounded with detail and connotation; he is available for looking at (he is a swimmer) and for pain (he is not much liked). The young narrator, at one point, describes him as looking like Jesus as he carried his skis on his back.[42] The boy is self-conscious about the way that he looks in front of Archer. He wants to impress him and not to seem like a child. Much of the memory seems to be about this.

Though he dines at the hotel, Archer lives off to himself in his own chalet, as though his liminal identity was expressed in a physical form. The boy begins to idolize Archer and to spend time with him in his room: "The room smelled mildly of Archer's sweat. I didn't mind at all."[43] There are sensual descriptions of the boy rubbing Archer's sore foot, bathing in his bath water, and scrubbing his back. There is a lot of physical contact between them, though Welch is careful to make the descriptions of the actions seem completely un-pederastic. Although older, Archer is presented as unaware of the possible sexual overtones of what he does with the boy and the story treads a fine line between showing a boy on the brink of discovery of his sexuality yet without the tools to understand it—or, most importantly, to identify it. Archer treats the boy as an equal, which flatters him, but is also a sign that Archer does not really know what he is doing. This fact is made clear when he allows the boy to ingest liquor and lager only to have the boy throw up. It never occurs to Archer that this is not appropriate.

Their Swiss idyll ends abruptly with the return of the older brother from a ski trip with friends. The brother, possibly repressed himself, beats the younger brother when he hears that he has been spending time with Archer. He attacks him in the washroom and water splashes everywhere, becoming symbolic blood.[44] The story ends with the brother yelling "'Bastard, Devil, Harlot, Bugger!'" The brother feminizes the narrator. Again, his knowledge of vocabulary gives away his innocence: he only knows the one non-sexual word, which ironically refers to his brother.

Welch's story leaves much unsaid and forces the reader to pay attention to the subtlety of language, detail, and description. It is an interesting exploration of when and how we first learn about sexuality. Did the boy ever understand what he was feeling? Did he ever realize his brother's—and society's—attempts to mold him? How do we know how to read the boy's feelings? How do we know to read this as fiction rather than as autobiography? The story is a classic example of one significant period in the life of any queer child. In that sense, it is a proto-coming out story about the brutality of adults and the damage done to the psyches of gay children. Like Burroughs, Welch creates an alternative version of his own history—one in which the older narrator, looking back, recognizes and embraces the queer child who will become the gay adult. Burroughs likewise, but especially in his late work, idealizes preadolescence—the moment between knowing and not knowing, innocence and experience, when he was straight by culture and gay by nature. That the story ultimately ends up not being about sex but about violence makes its own meaning fluid, like the notion of queerness itself, unknowable, outside of definitional boundaries, and ultimately personal and intimate.

* * *

The other major influence on Bowie on this album and others is the writer J. G. Ballard. If he did not influence Bowie as directly as Burroughs, he certainly acted as a parallel to him, often doing in words much of what Bowie was attempting to do in music. As different from Burroughs as someone possibly could be, Ballard lived quietly in the London suburbs where he raised his three children after his wife died unexpectedly while the family was on vacation. An early devotee of the science fiction genre, he eventually turned against what he called "outer space" for the pursuit of a science fiction of "inner space." A failed medical student, he had grown up in a crowded internment camp in Shanghai, the basis of his autobiographical novel *Empire of the Sun* (1984), and was drawn to the surreal sex and violence of everyday life. Like Burroughs and Bowie, one might say that he was attracted to perversity, but he came at it from the point of view of a pop genre, science fiction. In the 1970s he created a trilogy of books that perhaps best summed up his interests by channeling his thoughts on this subject through the description of urban cityscapes that have become, in Marc Augé's term, "non-places." In the book *Concrete Island* a wealthy architect crashes his Jaguar in the eddy of a freeway system that leaves him stranded and lost in a literal concrete jungle. In *Crash*, Ballard chronicles the merging of sex and violence, human and machine, in the form of a cult that reenacts car crashes as a way to create an erotic thrill that is beyond both gender and sexuality. In *High-Rise* a medical doctor living in an enormous steel and glass apartment complex has to struggle to survive as the inhabitants slowly become cut off from the world and resort to social and, ultimately, corporeal Darwinism to survive.

This last novel, though unpublished at the time of *Diamond Dogs* the album and the tour, is amazingly in tune with Bowie's own vision. The denizens of Ballard's apartment block slowly come unglued as the building's services—the high-speed elevators, central air-conditioning, and waste-disposal systems—stop working. Social order breaks down and chaos spreads as long-simmering disputes between the lower, middle, and upper floors of the residence spill over into violence. The residents of the complex, though all part of a professional class, divide themselves into clans and tribes and slowly devolve into animalistic parodies of humans, becoming more and more like literal animals as they enact their own sexual and violent desires.

The primitive "new world"[45] in which the inhabitants find themselves is a literalization of the dog-eat-dog world of late-Capitalist modernity. The opening image of the novel is of the doctor, Robert Laing, roasting and eating an Alsatian over an open fire. The dog, one of many in the book, belongs to the architect, Anthony Royal, who lives in the top-most apartment, and becomes, like many of the animals in the book, food to be hunted as the lower classes slowly make their way up the building's forty floors toward the penthouse. The animals are themselves, however, mere metaphors as it is the humans that devolve quickly past them. At one point Richard Wilder, a burly, heavily genitaled, ex-rugby player now television producer, encounters his neighbors and former drinking companions, Mr. and Mrs. Hillman, in their apartment on the seventeenth floor. He gives them the dog biscuits and pet food that he has with him, which elicits a sexual advance from Mrs. Hillman. Wilder taunts her like a dog-owner with a bone. Ballard writes: "Deriding her in front of her supine husband, he withheld the food from her until she broke down and retreated to the kitchen."[46] The scene ends with Wilder and Mrs. Hillman "sitting in the darkness on the floor of the sitting room . . . their backs to opposite walls, [as] they listened to the muted noises around them. The residents of the high-rise were like creatures in a darkened zoo lying together in surly quiet, now and then tearing at each other in brief acts of ferocious violence."[47] Ballard's characters all turn toward an animalistic state, becoming in the process half-humans—or humans behaving more like animals in the wild than the supposedly civilized denizens of humanity. The apartment building becomes a literal zoo of depravity. Wilder ultimately makes it to the thirty-fifth floor, where he encounters a young woman seemingly untouched by the tragedy. They barbeque a cat together and fall amiably asleep as she runs her fingers over the red stripes he has painted on his chest by dipping his fingers in a bottle of claret.

By the time we get to the conclusion, Wilder has been killed by a group of women on the roof, children run naked around a sculpture garden, and Laing, cooking the charred dog, has discovered the bones of humans in the swimming pool—the result of cannibalism, he suspects. The world that Bowie sketches in "Future Legend" when he describes how "the last few corpses lay/rotting on the slimy thoroughfare . . ./and red mutant eyes gaze down on hunger city . . .//fleas the size of rats sucked on rats the size of cats/and ten thousand peoploids split into small tribes/coveting the highest of the sterile skyscrapers/like packs of dogs assaulting the glass fronts of love-me avenue" he seems to be melding Burroughs with Ballard, forging a type of proto-punk poetry made up of Burroughs' tribal pastiche and Ballard's sterile architecture. The parahuman beings that populate this landscape are dog-like, scavenging, and horrific. The album cover painting of Bowie transforming into a half-man, half-dog creature, with its infamous airbrushed genitals, and the photo of Bowie on the inner sleeves with a dog in toe are emblematic of the "horrorshow" the album suggests.[48] The outsider identity that Bowie was to embrace in different ways frequently in his career was often based upon or paralleled by literary sources that he has begun in recent years to say more about. Beginning with his older half-brother Terry Burns' introducing Bowie to Jack Kerouac's *On the Road* (1957), Bowie took intellectual cues from the Beats and their subsequent generations. In this album, Bowie has, like us, embraced his inner animal and once again picked up on the zeitgeist of the time, only a couple of years in advance of the actual punk invasion itself and the real economic meltdown and resulting fascist response that was to come with it. The year of the diamond dogs referred to on "Future Legend" could be 1838, 1974, 1984, or today.

Ballard was to go on to write more novels about the effects of technology and architecture on people, often positing the notion that people are changed, for the worse, by the environments that they inhabit. One example of his later work in this area is the novella *Running Wild* (1988), in which the pampered teenagers living in a gated community kill their parents, and all of their support staff, then mysteriously disappear. As in *High-Rise*, the writing is as much about class as anything else—the decadence of having everything provided to you results in the destruction of the very giver of the luxuries. In this case, it is the parents, not the apartment block, who are reacted against. The series of deaths, pieced together by a witless detective, is served up by Ballard as a series of literal filmic images:

> The camera resumes its melancholy tour. By the time it reaches the third house, the Gropius-inspired home of a distinguished concert pianist, the sequence of entrances, deaths and exits begins to resemble a nightmare exhibition that will never end. House by house, the assassins had moved swiftly through the estate on that quiet June morning, killing the owners, their chauffeurs and servants, before abducting the thirteen children. Husbands and wives were shot down across their still-warm beds, stabbed in their shower stalls, electrocuted in their baths or crushed against their garage doors by their own cars. In a period generally agreed to be no more than twenty minutes, some thirty-two people were savagely but efficiently done to death.[49]

* * *

In his collection of essays and reviews, *A User's Guide to the Millennium*, Ballard expounds upon his concept of "inner space":

> I feel that the writer of fantasy has a marked tendency to select images and ideas which directly reflect the internal landscapes of his mind, and the reader of fantasy must interpret them on this level, distinguishing between the manifest content . . . and the latent content, the private vocabulary of symbols drawn by the narrative from the writer's mind. The dream worlds invented by the writer of fantasy are external equivalents of the inner world of the psyche, and because these symbols take their impetus from the most formative and confused periods of our lives they are often time-sculptures of terrifying ambiguity.[50]

As Ballard goes on to note about "the internal landscape," "It is particularly rich in visual symbols, and I feel that this type of speculative fantasy plays a role very similar to that of surrealism in the graphic arts. The painters Chirico, Dali and Max Ernst, among others, are in a sense the iconographers of inner space."[51] Ballard's writing builds on Burroughs' in the blurring of inner and outer realities in his writing, though unlike Burroughs, Ballard is careful to maintain a realistic rendering of the outside world, no matter how much it might reflect the desires and horrors of the inner mind. Like Bowie, his work focuses specifically on rendering visual effects. As he says in his autobiography:

> Ever since childhood I had a flair for drawing, and in the art department at The Leys I made plaster casts of the faces of friends (I called them "death" masks after those of Shelley, Blake, Napoleon and other heroes). . . . To my lifelong regret, however, I lacked the skill and facility to become a painter, whereas my head was filled with short stories and I had the beginning of a knack for expressing them.[52]

Also similar to Bowie, and in many ways distinct from Burroughs, Ballard's fiction deals with the minutiae of everyday life. Ballard rails against High Modernist writers for what he sees as their self-obsession and refusal to represent the mundaneness of contemporaneity. Ballard instead calls for an approach to fiction that "recognised a world dominated by consumer advertising, of democratic government mutation into public relations. This was a world of cars, offices, highways, airlines and supermarkets that we actually lived in."[53] He congeals his aesthetic into the following formulation: "I would interiorise science fiction, looking for the pathology that underlay the consumer society, the TV landscape and the nuclear arms race, a vast untouched continent of fictional possibility."[54] Ballard focuses, like Bowie via Warhol and other pop artists, on the artificial landscape of advertising and commercialization—the simulation, to use Jean Baudrillard's vocabulary, that has replaced the real, what Ballard refers to as the "multiplied body of the film actress—one of the few valid landscapes of our day."[55] Pop art makes the subjective and the objective one and the same. Ballard recognizes a change in Britain during the 1960s in which "emotion, and emotional sympathy, drained out of everything, and the fake had its own special authenticity."[56]

Ballard's multiple interests in the body, advertising, technology, and science come together in the novel that is arguably his masterpiece, *Crash*, first published in 1973. The origins of the novel lay with an unusual performance piece. Ballard has chronicled how he had earlier been involved in experimenting with the intersection of science and sex. One was an event at London's ICA "when we hired a stripper, Euphoria Bliss, to perform a striptease to the reading of a scientific paper."[57] He was asked to stage another event at the New Arts Laboratory in London. He assembled crashed cars from various parts of London and hired a woman to appear topless. The result of the mix of audience, wrecked cars, and the suggestion of sex was "huge tension in the air, as if everyone felt threatened by some inner alarm."[58] As Ballard later wrote, "*Crash* is set at the point where sex and death intersect, though the graph is difficult to read and is constantly recalibrating itself."[59] Ballard would eventually publish a novel-length fragmentary work on this topic entitled *The Atrocity Exhibition* (1970). This experimental work reaches its apotheosis with *Crash*, in which, as Ballard describes, "I would openly propose a strong connection between sexuality and the car crash, a fusion largely driven by the cult of celebrity."[60] The novel is, as he later notes, similar to Young British Artist's Tracey Emin's work *My Bed* (1999), where she displays her own bed, complete with soiled sheets, condoms, and cigarettes, "which reminds us that this young woman's beautiful body has stepped from a disheveled grave."[61]

In the novel, the character James Ballard lives with his wife, Catherine, in an open marriage filled with sex that is often wedded to some form of violence. At the beginning of the novel, Ballard is involved in a dangerous accident that leaves him scarred and in braces. The reaction to this change causes his wife to see him in a new light, sexually charging their relationship. For Ballard the character, "This obsession with the sexual possibilities of everything around me had been jerked loose from my mind by the crash."[62] Catherine becomes obsessed with his scars, which act as seams connecting the inside and outside of his body, riddling it with new orifices of sexual pleasure. As in a performance by Bowie, especially during the Ziggy period, but as late as the music videos for *Lodger* (1979), the sexual becomes, to some extent, unmoored and without bounds, palpable but difficult to define. The car crash scrambles genders and sexualities that, via technology, explode into new definitions that do not recognize the boundaries of the body. To some extent, this mechanization works in reverse. At one point, Ballard stares at himself in the mirror, a "pale, mannequin-like face, trying to read its lines. The smooth skin almost belonged to someone in a science-fiction film, stepping out of his capsule after an immense inward journey on to the overlit soil of an unfamiliar planet."[63] He later sees himself as "some huge jointed doll, one of those elaborate humanoid dummies fitted with every conceivable orifice and pain response."[64] For Ballard, "human inhabitants of this technological landscape no longer provided its sharpest pointers, its keys to the borderzones of identity."[65]

The novel is filled with images of bodily fluids—semen, salvia, vaginal fluid, excrement, and vomitus all play important roles in various sexual scenes and scenarios. Ballard takes pains to show men penetrating women vaginally, orally, and anally, but also Catherine placing her mouth on Ballard's scars, in a version of cunnilingus, and one character even placing his penis in the crotch of Ballard's arm. The entire body is sexualized and turned into a multi-gendered surface. This state is magnified by the technological parallels, the tears in the vinyl fabric of cars that can become makeshift orifices or fantasies about making love to dashboards. At the end of the book, Catherine and Ballard find Vaughan's beloved Lincoln in "derelict condition, the loosened body panels and fenders invited the hostility of passers by. A gang of youths smashed the windshield and kicked in the headlamps."[66] Much as happened at J. G. Ballard's art installation, the car attracts the most profound of passions. The final image in the book is of Ballard the character with Catherine in a police pound, masturbating and smearing his semen on the cars in an image that Ballard the author has said is distinctly meant to suggest fertility, the seeding of the galaxy with new types of sexuality. The ending of the novel is in some ways described in advance in *The Atrocity Exhibition*, when a character muses

> that automobile crashes play very different roles from the ones we assign them. Apart from its manifest function, redesigning the elements of space and time in terms of our most potent consumer durable, the car crash may be perceived unconsciously as a fertilizing rather than a destructive vent—a liberation of sexual energy—mediating the sexuality of those who have died with an intensity impossible in any other form.[67]

Ballard presciently foresaw the connection between the erotics of car crashes and the fetishization of the scarred or maimed human body. Ballard's novel looks ahead to cybererotics and the technicalization of sex, but also plumbs the depths of a subculture that attempts to recreate the sexual thrill of famous deaths by auto—whether James Dean or Jane Mansfield.[68] The novel, like the film's faithful rendering by David Cronenberg in 1996, is filled with moments where one character stares at another, seemingly unable to see the person for the scars, the surface outlining and eroticizing of the allocentric body in ways that the undamaged body never could. The protagonist in the book, also called Ballard, studies photographs of Gabrielle, a friend of the central character and ringleader for a subculture of people who recreate the car crashes of famous movie stars, who is named Vaughan:

> On her legs were traces of what seemed to be gas bacillus scars, faint circular depressions on the kneecaps. She noticed me staring at the scars, but made no effort to close her legs. On the sofa beside her was a chromium metal cane. As she moved I saw that the instep of each leg was held in the steel clamp of a surgical support. From the over-rigid posture of her waist I guessed that she was also wearing a back-brace of some kind.[69]

Ballard the character also notes that "in the later photographs the bruises that were to mask her face began to appear, like the outlines of a second personality, a preview of the hidden faces of her psyche which would have emerged only in late middle age."[70] The most physically damaged of the characters in the novel, Gabrielle is also the locus of extreme desire, becoming Ballard's lover and, ultimately, Dr. Helen Remington's, whom Ballard meets, naturally, at a car crash and who becomes, with him, a fan of this new subculture. This sexual fascination is carried further via the realm of fantasy a few pages later, where Ballard fantasizes about a woman in a photograph that Vaughan shows him of an auto accident:

> Without thinking, I visualized a series of imaginary pictures I might take of her: in various sexual acts, her legs supported by sections of complex machine tools, pulleys and trestles; with her physical education instructor, coaxing this conventional young man into the new parameters of her body, developing a sexual expertise that would be an exact analogue of the other skills created by the multiplying technologies of the twentieth century.[71]

These new technologies of the twentieth century create pleasure and horror. The body becomes a map on which to trace the actual or recreated traces left by automobile accidents. The most benignly dangerous of twentieth-century activities, driving a car, becomes eroticized by Ballard, who brings out the hidden death drive not only in sex but in the use of technology itself. The novel emphasizes the freeway, the airport hangar, the hospital, and television or film (Ballard the character is a producer): places and things that we might associate with transition, the liminal. Nothing could be more banal, pointless, or contemporary than dying by automobile. Ballard seems to suggest that such a death incorporates, in its very ordinariness, a desire to transcend the safe existence that we think we live, using technology to remove barriers of time and space that would have once kept us tied to actual places. An effect of this fascination with the reorganization of the body was the creation, as Ballard the character realizes, "of an entirely new sexuality."[72] Ballard recognizes the stirring within himself of homoerotic feelings for Vaughan that ultimately result in his sodomizing Vaughan, in a car, while under the effects of LSD. Before this happens, "In my fantasies, as I made love to Catherine, I saw myself in an act of sodomy with Vaughan, as if only this act could solve the codes of a deviant technology."[73] While Ballard recognizes that this act is "an event as stylized and abstracted as those recorded in Vaughan's photographs,"[74] it is also the one sexual act in the novel where a character most completely fuses with technology. When Ballard finally embraces him,

> Vaughan's skin seemed to be covered with scales of metallic gold as the points of sweat on his arms and neck fired my eyes. I hesitated at finding myself wrestling with this ugly golden creature, made beautiful by its scars and wounds. I moved my mouth across the scars on his lips, feeling with my tongue for those familiar elements of long-vanished dashboards and windshields.[75]

Vaughan becomes a car and the crashing into Vaughan, the collision of Ballard's penis and Vaughan's rectum, the central metaphor for the novel as a whole.

Before Ballard enters Vaughan, he opens his jacket, "exposing the re-opened wounds that marked his chest and abdomen." Ballard continues: "I ran my lips along his left-collar bone, and sucked at his scarred nipple, feeling the re-sectioned areola between my lips."[76] Vaughan becomes feminized as Ballard sucks at his nipple, much as Seagrave had played with his infant son in an earlier scene when he "unbuttoned his shirt and placed the child's mouth on his nipple, squeezing the hard skin into the parody of a breast."[77] Beyond gender, or the gender parody of camp, the men and the women in the novel mold their bodies into different bodily parts, sexualizing the body beyond its normative boundaries. Like the work of Burroughs or Monique Wittig in *The Lesbian Body* or *Les Guérillères*, the entire body is eroticized. Nothing is ugly or de-centered. All wounds are vaginal or anal, and all parts of the body are equally available for sexual function. By the end of *Crash*, almost everyone has had sex with everyone else, regardless of gender or previous sexual preference. A new mapping of the body is brought about via proximity to technology, automobiles and airplanes, especially, and to the technology of prosthetics as well: the outward sign of an inward transformation of a near-death experience.

The fusion of technology and the body via death and the erotic is linked autobiographically for Ballard to his semi-autobiographical novel *Empire of the Sun*. Though post-dating *Crash* by a decade, it contains a similar tale of someone whose identity is connected to a fusion of human and machine, in this case, the British boy Jim who lives in Shanghai but is separated from his parents amidst the chaos of the immediate aftermath of Pearl Harbor and lives part of his childhood as a Japanese prisoner. Jim, another stand-in for Ballard, learns to identify with the Japanese soldiers, especially the kamikaze pilots who fly the Zeroes. The connection between machines and death becomes a fantasy for young Jim of a double suicide with one of the pilots. His nascent pre-adolescent sexuality clearly linked to the much more adult and explicit sexuality of *Crash*, which likewise uses planes as machines that contain their own erotic fields, much like cars. As Takayuki Tausumi notes, Jim's fantasy is not only connected to the fusion of man and machine, but of Japanese and British identity as well. He is explicitly binational and open to the effects of multiple identities. When Jim sees the American B-29, for example, he knows the war is over.[78]

His allegiance is finally to technology, not to nation, just as the Ballard in *Crash* is more affected by cars than he is by gender. Tausumi vividly recounts how Ballard implored fans at a science fiction convention in 1982 to "do 'Pearl Harbor' in our imagination."[79] The implications are clear: Ballard's national identity is in part effaced by an American one. The love of cars, of technology, that is implanted in his mind is partly an American one, but this American imaginary inhabits a British body. The multiple, conflicting perspectives are what Tausumi calls "queer," and "makes us keenly aware that we Japanese have also ended up, unwittingly, with an imaginary hyperqueer version of Americanism, however hard we seem to have studied American culture."[80] Like Ballard, Bowie's album *Lodger* depicts someone who is always trying to move forward, as if from death itself. The song "Move On," for one, depicts Bowie as a constant traveler. Bowie is no longer of one nationality as the song name checks Russia, Japan, Africa, Cyprus, and Turkey. The song "African Night Flight" recounts a British pilot lost in the jungle near Mombasa dreaming of flying out and escaping from the bar where he has mostly gone to seed.

The film version by Cronenberg finds a cinematic way to represent Ballard's literary style. Mainly, Cronenberg films his scenes with a great deal of objectivity—avoiding close-ups, keeping the pacing slow and even, the performances flat and affect-less. We are often aware that what we are watching is a film—the camera angle carefully calibrated with a character's perspective, especially in an act of looking, staring, perusing. Though the novel takes place in London, the film, shot in Toronto, exists in a typical Ballardian non-place of artificial horizons. The film creates the look of a generic, even immaculate, topography of glass buildings, gleaming metallic surfaces, and comely bodies that suggest a near future in which all surfaces have been wiped of ugliness and difference. The only thrill, especially of a sexual kind, is tempting death itself. Into this upper-middle-class reverie walks Vaughan (Elias Koteas), who, after Ballard's car accident releases the sexual tension of imperfection, represents everything that sex might be. He is himself imperfect—scarred, pock-mocked, and dirty. He is also intelligent, well-hung, and the leader of a cult devoted to car crashes. He is everything that the character Ballard (James Spader), and his wife (Deborah Kara Unger), desires and he further unleashes the boundaries of their death-wish, ramping it up in literally dangerous ways. Cronenberg is able to get across the seamlessness of this idealized world—one only slightly exaggerated from our own—and the ways in which sex, death, and technology flow into each other so that the characters are in a constant state of arousal. As in the novel, gender and sexuality cease to function in the usual ways as Cronenberg creates his own softly pornographic scenes, some of them from the novel and some not, including Ballard having anal sex with Catherine while she fantasizes about him having sex with Vaughan.

Throughout the film, Cronenberg frames images of peoples' wounds and injuries, often fetishizing them, especially their orifice-like characteristics. The visual is put with the tactile, scars and wounds put near hands, braces, and clothing to frame them and further eroticize them as objects to be seen, felt, and touched. Slowly the film sets these bodies, and body parts, into circulation as part of the sexual availability and as new definitions of what we might find erotic. Playing against the perfect surface of the actors James Spader and Deborah Kara Unger, they take on their own beauty, one born of the violence that they continue to reflect. As Pansy Duncan points out, the film can be read via standard postmodern theory as an elaborate attempt to "marry the rough surface of genuine emotion and the glossy surface to emotional inauthenticity."[81] In that sense, the rough surface is equivalent to "Barthes's panegyric to the photographic *punctum*, which, in a miracle of metaphoric efficiency, places the rough, 'punctured' surface of the photograph and the state of being moved by that photograph under the semiotic umbrella of one word."[82] We might say, musically, that the *punctum* is similar to Barthes' notion of the *geno-song*—the performance that leaves the material traces of the body in it.[83] Duncan ultimately sees the film as creating a sense of *fascination*, a distancing effect or "'zombie' emotion" that also manages to snare the viewer.[84] While the gleaming interiors and beautiful cars and airplanes in the film are themselves a part of the effect, the crash subculture and thrill of car crashes are as well. Finally, the film itself is designed, for Duncan, to fascinate the viewer in the same way—you are uncomfortable, but you also cannot look away. The process of fascination is "an eerily triangulated emotion but also . . . the film's no less triangulated narrative trajectory, which seems to multiply continuously into new couplings and new permutations of mimetic desire."[85]

In her book *Crash: Cinema and the Politics of Speed and Stasis*, Karen Beckman notes that Ballard's novel is, in a way, an attempt to make a pop art painting, to assemble a novel as a pastiche of found objects from popular culture that are put together, like one of Burroughs' cut-ups, to make a commentary on what fiction in general and science fiction in particular could go if it allowed itself the freedom to move beyond realist fiction and the usual subject matter we associate with the genre.[86] In particular, she notes that Andy Warhol saw pop art as "just like taking the outside and putting it on the inside, or taking the inside and putting it on the outside,"[87] a concept not dissimilar to Ballard's interest in "inner space" and in using wounds and scars to bring the inside and the outside of the body into a kind of alignment as one continuous surface. For Ballard's book and Cronenberg's film, the avenues that lead into the body are privileged—wounds, the vagina, the anus, the opening of the penis. As Acker writes about the film:

> For me, the central shot of the film, a few seconds long, is one of a penis, I remember that it's Vaughan's, next to Katherine's [*sic*], Ballard's wife's, cunt. The image immediately repeats itself as a finger in the same position on the cunt. What interested me most was that, contrary and probably antagonistic to all porn conventions, the cock is not hard. Through sexual desire, both his own and that of his characters, Cronenberg has reenvisioned the dominate and always rigid phallus of the old the king-must-not-die world as other, soft, another body part, by the end of the film as metal, a car, death, a kiss.[88]

In addition to a new role for the penis as an often-flaccid organ, sexual fluids leak throughout the novel. As Beckman recounts: "James comes inside of Helen, and she lets the semen fall back onto his crotch; Catherine allows James's semen to run out of her vagina into James's hand; and Vaughan allows James's semen to 'leak' from his anus 'across the fluted ribbing of the vinyl upholstery' of his car.'"[89] The film manages to convey the same sense of stasis in motion, or fluid immobility, drawing the reader forward by the same sense of dread and desire. Key sexual scenes from the novel are intercut with scenes of driving that create a different sense of dangerous desire, one that equally defamiliarizes the viewer, though in a different register. Sex becomes non-normative, perverse in a positive sense, while the banality of driving is shown for what it is: a willingness to die, the ultimate vulnerability.

If one agrees with Beckman that Ballard's novel is a commentary on pop art, then he is willing to sexualize that school of painting. He also, as she explains accurately, "expands the space of sexual difference beyond the limits of the material body, imagining movements and intersections that a biologically based conception of sexual difference might foreclose."[90] Finally, she thinks that Ballard purposefully combines media, or "allows the possibility of folding the newly imagined movements and intersections of mediums back onto the body, perhaps transforming the seemingly fixed limits of that body in the process."[91] As with Warhol's *Empire* (1964), Ballard's novel becomes an example of a painting in words, or a film as sculpture. Ultimately, for Beckman, it goes beyond Warhol's experiments to illustrate the mechanics of the medium of film: "Freed from the material, chemical, and perceptual constraints of the medium, Ballard's translation of film takes it well past the point of projectability . . . allowing film to fall apart into language so that he might examine its otherwise inseparable components in relation to one another."[92] Like Burroughs' collages made up of small parts of photographs arranged like stills from a film, or Warhol's late *Piss and Sex Paintings*, or Bowie's planned films for the Diamond Dogs tour, Ballard intermixes media to create a new effect and to use his own medium of words to comment on film and its limits.[93] Perhaps to answer Duncan's claim that the film version to some extent repeats the glossiness of the winking reflected surface of postmodernism, Beckman would say that it deconstructs the medium of film, becomes that surface, with its glossy cars ("varnished," as Beckman points out), reflective glass, and emphasis throughout on film stars, cameras, and objectivity.

Ultimately, Cronenberg's film, like Ballard's novel, might be called *post-queer*. It exists outside the usual boundaries of sex and desire and attempts to embody a new materiality. Like the work of Bowie on sexuality, it does not fully explain the shape of this new desire, but it does enact its materiality and suggests that it is dependent upon the media of pop culture for its shape and existence. Ballard's novel, like Bowie's personae, is about erasing identities. In the same way that transgendered identity, or, say, the notion of queer heterosexuality challenge the very definition of queer, especially as a synonym for non-normative or an antonym for heterosexuality, Bowie's sexuality is shaped by a radical refusal to be categorized and an attempt instead to define for himself, like Burroughs and Ballard before him, a new space in which to exist. Cronenberg's film does not end, like the novel, with a scene that suggests the seeding of this new sexuality and its transportation out into the universe via airplanes and cars. Rather, the film ends with James driving Vaughan's car and running Catherine off the road. Her car jumps an embankment and slides down it. James stops, backs up, and rushes down the hill to her. James bends over her, then positions himself next to her on the ground. Fascinated and concerned, he touches her at the moment of her greatest fragility and most alluring pose—envying her experience and wishing it was happening to him. "Are you hurt?" he asks. "I'm all right," she answers. As Cronenberg explains in the commentary on the 1997 Criterion version of the film, Catherine's answer is one of disappointment. She begins to cry. "Maybe the next one, darling," Ballard says. They then proceed to have sex there, in the shadow of the overturned car, ending the film. This scene echoes the first scene of the movie and creates a Möbius loop in which the same line is repeated almost verbatim. The film opens with Catherine having anal sex with her flying instructor in a private aircraft hangar. James is almost simultaneously doing the same with the camera girl on his set. When he returns home to their apartment, he asks her if she came. "No," she says. "Did you?" "We were interrupted," he says. "I was called back to the set." "Poor darling, maybe next time." They then have anal sex on the balcony while looking out into the city, at the traffic, at all the cars streaming down below.

In the same commentary track, Ballard recounts a moment at Cannes when, after the screening, a reporter stated that the film did not go far enough and did not equal the novel in terms of its willingness to take risks. Luckily for Cronenberg, Ballard was at hand, took the mike, and said with no hesitation that the film went even further than the novel, that indeed the film begins where the novel ends. While perhaps not recreating the hallucinatory, surreal quality of the novel, the film definitely succeeds at crafting an accurate visual representation of the erotic nature of the novel. It focuses on the sex, but it also gets it right and manages to succeed where few films do: to be true to its source material and itself and not to flinch in its representation of human nature—even one transformed by machines.

* * *

J. G. Ballard's work on the fusing of the human and the machine can also be related to Bowie's interest in disability. Bowie's own representations of disability are, like many things in his corpus, a rich nexus of influences on him and subsequent influences he has had on others. In terms of the latter, Lady Gaga's notion of the "monster," as, in part, both queer and cyborgian, runs throughout her stage performances—concerts, MTV Video Award broadcasts—and her famous music videos as well (up to the recent "You and I"). Gaga dons new personas and masks at a dizzying rate—seemingly with every new news cycle—in a manner linked to Bowie's trend-setting manipulation of the body in the 1970s and 1980s, as she seems most explicitly to acknowledge by wearing a lightning bolt across her face in her video for "Just Dance."[94] To use F. Scott Fitzgerald's famous phrase, Gaga reflects a tradition in Bowie's work that emphasizes the notion of "the crack-up." Much like Malcolm McDowell's portrayal of Alex DeLarge in Kubrick's *Clockwork Orange* with a false eyelash on only one eye, the physical sense of grotesquerie suggests that her characters have a cracked psyche, a mental state of fragility or vulnerability and an anti-normative resistance to society as it is expected to be lived.

In Bowie's work, these characters are often used to reference either Bowie himself ("When it's good, it's really good; when it's bad, I go to pieces") or his half-brother Terry Burns who was a major intellectual influence on Bowie as well as a frequently institutionalized schizophrenic whose illness was turned into a dark secret by Bowie's family. Bowie's representations of Terry's mental state range from the obscure, the song "Bewlay Brothers" on the album *Hunky Dory* in 1971, to the explicit in "They Say Jump" on 1993's *Black Tie, White Noise*. The mixing of fictional character and real life is, of course, an important trope within Bowie's work that he used as a way to express ambivalence about his own past, often reflected via a doppelganger or a dark twin, especially on his album *Scary Monsters* from 1980. In the video for this song, Bowie jumps from the roof of a television tower in Germany recreating one of his brother's suicide attempts. Bowie's character is pursued by the paparazzi as a pack of senseless spectators who examine him and his life in the minutest detail, causing the fatal leap. Burns' illness seems to be explicitly referenced in the lyrics when Bowie sings "They say, 'he has no brain.'" And again, later, "They say, 'He has no mood.'" Bowie appears at different times in the video battered and bruised.

While images of madness crop up in a number of Bowie's songs—from the mid-sixties onward—various critics have speculated about which ones might be images of Terry specifically. In "The Bewlay Brothers" the song's lyrics are so obscure and obtuse, like many on this album in particular, that it is difficult to know what the context is. While the atmospherics and the music create a sinister mock-Victorian feel, the lyrics avoid specificity. Still, two striking images seem to prefigure Terry's death: "Now my brother lays upon the Rocks/He could be Dead, he could be not/He could be You." And the line, "In the Crutch-hungry Dark." Almost ten years later, while a patient at Cane Hill, Terry did try to kill himself by jumping from a window. He became a cripple after that, with a damaged right arm and a limp. When he finally took his own life, it was by lying in front of a train. He stopped on the first attempt, December 27th, but succeeded on January 16, 1985. Until the end, Burns apparently idolized his younger brother. Bowie, however, rarely responded to his brother's entreaties or visited him. Bowie and Burns' mother was distant, in part, because of her perception that Bowie was unavailable to Burns and/or could have done much more for him.[95]

Bowie's use of the trope of brokenness and the notion of some sort of disability was never limited to his half-brother. Bowie's own primary identity seemed to be as one who was himself disabled in some way with Burns acting as the dark twin that showed up or mirrored the disability in Bowie himself. Many of Bowie's songs, from throughout his career, reference this sense of disability as a mental illness. This fear came not only from Burns' schizophrenia but from a general history of mental illness on Bowie's mother's side of the family. Seemingly casual lyrics in Bowie's oeuvre such as "I know that people think/that I'm a little crazy" from "Fascination" are not as innocent as they might seem. By the time he got to *Scary Monsters* and the imagery of a battered Major Tom in a padded room, Bowie was playing with the self-help books of pop psychology, especially *I'm Ok, You're Ok*, a 1969 book by Thomas Anthony Harris that made the *New York Times* best-seller list in 1972, and gets referenced twice on the album when Bowie sings "I'm ok, you're so-so" on "Up the Hill Backwards," a song that also includes the line, "We're legally crippled," and on "Ashes to Ashes," when Bowie plaintively claims "I'm happy, hope you're happy too." Bowie's sense of brokenness was not limited to the inside, however, and some of his most famous portrayals are based upon physical rather than mental disability. While this fact is most obvious in his Broadway portrayal of the Elephant Man, it can also be seen in his performance of Jerome Newton in *The Man Who Fell to Earth* (1976), especially that character's inability to deal with earth's atmosphere—whether riding in an elevator without fainting or, ultimately, drinking without becoming an alcoholic. Bowie is literally differently abled in the film and in his performance Bowie frequently calls attention to it—from the way he plays with his glasses to the many scenes in which he appears prone or supine, unable to deal with the physical demands of earth's gravity. At a more subtle level, even Bowie's most famous performance, the concert version of Ziggy Stardust, is based in part upon C-list rocker Vince Taylor, who not only suffered from a mental condition, but who Bowie saw perform live wearing a leg brace. Bowie recalls: "He had to shove his injured leg out behind him to, what I thought, great theatrical effect. . . . This rock stance became position number one for the embryonic Ziggy."[96]

The sense of brokenness has also been widely influential—from Marilyn Manson's *Mechanical Animals* to, of course, Lady Gaga's first two albums. Bowie's images of falling and being broken also influenced fashion designer Yoji Yamamoto, who paid homage to the cover of *Lodger* in his Tokyo boutique (Y's) in 1980.[97] Yamamoto was himself influential on playwright Heiner Müller and fellow Bowie collaborators Pina Bausch and Takeshi Kitano. The fusing of fashion and rock, pain and pleasure, that is the hallmark of Lady Gaga's oeuvre so far, mines this rich vein of interrelated "high" and "low" art phenomena. Other examples of the representation of queer disability in popular music can be seen in Lady Gaga's recent video work, especially as it eroticizes the body of the differently abled. In particular, the long video for her song "Paparazzi" (2009) from her debut album, *The Fame* (2008), references her own struggles with fame, especially the attempt to balance it with a love life. The elaborate music video is given a markedly cinematic treatment, referencing the look of films from the 1940s, especially melodramas like *Mildred Pierce* (1945). There are also specific references within the video to *Vertigo* (1958) and *Metropolis* (1927). The ten-minute video tells the story of a Gaga-like starlet who struggles on the balcony of her fabulous mansion with her boyfriend, who attempts to kill her by pushing her off the balustrade just as a member of the paparazzi begins to shoot their pictures. Most of the video illustrates the revenge of the protagonist as she returns to the mansion, *Vogue*-like dancers in tow, to kill the servants, whose dead bodies we see in flashback, and ultimately poison her nefarious boyfriend, played by Swedish boy-toy Alexander Skarsgård of *True Blood* fame. What is most striking about the video is the way that the song's infectious dance beat is used to reflect the halting steps that Gaga's character takes as she first rises from a chair upon being taken into the foyer by her servants. Her avant-garde dance steps emphasize the mechanical nature of the music. The halting, almost-unsteady beat is given a positive connotation, her disability seen as a strength as she pushes herself forward through space and toward, one presumes, a reclamation of her former life. Her metal braces and crutches are seen as fashion accessories; her damaged body something in which to take pride. Her boyfriend even sports a metal eye patch in the scene of his death—almost as though her own near-death experience is seen as sexy and titillating. This theme of sexy disability continues in the live performances that Gaga was to give of this hit, especially at the 2009 MTV Music Video Awards. In her next video, for the song "Bad Romance," Gaga is to some extent a sequel in that it continues some of the same themes by turning the monstrous into an emblem of sex and power. "I want your ugly/I want your disease," she sings, and "I want your horror/I want your design." She even discusses revenge (again) and references *Psycho* (1960) and *Rear Window* (1954). Her cinematic investigation of fame and the bad romances that it brings seems to be related to the notion of disability, of life no longer working as it once did but being all the more fabulous because of it.

Most significantly, Gaga's film references Bowie's video "Jump They Say" (1993). Bowie's video seems similarly cinematic, though the sources are clearly the sterile environments of futuristic films, whether Jean-Luc Godard's *Alphaville* (1965), Chris Marker's "Le Jeteé" (1962), Orson Welles' *The Trial* (1962), Kubrick's *2001*, or Ernie Gehr's "Serene Velocity" (1970). Bowie's version also includes someone being photographed, but it is a corporate businessman who is being watched from within the interior of his own company. The setting could be a reference to the sterility of institutions as well as to some sort of vision of the future as film screen. Performance takes on a sinister tone as the character that Bowie plays feels compelled to jump by the people who surround him—his audience, or perhaps, someone who is trying to control him like a lab rat. Bowie ends up smashed on the street below, much like the image from his album *Lodger*, where he is seen from above as he rushes toward the immaculately white tiles of a bathroom interior. In both images, the geometric perfection of his environment emphasizes the crushed, asymmetrical, disheveled, and broken condition of his body.

The *Vertigo*-like photograph for the album cover was created by British pop artist Derek Boshier, who had attended the Royal Academy of Art with David Hockney.[98] Bowie was filmed with a special table that supported him while he seemed to plummet through space. The interior sleeve of the album includes photographs of the body of Che Guevara, a supine infant, a painting of a foreshortened Christ (Andrea Mantegna's *Lamentation over the Death of Christ*, 1480), a photograph of Bowie being prepared for the shoot, and two men's watches. Water spurts out of a lavatory basin, looking similar to an image from an accompanying video for a song on the album entitled "D.J." The final cover looks purposefully grainy, as though it were taken with a Polaroid SX-70. The album artwork seems to document someone's suicide attempt, or perhaps damage done to them. In the twisted stance of the body, it also recalls the Expressionist paintings that had so influenced Bowie and Iggy Pop in Berlin, perhaps especially Egon Schiele *Self-Portrait Standing* (1910). In this ambivalence, perhaps, it most reflects a homage to Roman Polanski's film *The Tenant* (*Le Locataire*, 1976), which chronicles the tale of a man who moves into an old apartment in Paris slowly to take on the characteristics of its previous tenant, Simone Choule, an Egyptologist. The lead character, a lonely Pole named Trelkovsky played in an uncredited role by Polanski himself, is berated by the landlord (Melvyn Douglas), concierge (Shelley Winters), and fellow tenants until he begins to suspect that he may be mad. In the end, he seems to take on the characteristics of the former tenant, including attempting to look like her by wearing makeup and women's clothing. The film ends ambiguously with the idea that maybe Trelkovsky was Choule all along.

The packaging of Bowie's album seems to refer to this film, even though the contents of the album itself do not. The video "Jump They Say," however, channels the paranoia in Polanski's film and the real danger of being hounded by a group. At the time Polanski made *The Tennant* he had already been forced out of the United States on charges of raping a minor and had had to relocate to Paris, the setting for the film. *The Tenant* completes his "apartment trilogy" of *Repulsion* (1965), *Rosemary's Baby* (1968), and *The Tenant*, with the most personal film among them and the only one starring himself. It is difficult not to imagine that Polanski saw himself hounded out of California to France where he was hounded still by another chorus, symbolic, perhaps, of the paparazzi who follow Bowie and Gaga like the voices in the head of Bowie's half-brother.

Bowie references Burns' suicide eight years earlier obliquely in the way in which the protagonist in the song is encouraged to jump. The video could just as easily be a reference to Bowie himself, to the constant attention that he receives, the lack of privacy and the maddening aspects of extreme fame. The cinematic references are definitely views into Bowie's own interests. The sterility of the sets mirror not only *2001*, with flight attendants dressed in the same costume used in the film, but Gehr's "Serene Velocity" in the use of fluorescent lights that are turned on an off much like the fluorescent lights of the hallway of a classroom building at the State University of New York, Binghamton, which Gehr filmed with a stationary tripod. The most important filmic reference, however, is to Marker, with Bowie himself recreating the image of the protagonist of that time-travel film lying in a hammock with his eyes covered. Here, it seems to be a reference to being tortured or in extreme pain for some reason, though in Marker's original it is the representation of part of the process of time travel. The end of the video, when Bowie lies crumpled on top of a car after jumping, while a reference to both Polanski and to *Lodger* also echoes *Crash*. Repeated throughout the novel is a reference to a gloved hand. Ballard's novel opens with Vaughan's death and his dead body being comforted by Elizabeth Taylor, one of his idols; the very first paragraph ends: "As I knelt over Vaughan's body she placed a gloved hand to her throat."[99] This gesture, which also appears prominently in the music video, repeats throughout the book. After Vaughan comes upon the victim of a head-on collision, Ballard writes, "When Vaughan had taken the last of his pictures he knelt down inside the car and held her face carefully in his hands."[100] Later, when present during the filming of a crash, James spies "a woman's dusty suède glove"[101] in the crashed car that the actress will be filmed in post-crash. James muses, "Did the actress sitting in the car under her death-paint visualize the real victim injured in the accident that had crushed this vehicle? Did she instinctively mimic the postures of this injured woman, transforming in her own magnificent person the injuries of a commonplace accident, the soon-forgotten bloodstains and sutures?"[102] Later in the novel, when James and Catherine come upon a couple trapped in a limousine after another serious crash, Ballard notes that the woman's "left hand held the window strap, the white glove marked with blood from her small fingers. She gave the policeman a weak smile, like a partially disrobed queen beckoning a courtier to touch her private parts."[103] The gloved hand, here and in the short film, does indeed invoke one of the trademarks of Elizabeth II. It also appears like an almost anachronistic detail in the midst of the sci-fi context of the novel, but suggests the emphasis on the tactile, on touch, and on the melding of hard and soft, covered and uncovered, seen and not seen that the non-touching touching of the gloved hand suggests.

Ballard the author discusses the notion of the "cripple" throughout the book. Frequently the body of a crash victim bears the literal marks of the car they were in during the crash—the body becoming realigned by the violence and the movement of the body against the car, especially the dash. The crippled or disabled victim is in some ways the novel's ideal. Vaughan and James have begun the process of changing their bodies into something else, something purposefully altered and no longer able-bodied in the normative sense. Gabrielle is the most prominent example in the book of this process of transformation. She is described in details that suggest a transgendered or transsexed process in which she is turning her body from human into machine. In the scene described earlier when James looks at pictures of victims of crashes with Vaughan, one victim in particular catches his attention. She first appears in photographs "lying in the crashed car . . . a conventional young woman whose symmetrical face and upstretched skin spelled out the whole economy of a cozy and passive life . . . without any sense of the real possibilities of her body."[104] She moves from "chromium wheelchair" to later being "reborn within the breaking contours of her crushed sports car. Three months later, sitting beside her physiotherapy instructor in her new invalid car, she held the chromium treadles in her strong fingers as if they were extensions of her clitoris."[105] For in fact, "the crushed body of the sports car had turned her into a creature of free and perverse sexuality, releasing with its twisted bulkheads and leaking engine coolant all the deviant possibilities of her sex."[106] Later, Helen Remington learns to drive her car in such a way that "her body formed an awkward geometry with the windshield pillars and the angle of the steering column, almost as if she were consciously mimicking the postures of the crippled young woman, Gabrielle."[107]

By using images of the disabled, Bowie and Gaga connect themselves to what Robert McRuer has termed the politics of "crip," a word he sees as having roughly the same connection to the notion of "disability" that "queer" has to "homosexuality" or "gay."[108] Like *queer*, *crip* can be claimed by almost anyone, including the non-disabled McRuer himself, as an identity that forces both an awareness of the privileges of able-bodiedness and a destabilizing of the assumed natural hierarchy of nondisabled and disabled as opposed to the universalizing of the latter.[109] The inherent danger in an able-bodied person's taking on the mantle of crip, as he notes, is not only the possibility of "appropriation" but, ultimately, liberal "patronizing tolerance."[110] Despite these caveats, however, McRuer ultimately advances crip theory as a way to "counter neoliberalism and access alternative ways of being."[111] It is in this spirit that Bowie and Gaga, I would argue, could be seen to take on this identity, as fraught with danger as it is. With its seeming dependence upon identity theory, disability studies might seem like one of the last vestiges of the real, one of the last places where identity must be immutable. In their own ways, Gaga and Bowie attempt to inhabit and extend the notion of crip much as queer does sexuality, by dissolving boundaries and expanding the possibility of identity, to bring to it a form of "fluidity."[112]

If crip can be claimed as a fluid identity, then it can perhaps also be claimed as a more modern one. The number of veterans who have returned from wars with prosthetic limbs has increased astronomically since the various gulf wars. But prosthetics, such as those sported by Lady Gaga in "Paparazzi," have been a part of male veteran identity at least since the First World War when the technology of warfare became so very efficient at killing and the concomitant rise in artificial limbs and ancillary technology began to keep pace. On HBO's series about prohibition in Atlantic City, *Boardwalk Empire*, the character of Richard Harrow (Jack Huston) is a returning vet who is missing the left side of his face and wears a mask attached to his eyeglasses to conceal the wounds he has sustained. The most erotic moment of season two was one in which viewers got to peek beyond the mask to see the vagina-like wound that lay beneath. That this moment took place in front of his best friend's lesbian wife, a painter (Angela Darmody played by Aleksa Palladino), during a portrait sitting only added to the tension. The vulnerability of the scene completed the feminizing of Harrow, a tough henchman for Jimmy Darmody (Michael Pitt), also a war veteran, who had earlier been shown to secretly dream about having a normative family and to keep a scrapbook filled with images from advertising of perfect American families. After the First World War the notion of "rehabilitation and engineering," as McRuer terms it, took off as rehabilitation replaced "degradation" to bring to the soldier "a restored marketability."[113] Masculinity, work, and able-bodiedness were ultimately brought together in the invention of prosthetic limbs by Henry Dreyfuss and others for the Veterans Administration in the 1950s.

Identifying Bowie as "crip" complicates his identity by adding a layer to the usual non-normative aspects of his constructed identity. If he was considered a sexual "alien" or an "outsider" artist, then we can also add "disabled" or "crip." Though obviously charismatic and handsome, Bowie is also known for his seemingly mismatched eyes, his sometimes "freakish" appearance in the 1970s, his drug dependence, and his physical problems since his heart attack. When he appeared in a Liverocks performance in 2006, his first since his heart attack, he sported a painted on bruise by his right eye and a bandage on his left hand—make-up and costume that referred to his recent brush with death. In this performance, in which he appeared classically restrained, bowing to the audience before singing "Life on Mars" with Mike Garson at a concert grand piano, the references to his newfound fragility appeared almost surreal within this context. The crip aspects of Bowie's persona have always been present—especially in terms of his fear of inheriting his family's history of mental illness—but his heart trouble made it clear that that part of his identity was now essential to him.[114]

The notion of able-bodiedness is especially important to masculinity, with feeling that one's masculine identity is connected to wholeness. As Susannah B. Mintz argues, "The 'traditional account,' according to [Tom] Shakespeare, assumes a contradiction between disability and masculinity, a view that fails to challenge masculine ideals and disregards the ways in which disabled men might 'depart from tradition' by 'reformulat[ing]' hegemonic masculinity."[115] Rather than seeing either identity as monolithic, it is important to see how masculinity, like disability, is in fact something where men must "reformulate for themselves what maleness means, repeatedly crossing the border of those paths, complicating the line between alternative and natural order and depicting instead . . . a divergent sense of masculinity."[116] In that sense, Bowie's performance of a complicated masculinity mirrors and even predates his complex relationship to disability, both of which, as Mintz argues, must be seen as composed of "a community of highly unlike individuals." Masculinity, like disability, "must be understood as no less fluid and changeable a term."[117] It is not surprising that Bowie has often kept the two identities related. When he appeared as John Merrick in Bernard Pomerance's 1979 play *The Elephant Man* on Broadway in 1980 he commented directly on masculinity and physical disability.[118] Winning over critics with his minimalist performance, Bowie eschewed makeup, unlike John Hurt in David Lynch's 1980 film on the same subject, and suggested Merrick's physical reality via his voice, posture, and choreographed movement on the stage. Bowie's presentation of disability in the play and in the video and elsewhere on songs about his brother or his own problems resists making it maudlin or sentimental.

Recent disability studies sees disability as existing in a binary with able-bodiedness as its "other"—necessary for the able-bodied to have an identity, or understand it. Yet why is it not the primary identity in that binary—especially since most people will be, at some point in their lives, disabled? As with the Deaf community, it is important that we not see disabled as meaning people who desire to be able-bodied. It is a mistake to think that everyone who is not bodily whole sees themselves as somehow lacking. They may indeed see the able-bodied that way. Technology and fashion are also slowly changing the way people think about bodily wholeness. As prosthetic technology becomes increasingly better, some people choose to amputate limbs and replace them with synthetic versions that not only work better but allow them in some cases to avoid the pain or discomfort that they had with their original body parts.[119] Likewise, there exist entire subcultures devoted to identifying with disabled bodies, sexually fetishizing them much as Ballard's characters do car crash victims, or who see trapped within themselves a disabled person. Some people choose electively to remove limbs or radically alter their bodies in other ways in order to be what they see as their true selves—not unlike someone who changes their body via some version of transsexuality.[120] Disability, in other words, parallels queer and racial identities in being seen as not only the "other" of able-bodiedness but as

go[ing] beyond minority status by providing a use value for a fearful sense of instability in the supposedly normal. For example, when able-bodied people stereotype people with disabilities as bitter or self-pitying, the able-bodied people try to separate themselves from their own fears about themselves by projecting what they fear about themselves on the disabled other. In such ways, the able use the disabled to deny the vulnerability of the abled and to construct the able sense of self as normal.[121]

Like Gaga, Bowie seems to recognize the crip identity as one in which the self dissipates and becomes lost in a collective identity that is powerful in its negative definition, its communal borders that refuse to recognize the normal state of things.

The fusion of man and machine that we see so often in Lady Gaga's videos and stage performances suggests a sort of steampunk version of the fusing of people with machines before the rise of more seamless cyborgian technologies. While the video for "Bad Romance" echoes Stanley Kubrick's *2001*, like Bowie's "Jump They Say," the "Paparazzi" mini-movie seems to suggest more primitive prosthetics instead—metal, braces, and pulleys. It eroticizes the body in its literal fusion of the human body and a metal support system. Bowie's song is a precursor to his album *Outside*, which introduced the idea of the "Death Artist." By the mid-1990s Bowie has changed as a star. In *The Hunger* from 1983 we see him aging suddenly as the vampire lover John Blalock. He is, in this film, passive, a role that he takes on in *Outside* as well: a reporter relaying what has happened as opposed to someone actively involved in it. Like Marina Abramović's *The Artist Is Present* (2010) at the Museum of Modern Art, in which she sat and gazed into people's eyes as long as possible, or Tilda Swinton's *The Maybe* (2013), where crowds at the same museum could watch her sleep, people are switching from the physical to the visual—from the actual body, to representations of it.[122] We remember the body now through pornography, YouTube, Facebook, Twitter, and in all of the many electronic representations of it that we use to mimic it and, we think, expand it into a new realm of instant hyper-sensation.

Death artist

Bowie carries the notion of death and schizophrenia we find in "Jump They Say" even further in *Outside* via the return of the retro-aesthetic first used, arguably, in *Diamond Dogs*. Bowie's own forays into the visual arts became more literal in the 1990s and *Outside* is the symptom of this newfound seriousness. Not only does the album include a self-portrait, but, as Paolo Hewitt notes, "in 1994 he contributed a multimedia narrative, titled *We Saw a Minotaur*, to Brian Eno's Warchild fundraising exhibition, *Little Pieces From Big Stars*. It was subsequently included alongside works by Francis Bacon and Pablo Picasso in the *Minotaurs, Myths and Legends* exhibition at Berkeley Square Gallery, London."[123] He has claimed that he was close to becoming a painter in the 1980s and, by contributing seriously to the British magazine *Modern Painters* in the 1990s, Bowie did his part to support the Young British Artists movement by publishing serious interviews and essays on those artists as well as such established ones as Balthus and Roy Lichtenstein. He starred in Expressionist artist Julian Schnabel's *Basquiat* (1996), about the Haitian-born painter who flamed out in New York's art world in the 1980s, playing his sometimes collaborator and fan, Andy Warhol. In 1995 Bowie had his own solo exhibition, which opened to mixed reviews, and further ones in 1996 in New York. While Bowie continued to collaborate with a number of artists, as he had always done, including Tony Oursler and Floria Sigismondi on the videos for *Earthling* (1996), most significantly, he worked with Damien Hirst.[124] The dean of the Young

British Artists, Hirst rose to fame in the 1990s by making art out of the bodies of animals, insects, and even a human skull. It is difficult not to see in Hirst's work at least one possible genesis for *Outside*. In an interview with Hirst that Bowie published in *Modern Painters*, they discuss Thomas de Quincey's "Murder Considered as a Fine Art." Hirst's comments, while referring to his fame for suspending sharks, sheep, and pigs in formaldehyde, could also refer to Bowie's intentions in *Outside*: "I suppose if you consider the law as a set of disciplines, then murder is an ultimate test of those disciplines as art. For me, it's a way to stretch things to the limit, to go beyond the law. That, I would guess, is what I do as an artist."[125] As Bowie goes on to say, "Our past and future, rather than melting away in the bliss of transcendence, were hacked off like rotting limbs, gangrened and snow-bitten by indifference. The pain must be all over now, Baby Blue."[126] The victim within the album's narrative is fourteen-year-old Baby Grace Blue whose limbs are found stuck into poles and rearranged as a work of "art." "It seems like confessions," continues Bowie, "of a fine art as a set of murders." Bowie seems to give other clues to his own album here. He refers to the notion of a larger "Hirstian Gesam-Kunstwerk" as a "'social sculpture'" à la Bret Easton Ellis' *American Psycho* (1991).[127] While Bowie separates this murderous edge from Hirst's work, his album, as a whole, does paint its own social or cultural portrait of a murder—not just as a singular body but as an interrelated portrait of a cultural moment in time.[128] As Bowie later asks, "In some cases the critique itself is seen as the work of art, the physical work merely an explanation or appendage to the critical essay. The depth of analysis is measured by the sculpture or paining. Do we need the actual physical work now that art-philosophy is a genre worth analysis?"[129] Is it just the idea of murder as art that is really necessary? The concept? Or the concept album?

In many ways Bowie is clearly going further and darker than Hirst is to ponder the true meaning of the idea of art as murder. While Hirst, in the interview, resists seeing art as "metaphor" and thinks that his work, while seeming whimsical at first, might ultimately yield a deeper meaning, Bowie seems more interested in the human body itself seen as an object of analysis, taken apart, literally, and put together, at least conceptually, if not really as an actuality. As David Buckley notes, Bowie collected Hirst's paintings, collaborated with him on one, and seemed to share at the time Hirst's "paranoiac denial of death that permeates our culture."[130] This point is made clear in the video for the album's first single, "The Heart's Filthy Lesson." Directed by Sam Bayer, it is clearly modeled on Mark Romanek's seminal video for Trent Reznor's hit "Closer" for the album *The Downward Spiral* in 1994. Bayer creates a similar sense of an old found film. Whereas Romanek used a hand-cranked camera from 1919, Bowie's video has a similar sepia feel, quick editing, and a prolific use of body parts. What is different is the emphasis on ritual in Bowie's video—references to a group of people coming together to perform some sort of artistic rite in which they construct a Minotaur. While this figure references the supposed murderer on the album, it is also obviously a reference to Picasso's interest in it, which is itself an important part of Greek legend and myth. While Bowie seems to see it as indicative of both murder and sex, he imbues it with a mostly dark meaning, one that is never completely explained within the context of the album. The rituals and the suggestions of animal sacrifice that suggest the Aktion school of performance art, they also call on the millennial anxiety of the album's original temporal context.[131] Conceived as the first of five albums to mark the end of the century and of the millennium, the series was designed to expose the feel of the end of the 1990s—one in which paranoia, violence, and anxiety were supposed to reign. The modern primitivism of the late twentieth century is intensified—as though the nineties would continue into the twentieth-first century and just become more extreme, linking the body-denying age of AIDS in the 1980s with a new reaction to it—one in which blood would rebound, flesh would be torn, and the horror of the inside would be made manifest on the outside.

Complementing this emphasis on murder is an equal focus on art. The video is not just about the dismantling of a body or bodies and the creation of a new one, but about the power of the artist. It is clear from the video that what we are seeing could just as easily be taking place in an artist's studio—white cloths are used as a backdrop and are arranged on the floor. The Minotaur is a life-size artist's dummy that has its head replaced with the Minotaur's head (much as a bull's skull is worn by a naked female figure in Reznor's video). While Bowie's video shows piercings and body parts, it also includes a baptismal moment in a bath tub and ends with a reenactment of the *Last Supper* (1494–98), though one closer in spirit to Buñuel's *Viridiana* (1961) than to Da Vinci's.[132] While dark and despairing, what is also taking place is a creation of sorts. The video does not seem to refer specifically to the lyrics of the song but to the overall idea of the album—that artistic creation could come from death, or even murder. This level of self-consciousness undermines some of the seriousness of the idea while also pointing interested viewers toward yet more associations that Bowie is trying to make. On the Outside tour with Reznor, and again later, on the Earthling tour, Bowie used these white cloths as part of the set—similar ones had been used in the studio where the band originally composed the album with Bowie—suggesting that what we are hearing is about art, about how we might take an idea, however uncomfortable, and develop it in an artistic way. By the 1990s performance for Bowie was no longer the actual body, Ziggy in a futuristic, gendering-scrambling spandex suit, but in the manipulation of the art-historical references that could be made into a new form of performance—performance as painting and sculpture crossed with the millennial anxiety that he was picking up from the culture at large.[133]

Tall women

In many ways the various strands of David Bowie's interests in the body and machines, disability and the marionette, come together in the work of Helmut Newton, a German-born fashion photographer who snapped not only famous images of Bowie but created some of the most arresting fashion photos of the latter-half of the twentieth century. Newton was famous for photographing for *Vogue* and his images, which could often court controversy, frequently returned to themes that obviously fascinated him: tall, Amazonian women; women and fetish gear; women in partially surreal settings—with subtle changes in scale affecting the reality of what we are seeing.[134] In his emphasis on the naked body, often completely in lieu of clothes even for fashion shoots, Newton made his work seem to be more about the body than what covered it. Clothes never seemed so much on display as merely of a part of another goal, that is, the photograph itself. While others might photograph clothes, Newton seemed to photograph provocation.

As Karl Lagerfeld notes, Newton's photographs age much better than the clothes he photographed.[135] Newton's sensibility, which embodied and continued the 1920s Berlin where he was born, often evoked darkly erotic work. While Newton claimed not to care for either surrealism or narrative, his work often contained bits of both.[136] In terms of the latter, his images often seemed staged and stylized, as though the viewer is stumbling upon a tableau in which a story has been stopped and the characters, in the middle of an action, have suddenly frozen. His photographs with two or more people in them always contain a sense of drama, as though he is trying to capture within the photo a representation of a whole world, not just an image. Newton himself claimed that his photos were about unique moments and that he was a photographer of "reality."[137] That reality, which he claimed as his own, was of a particular jet-set that was composed of wealthy people who, like him and his wife and business partner, photographer Alice Springs (June Browne), summered in Monte Carlo and wintered in Los Angeles. The reality that is on display, however, is really more internal—statuesque, often nude models arranged in settings and scenarios that suggest bondage fantasies, or some other sort of erotically charged situation. A lot of his various sexual interests came together in photographs he took for *Playboy* as motifs that returned several times in his work—mannequins, who were often staged with living models who were made to look like their twins to create a "Doppelganger" effect, for example.[138] Mannequins were eventually replaced with high-end sex dolls that were used to create a double take on the part of the viewer in which, like the mannequins, might often appear at first glance to be real women. The movement back and forth between reality and artificiality delighted Newton, as did the notion of people behaving like dolls or puppets, and vice versa. Newton, like Ballard, even used crash-test dummies as his subject matter.

While women are the almost exclusive topic of Newton's photography, the erotic investment in them often created a disruption in the notion that they are the object of male spectatorship. The female models in his work were almost always presented as strong and confident, literally so in images of weight-trainer Lisa Lyon, for example, or in the tall models of his series *Big Nudes*, but also women were often shown to be in control in the various scenarios that his photos suggested. It is not by accident that Newton entitled one of his books *World Without Men*, as women are frequently the only sex featured in his photographs. In one series, shot in Paris, Newton photographs two female models, one in male evening dress and short hair, paired with a model dressed conventionally as a woman. The notion of female control comes across in the attitudes of the models, who seem to radiate the attitude of the "cool girls" that he preferred— pale, Nordic, and ironically aloof.[139] The models are either very pale or very tan, but always distinctly fleshy—not the waif-like or skeletal models one might associate with the 1960s or the 1990s. His obsession with female power is made explicit in his interest in bondage—sadomasochistic imagery that involves women with whips and chains (or in them), extremely long boots, fishnet stockings, riding crops, and saddles. One of Newton's own personal obsessions was with director Max von Stroheim's use of the neck brace in Jean Renoir's *La Grande Illusion* (1937), a prop that shows up often in Newton's Prussian-themed photos.

Braces and sadomasochistic imagery point up yet another aspect of Newton's biography—not only his early years in Berlin, and interest in bordellos, but also the way that imperfection works with perfection to set each other off. Most of the bondage photos blend into the photos of disability. The images of braces are also connected to his heart attack in 1972 and his images documenting the aftermath when he was connected to wires and tubes. Newton photographed models who were amputees in ways that extended the use of braces or supports beyond the prosthetic to create alternative notions of identity or subjectivity—women who were sexy and attractive as women outside the bounds of normative able-bodiedness.

Newton frequently touched on the Freudian aspects of his representation of sexuality, citing, among others, Arthur Schnitzler, who wrote *Traumnovelle*, the basis for Stanley Kubrick's *Eyes Wide Shut* (1999). According to Kubrick's co-screenwriter on that film, Frederic Raphael, Kubrick used Newton's photographs as a basis for his screenplay. One can assume that Kubrick might have used Newton's photos in particular for the central orgy sequence in the film, the "masquerade ball" in the story, which contains the very Newtonish image of clothed men observing nude women, all of a particular body type that would not be out of place in a Newton photograph. Raphael describes his impressions:

> Newton's photographs were divided between fantasies, set in extremely elegant surroundings, and shots of whorish women in the style of stills from low-life documentaries. Sometimes the desire to be perverse became comic: one shameless brunette, rising from a rumpled bed, bent her seductive smile on the photographer although she was leaning on a black cane, wearing a neck brace and a cast on her left leg. Newton seemed obsessed . . . by male voyeurism: his composite pictures often featured a naked woman or women . . . being watch by evening-dressed males. The shamelessness of the women was in contrast to the furtive dignity of the men who watched them.[140]

While it says more about Raphael's attitudes toward women than Kubrick's, Raphael's "whorish" women are presumably the models used in the Los Angeles series set in desolate motels. Kubrick's infamous sequence, in which prostitutes have sex with men who are a part of a secret society while other members, male and female, watch, is itself un-erotic, which may be Kubrick's point—that from inside an obsession, in this case the desire for sex outside of marriage as a form of revenge, sex is mechanistic, machine-like, and ultimately even off-putting. While Newton himself did two series based on pornography, the images in these series were criticized by one collector as "not hard enough."[141] Indeed, Kubrick's version of the pornographic actually contrasts with Newton's "erotic fantasies."[142] As Michael Stoeber notes, the reflections of reflections that Newton uses, especially models who look like each other, recalls Heinrich von Kleist's *Über das Marionettentheater* when he observes that marionettes seem like humans before the fall into "self-consciousness." Newton's puppets, by contrast, seem to already display that grace.[143] Like Kubrick's nude women in the film, Newton's often wear masks, but they do so with a knowingness that belies their missing identity. As one critic notes, Newton's women "have been stripped of humanity—no longer persons, they become *personae*."[144] They are, in a sense, the living embodiment of Bowie's characters—shards of Newton's personality, they make up a world of alternative beings.

Like Bowie, Newton radiates an image of consummate sophistication and cosmopolitanism. He has similar obsessions with puppets, disability, and gender, living easily all over the world—from Berlin to London to Paris and Monte Carlo to LA. Like Bowie, his work shows the intersecting interests of a number of obsessions that keep reappearing never to be vanquished completely by his art. Like Bowie, he was only beginning to be appreciated at the end of his long career as the public caught up with what he had accomplished and began to realize the extent to which it would not only endure but had changed the way that other artists work—the way that they look at their medium. His view has become their view because they are now the same.

I consider myself responsible for a whole new school of pretensions.[145]
—David Bowie, February, 1976

Matthew Biro makes the following conclusive statement about the "the influence of mass culture on the avant-garde":

> The ever-intensifying dialectic between "high" and "low" culture that characterizes the present day is nothing new—a fact that has important implications. If, in other words, the emergence of the "historical avant-garde" manifests many parallels with the subsequent emergence of "postmodernism," then the initial history of the avant-garde, the help it gave to the development of both consumer culture and the technique of fascist and totalitarian propaganda and spectacle, should signal what is at stake today. Although it was not achieved, the promise that the avant-garde made to transform society is something that remains in the present.[146]

While we may not have a new avant-garde that can battle the inherent effects of fascism that Theodor Adorno feared, we do and have had an avant-garde that attempts to use consumer society to ameliorate the effects of brainwashing and society becoming the spectacle by embracing the division between the everyday life of the consumer object and the romantic or modernist role of the artist. As Susan Sontag has stated, "People say a lot of stupid things about the fifties, but what *was* true about that time was that there was this total separation between those who were tuned into popular culture and those who were involved in high culture. There was nobody I ever met who was interested in both, and I always was, and I used to do all sorts of things by myself because I couldn't share this with anybody else."[147]

While Sontag enjoyed popular culture, she also defended the high-cultural tools that she used to analyze it:

> The so-called Romantic revolutionary period—and we're essentially still dealing with expectations and feelings that were formulated at that time, like ideas about happiness, individuality, radical social change, and pleasure. We were given a vocabulary that came into existence at a particular historical moment. So when I go to a Patti Smith concert at CBGB, I enjoy, participate, appreciate, and am tuned in better because I've read Nietzsche.[148]

I would similarly argue that Bowie's own work, his pulling down of high culture into low, can best be understood if we have a critical analytical vocabulary and set of theoretical paradigms with which to view him in order to be able to explain and understand how his art works. He came along at a specific historical and cultural moment, the 1970s, when his interest in combining media, experimenting with gender and sexuality, and building upon the best work of the rock music of the 1960s could come together to create a new school of "artistic pretentions." As Sontag argued:

> What is essentially different in the seventies is that there isn't the illusion that a lot of people think the same as you do. I mean, one is restored to one's position as a freelance person. . . . All throughout the sixties, I was horrified by the anti-intellectualism of the movement and the hippies and the bright-thinking people whom I stood shoulder to shoulder within various political situations. I couldn't stand how anti-intellectual they were.[149]

Bowie was one who also came along and fought against the anti-intellectualism of the sixties, helping to deepen rock music and to make it a place for not just the insider but the outsider as well, a different type of rebel, one who is not named, frequently misunderstood, and hiding in plain sight. Bowie brought us to the brink of understanding a new notion of cool, and now that idea is commonplace, in large part thanks to him.

Notes

1   See, for example, "Bowie's Top 100 Books—The Complete List," October 1, 2013 to October 7, 2013. http://www.davidbowie.com/news/bowie-s-top-100-books-complete-list-52061.
2   Cf. my comments on the style of post-Second World War youth subcultures in Chapter 2, especially the work of the CCCC and of Dick Hebdige.
3   Craig Copetas, "Beat Godfather Meets Glitter Mainman," in *The Bowie Companion*, ed. Elizabeth Thomson and David Gutman (New York: Da Capo, 1996), 108.
4   Copetas, *The Bowie Companion*, 108.
5   Copetas, *The Bowie Companion*, 197.

6 There seem to be contradictory reports on when Bowie was first exposed to Burroughs' writing. Bowie says in one interview that he was reading him in his teens. Dominic Wells, "Boys Keep Swinging," *Time Out*, August 23–30, 1995 to October 20, 2014. http://music.hyperreal.org/artists/brian_eno/interviews/Bowieno.html. Malins, as well, assumes that Bowie always used Burroughs as an inspiration:

> [Gary] Numan had been writing short stories since the age of four, and as he took his material more seriously he started to flesh out his lyrics and ideas stolen from sci-fi magazines and authors such as Philip K. Dick and William Burroughs. The surreal scene writings, bizarre characters and futuristic themes of these novels offered oblique, otherworldly locations for him to express his own feelings. Although David Bowie stole freely from the same sources, Numan created his own unique style. (Gary Numan and Steve Malins, *Praying to the Aliens: An Autobiography by Gary Numan with Steve Malins* (London: Andre Deutsch 1997), viii–ix)

   According to Stevenson, "After the meeting Bowie is reported to have read extracts from Burroughs's novel *The Wild Boys* (1971) to some of his concert audiences." Nick Stevenson, *David Bowie: Fame, Sound and Vision* (Cambridge: Polity, 2006), 67.

7 Copetas, *The Bowie Companion*, 106–07.

8 David Bowie Is, Art Gallery of Ontario, Toronto, November 20, 2013.

9 The 1980 Floor Show is also mentioned in the interview and is also a prototype of the later Diamond Dogs tour.

10 Barry Miles, *William Burroughs: El Hombre Invisible: A Portrait* (New York: Hyperion, 1993), 231.

11 Qtd. in Miles, *William Burroughs*, 235.

12 Ibid.

13 In the liner notes to the European edition of his album *Buddha of Suburbia* (1993), Bowie significantly wrote: "A major . . . obstacle to the evolution of music has been the almost redundant narrative form. To rely upon this old war-horse can only continue the spiral into British constraint and insularity. Maybe we could finally relegate the straightforward narrative to the past." David Bowie, "The Buddha of Suburbia—Liner Notes," Teenage Wildlife, July 14, 2014. http://www.teenagewildlife.com/Notes/Albums/TBOS/linernotes.html.

14 As David Pattie describes Kraftwerk:

> The robots might gesture . . . *towards* the cyborg or the posthuman, as they occur both in Harraway and Hayles, and in popular culture; but the performance as a whole is configured as a network—the kind of integrated but distant communicative framework created by our interaction with the technologies that we have shaped, and which shape us in their turn. (David Pattie, "Kraftwerk: Playing the Machines," in *Kraftwerk: Music Non-Stop*, ed. Sean Albiez and David Pattie (New York: Continuum 2011), 133)

15 As he did on other seventies albums, even *Low*, Bowie was able to make synthesized music sound almost human:

> This combination comes out again on his nineties albums. The entire process of working, where computers and samples played as great a role as live music, reminded him of his attitude in the 1970s, taking technology "and combin[ing] it with the organic. It was very important to me that we didn't

lose the feel of real musicianship working in conjunction with anything that was sampled or looped or worked out on the computer." (Qtd. in Dave Thompson, *Hallo Spaceboy: The Rebirth of David Bowie* (Toronto: ECW Press, 2006), 166)

16 Qtd. in Nicholas Pegg, *The Complete David Bowie*, 6th ed. (London: Titian Books, 2011), 68.

17 Qtd. in Pegg, *The Complete David Bowie*, 68.

18 William S. Burroughs, *The Soft Machine; Nova Express; The Wild Boys: Three Novels* (New York: Grove Press, 1980), 147.

19 Burroughs, *The Wild Boys*, 153–54.

20 Burroughs, *The Wild Boys*, 155.

21 Burroughs, *The Wild Boys*, 159–60.

22 As Nick Stevenson notes, the *Diamond Dogs* cover "bears a close relationship to Burroughs's . . . own description of a Penny Arcade Peep Show in . . . *The Wild Boys*. The arcade is located in a funfair and is populated by decadent young men." As I note in relation to this novel as well as Burroughs' first two, Burroughs was trying to create a hyper-masculine world, to make butch the gay world and to rebrand it as "queer." As Stevenson continues, "The freakishness of the utopian and dystopian worlds of Bowie and Burroughs is intended to undermine dominant ideas of homosexuality and introduce alternative masculine sexual pleasures. The freak show has a long history as a form of troubling and disruptive sexual fantasy." Nick Stevenson, *David Bowie: Fame, Sound and Vision* (Cambridge: Polity 2006), 68. As he later notes, "Both Bowie and Burroughs are welcoming us to a carnivalesque freak show. Arguably both in different ways are asking us to imagine a new queer utopia where femininity is permanently displaced and an aggressive male sexuality affirmed." Stevenson, *David Bowie*, 69.

23 The section entitled "Sweet Thing" is one of his greatest achievements and, like much of this side of the album, blurs songs and images together and demonstrates many of the album's innovative techniques. We are in a city landscape that has been changed by some sort of disaster in which people seem to have mutated in some way. We get a story about drugs and sex, but also about the star/fan relationship once again. Bowie seems to sing as a hustler talking to a prostitute, or trying to score a new one, but Bowie also sounds like a politician, which echoes the novel, while also commenting on himself—on his own now complex history in the rock-and-roll business. The "poisonous people" who are "spreading rumors and lies" may well be from the point of view of inside the industry, especially for someone so paranoid and drug-addled as Bowie would have been then. The only answer might be to don "bullet-proof faces." The shop on the corner selling papier-mâché masks, then, references the Kabuki mask Bowie uses at one point in the concert and the many masks he has always worn as a performer. If at one level the song is autobiographical, perhaps he is ashamed of his own sexual indiscretions: "On the street where you live I could not hold up my head/for I put all I have in another bed/on another floor/in the back of a car/in the cellar of a church with the door ajar." When he desperately intones, "I want you, I need you! Anyone out there?" he admits his need of fans, but also creates one of several self-conscious moments in the concert. Here, he is being literal: is there anyone out there in the audience, outside of the proscenium arch? His desperation is raw, but his theatricalization is keen. He also notes that his "set is

amazing, it even smells like a street." He finally notes the smile on the fan/prostitute/ lover's face, he asks, "isn't that me?" Indeed, the real and the artificial, the fan and the star distinction at this point collapses.

24 On the misogyny of his texts, especially the absence of women, Burroughs said:

> I was merely proposing this as one experimental line that I would be most interested to follow, in the direction of mutations from the present humanoid form. . . . That is boys who had never had contact with women would be quite a different animal. We can't imagine what they would be like. I certainly have no objects if lesbians would like to do the same. (Qtd. in Miles, *William Burroughs*, 184)

In *The Western Lands* he makes clear that evolution stopped because of women who need a human host in which to exist in physical form. Men were never able to realize their destiny. Miles, *William Burroughs*, 222. In Burroughs' universe, it is men, not women, who are magical, spiritual, and fluid. Women are connected to everything Burroughs abhors: "rigid authoritarian structures of state and the military." Miles, *William Burroughs*, 223.

25 Burroughs recycled material from the *Wild Boys* in his next book, a sort of sequel to it, entitled *Port of Saints* (1980). Much of what is in this book repeats scenes and details from the *Wild Boys*, but with less linear narrative and more dependence upon imagery and pornography to carry the reader through. The novel provides a sort of origin story for the Wild Boys, giving the reader a mythical backstory for them:

> According to the legend an evil old doctor, who called himself God and us dogs, created the first boy in his adolescent image. The boy peopled the garden with male phantoms that rose from his ejaculations. This angered God, who was getting on in years. He decided it endangered his position as CREATOR. So he crept upon the boy and anesthetized him and made Eve from his rib. Henceforth all creation of beings would process through female channels. But some of Adam's phantoms refused to let God near them under any pretext. After millennia these cool remote spirits breathe in the wild boys who will never again submit to the yoke of female flesh. And anyone who joins them must leave woman behind forever. (William S. Burroughs, *Port of Saints* (Berkeley: Blue Wind Press, 1980), 97)

26 One example of Wittig's description of the lesbian body shows the mix of scientific objectivity and poetic beauty that one finds in so much of Burroughs' writing on the young male body:

> After the sun has risen they anoint their bodies with oil of sandalwood curcuma gardenia. They steady one foot on a tree-trunk. Their hands rub each leg in turn, the skin glistening. Some of them are lying down. Others massage them with their fingertips. The bare bodies gleam in the strong morning light. One of their flanks is iridescent with a golden lustre. The rising sun does likewise when it sends its rays slanting across the erect rounded tree-trunks. The arcs of the circles so touched reflect a little of the light, their outlines are blurred. (Monique Wittig, *Les Guérillères*, trans. David Le Vay (New York: Avon Books, 1973), 15)

27 Scott Bukatman, *Terminal Identity: The Virtual Subject in Postmodern Science Fiction* (Durham: Duke University Press, 1993), 77.

28 Bukatman, *Terminal Identity*, 77–78.

29 Bukatman, *Terminal Identity*, 78.

30 Bukatman, *Terminal Identity*, 79.

31 Kathy Acker, *Bodies of Work: Essays* (New York: Serpent's Tail, 1997), 2.

32 William S. Burroughs, *Junky*, ed. and intrd. Oliver Harris (New York: Penguin, 2003), 60.

33 Burroughs, *Junky*, 60.

34 Burroughs, *Junky*, 82.

35 Burroughs, *Junky*, 93.

36 Jorge Garcia Robles, *The Stray Bullet: William S. Burroughs in Mexico*, trans. Daniel C. Schechter (Minneapolis: University of Minnesota Press, 2013), 131.

37 William S. Burroughs, *Queer* (New York: Penguin, 1987), 27.

38 William S. Burroughs, "Introduction," *Queer*, xiv.

39 Burroughs, "Introduction," xviii.

40 Ibid.

41 Miles, *William Burroughs*, 179.

42 Denton Welch, "When I Was Thirteen," in *The Faber Book of Gay Short Fiction*, ed. Edmund White (Boston: Faber and Faber, 1991), 77.

43 Welch, *The Faber Book of Gay Short Fiction*, 81.

44 Welch, *The Faber Book of Gay Short Fiction*, 88.

45 J. G. Ballard, *High-Rise* (New York: Liveright, 2012), 207.

46 Ballard, *High-Rise*, 152.

47 Ibid.

48 Some of Bowie's transformation here might well echo a comment he made once in an interview, that the first time he considered the possibility of madness "was when he was reading *Metamorphosis*, Franz Kafka's tale of psychological and physical transformation, with its suggestion that our shared humanity might be ripped away in a night's sleep, to reveal a bestial creature within." Peter Doggett, *The Man Who Sold the World: David Bowie and the 1970s* (London: The Bodley Head), 26.

49 J. G. Ballard, *Running Wild* (New York: Farrar, Straus, and Giroux, 1998), 12.

50 J. G. Ballard, "Time, Memory and Inner-Space," in *A User's Guide to the Millennium: Essays and Reviews* (New York: Picador, 1996), 200.

51 Ballard, *A User's Guide*, 200.

52 J. G. Ballard, *Miracles of Life: Shanghai to Shepperton: An Autobiography* (London: Fourth Estate, 2008), 134–35.

53 Ballard, *Miracles of Life*, 166.

54 Ballard, *Miracles of Life*, 167.

55 J. G. Ballard, *The Atrocity Exhibition* (London: Fourth Estate, 2006), 86.

56 Ballard, *Miracles of Life*, 208.

57 Ballard, *Miracles of Life*, 210.

58 Ballard, *Miracles of Life*, 239.

59 Ballard, *Miracles of Life*, 242.

60 Ballard, *Miracles of Life*, 238.

61 Ballard, *Miracles of Life*, 242.

62 J. G. Ballard, *Crash* (New York: The Noonday Press, 1973), 29.

63 Ballard, *Crash*, 36.

64 Ballard, *Crash*, 40.

65 Ballard, *Crash*, 48–49

66 Ballard, *Crash*, 221.

67 Ballard, *The Atrocity Exhibition*, 26–27.

68 The idea of smashed cars as art can be seen to exist in forms other than Ballard's installation and in his novel. John Chamberlain was a sculptor who created "hard-wrought automobile work as a sculptural version of gestural Abstract Expressionist painting, his shredded and smashed metal pieces sharing the explosive visual energy of painters like Willem de Kooning and Jackson Pollock. . . . Others likened his approach to the 1960s pop artists, citing Mr. Chamberlain's use of commonplace industrial materials." Andrew Rosseth, "John Chamberlain, Sculpture of Crushed, Shredded Automobile Parts, Dies at 84," *New York Observer*, December 21, 2011 to December 22, 2011. http://www.galleristny.com/2011/12/john0chamberlain-dies-at-84-12212011/?show=print.

69 Ballard, *Crash*, 94.

70 Ballard, *Crash*, 97.

71 Ballard, *Crash*, 100.

72 Ballard, *Crash*, 102.

73 Ballard, *Crash*, 194.

74 Ballard, *Crash*, 103.

75 Ballard, *Crash*, 201.

76 Ibid.

77 Ballard, *Crash*, 104.

78 Takayuki Tatsumi, *Full Metal Apache: Transactions Between Cyberpunk Japan and Avant-Pop America* (Durham: Duke University Press, 2006), 90.

79 Tatsumi, *Full Metal Apache*, 91.

80 Ibid.

81 Pansy Duncan, "Taking the Smooth with the Rough: Texture, Emotion, and the Other Postmodernism," *PMLA* 129, no. 4 (2014): 209.

82 Duncan, *PMLA*, 209.

83 While useful, this essay is ultimately about the aesthetics of postmodernism and theories of affect and emotion. The latter has begun to make some headway in works of realist fiction and film—see, for example, Fredric Jameson's discussion of emotion in *Antinomies of Realism* (New York: Verso, 2013). But I do not agree with Duncan's assertion that the uneven surfaces in the film represent modernism and the smooth, textureless surfaces postmodernism. This is not a useful distinction to make about the film and is a reductive way to talk about the content of the film's images.

84 Duncan, *PMLA*, 210.

85 Duncan, *PMLA*, 213.

86 While Beckman is grudging at best in what she sees as Ballard's "failed" attempt at experimenting with the politics of gender, she fails herself fully to appreciate the importance of the book to masculinity studies, in particular to the rare queering of a straight white male character. The whole point of the novel, which she resists, is the notion of a new gender or sexuality. I do not agree with her that "throughout *Crash* . . . James tends to transgress boundaries through the penetration of the wounds of others while his own body remains largely intact. The boundaries of female bodies . . . often seem more porous and fluid than those of James's body." Karen Beckman, *Crash: Cinema and the Politics of Speed and Stasis* (Durham: Duke University Press, 2010), 177.

87   Qtd. in Beckman, *Crash*, 161–62.
88   Acker, *Bodies of Work*, 175.
89   Beckman, *Crash*, 164.
90   Beckman, *Crash*, 166.
91   Ibid.
92   Beckman, *Crash*, 172.
93   Ballard sets the novel near Shepperton, famous for its film studios. He lived in Chiswick.
94   One might argue that Madonna also learned the art of the persona from Bowie and that Lady Gaga simply sped the process up. As Alastair Williams says of Madonna, echoing the work on her by John Fiske: "She has been likened to a corporation that produces images of herself in various media, thereby repudiating the non-commercial claims of rock authenticity. Instead of trying to embody a particular identity, as most rock performers typically do, she slips in and out of subject positions from song to song and within songs." Alastair Williams, *Constructing Musicology* (Aldershot: Ashgate, 2001), 93.
95   For a muckraking, but detailed, account of Bowie's relationship to his half-brother, see Peter and Leni Gillman, *Alias David Bowie: A Biography* (New York: Henry Holt and Co., 1987).
96   Qtd. in Mikal Gilmore, "How Ziggy Stardust Fell to Earth," *Rolling Stone* (February 2, 2012): 42.
97   Bowie has often been on the forefront of fashion. The "David Bowie Is" show makes this connection clear with Bowie's costumes from his concerts and music videos acting as a who's who of famous clothing designers with whom he has worked to create costumes that continually push at the boundary between the sexes.
98   Boshier went on to do some cubistic set designs for Bowie's 1978 world tour.
99   Ballard, *Crash*, 7.
100 Ballard, *Crash*, 11.
101 Ballard, *Crash*, 109.
102 Ibid.
103 Ballard, *Crash*, 154.
104 Ballard, *Crash*, 99.
105 Ibid.
106 Ibid.
107 Ballard, *Crash*, 121.
108 Robert McRuer, *Crip Theory: Cultural Signs of Queerness and Disability* (New York: New York University Press, 2006), 34.
109 McRuer, *Crip Theory*, 36–37.
110 McRuer, *Crip Theory*, 37.
111 McRuer, *Crip Theory*, 42.
112 McRuer, *Crip Theory*, 34.
113 McRuer, *Crip Theory*, 114.
114 Bowie and his personae are used as the symbol of freakishness on the cable television series *American Horror Story*. In the fourth season of this anthology series, set in a traveling sideshow of freaks in winter camp in Florida, Bowie is invoked in some way in nearly every episode. Jessica Lange plays the character Fraulein Elsa Mars, the impresario of the troupe, who sings "Life on Mars" during every evening's

public performance. She is dressed in a tattered version of Bowie's powder-blue suit from Mick Rock's music video for the song. Almost every character in the show is "freakish" in some way—from pin heads to lobster-claw hands—or embody the extremes of normality—the overweight woman, the giantess, the world's smallest woman, etc. Some of the abnormalities are hidden—the man with the largest penis, for example, played by Denis O'Hare—some are mental (there are two serial killers). Bowie's past interests in clowns and sexual ambiguity are themes on the show and the producers often invoke him indirectly by including songs other than "Life on Mars" in an anachronistic way—whether Fiona Apple's "Criminal" or Nirvana's "Come As You Are." Lange's character traces her backstory to "Weimar Republic 1932" when she was a famous prostitute who was drugged and placed in a snuff film, where she lost both her legs on camera. She is clearly a version of Marlene Dietrich via Bowie. Bowie's own outsider nature is the touchstone for the show, which rereads freakishness as empowering and positive. The series finale features Lange reproducing Bowie's video for "'Heroes'" where she is dressed in a white suit in contrast to Bowie's all-black ensemble.

115   Susannah B. Mintz, "Lyric Bodies: Poets on Disability and Masculinity," *PMLA* 127, no. 2 (March 2012): 249.

116   Mintz, *PMLA*, 261.

117   Ibid.

118   Bowie joins Bill Crudup, Mark Hammill, and Bradley Cooper as handsome men who have played the deformed but debonair historical figure. See Eric Grode, "A Twist of Art: Handsome as Disfigured," *New York Times*, July 19, 2012 to July 19, 2012. http://www.nytimes.com/2012/07/22/theater/bradley-cooper-takes-on-the-eletphant-man.html?partner=rss&emc=rss.

119   See, for example, Alexis Okeowo, "A Once-Unthinkable Choice for Amputees," *New York Times*, May 14, 2012 to May 15, 2012. http://www.nytimes.com/2012/05/15/health/losing-more-to-gain-more-amputees-once-unthinkable-choice.html?pagewanted=all&module=Search&mabReward=relbias%3As&_r=0.

120   See, for example, Jennifer Chambers Lynch's film about the sexual obsession of disability, *Boxing Helena* (1993), or the plastic surgeries filmed as performance art of Orlan. Bowie talked about her, Stelarc, and other contemporary performance artists throughout his art-obsessed phase in the 1990s. Thompson, *Hallo Spaceboy*, 124.

121   Robert Dale Parker, *How to Interpret Literature: Critical Theory for Literary and Cultural Studies*, 3rd ed. (New York: Oxford University Press, 2015), 374–75.

122   James Westcott, "A Culture of 'Perform Yourself,'" *New York Times*, August 18, 2011. http://www.nytimes.com/roomfordebate/2011/08/18/did-youtube-kill-performance-art/a-culture-of-perform-yourself?module=Search&mabReward=relbias%3Aw%2C%7B%221%22%3A%22RI%3A10%22%7D.

123   Paolo Hewitt, *Bowie: Album by Album* (London: Carlton, 2012), 218.

124   Oursler has been experimenting with art composed of projections and puppets since 1991. He was hired by filmmaker Stanley Kubrick to try to make a prototype of a believable puppet boy for the project *AI* (2001), which was ultimately realized by Steven Spielberg without actual robots. Oursler's projections were used extensively by Bowie in the videos for *Earthling* and on the accompanying tour. Bowie turned to Oursler again for the video to "Where Are We Now?" from *The Next Day*. Oursler

projects faces onto curved surfaces that look like the head of an artist's dummy. The chattering disembodied heads can seem like the dehumanized characters from a Samuel Beckett play. Oursler seems to comment on and play with multiple personalities and passive-aggressive behavior. Sigismondi would direct Bowie and Tilda Swinton in the video for the single "The Stars (Are Out Tonight)," also from *The Next Day*.

125 David Bowie, "(S)now: David Bowie Interviews Damien Hirst," *Modern Painters* 9 (Summer 1996): 38.

126 Bowie, *Modern Painters*, 38.

127 Bowie, *Modern Painters*, 39.

128 Bowie earlier separates Hirst from "the severer side of body-part art—Kiki Smith, Joel Peter Witkins's human-corpses in *tableaux*, or Beth B's wax sculptures of female circumcision . . ." (36).

129 Bowie, *Modern Painters*, 39.

130 Qtd. in David Buckley, *Strange Fascination: David Bowie, The Definitive Story*, rev. ed. (London: Virgin, 2001), 497.

131 For more on this school of art, see my discussion in the introduction to this volume.

132 A Minotaur also figures in his video for "Seven Years in Tibet" for *Earthling*.

133 For more on Bowie's use of art history on *Outside* see my discussion in chapter 5 of *The Aesthetics of Self-Invention: Oscar Wilde to David Bowie* (Minneapolis: University of Minnesota Press, 2004).

134 Other interests included a fascination with swimming pools, like David Hockney— see, for example, *Piscine III* (1973)—and a love of hotels, which he considered "like a movie set," erotic and mysterious.

135 Karl Lagerfeld, "Nordfleisch (Introduction)," *Big Nudes*, by Helmut Newton (New York: Xavier Moreau, 1982), 9.

136 Hugh Hefner and Edward Behr, among others, have pointed out the surrealism of Newton's work, though Newton himself denies it. See, for example, Hugh M. Hefner, Foreword, *Playboy: Helmut Newton*, by Helmut Newton (San Francisco: Chronicle Books, 2005), 7; Helmut Newton, *Sleepless Nights* (New York: Congreve, 1978) N. pag.; Helmut Newton, *Autobiography* (New York: Nan A Talese, 2003), 187.

137 Helmut Newton, *Helmut Newton* (New York: Pantheon Books and Paris: Centre National de la Photographie, 1987) N. pag.

138 Newton, *Autobiography*, 222.

139 Lagerfeld, *Big Nudes*, 7.

140 Frederic Raphael, *Eyes Wide Open: A Memoir of Stanley Kubrick* (New York: Ballantine, 1999), 111–12.

141 Qtd. in Newton, *Autobiography*, 262.

142 Lagerfeld, *Big Nudes*, 13.

143 Michael Stoeber, "Woman As Will and Idea: Beautiful, Self-Confident, Strong and Independent," in *The Artificial of the Real: Anton Josef Trčka, Edward Weston, Helmut Newton*, ed. Carsten Aherns (Zurich: Kestner Gesellschaft/Scalo, 1998), 137.

144 Helmut Newton, *White Women* (New York: Stonehill, 1976) N. pag.

145 Reprt. in *Bowiepix* (New York: Delilah Books, 1983) from an interview April, 1971.

146 Matthew Biro, *The Dada Cyborg: Visions of the New Human in Weimar Berlin* (Minneapolis: University of Minnesota Press, 2009), 22.

147   Susan Sontag and Jonathan Cott, *Susan Sontag: The Complete* Rolling Stone *Interview* (New Haven: Yale University Press, 2013), 37.
148   Sontag and Cott, *Susan Sontag*, 34. Combining the "high" and "low" is something that Sontag would do brilliantly in her first book of essays, *Against Interpretation* (1966), which would take the Supremes as seriously as Sartre.
149   Sontag and Cott, *Susan Sontag*, 32.

General Bibliography

Acker, Kathy. *Bodies of Work: Essays*. New York: Serpent's Tail, 1997.

Acker, Kathy. *Pussy, King of the Pirates*. New York: Grove Press, 1996.

Adorno, Theodor. "On Popular Music." In *Cultural Theory and Popular Culture: A Reader*, edited by and Introduction by John Storey, 202–14. New York: Harvester Wheatsheaf, 1994.

Agamben, Giorgio. *Stanzas: Word in Phantasm in Western Culture*. Translated by Ronald L. Martinez. Minneapolis: University of Minnesota Press, 1993.

Augé, Marc. *Non-Places: Introduction to an Anthropology of Supermodernity*. Translated by John Howe. New York: Verso, 1995.

Auslander, Philip. *Performing Glam Rock: Gender and Theatricality in Popular Music*. Ann Arbor: University of Michigan Press, 2006.

Babcock, Daniel. "Sex Fantasy #68: Yo Ho Ho." In *Discontents: New Queer Writers*, edited by Dennis Cooper, 50–55. New York: Amethyst Press, 1992.

Ballard, J. G. *The Atrocity Exhibition*. London: Fourth Estate, 2006.

Ballard, J. G. *Concrete Island*. New York: Vintage Books, 1985.

Ballard, J. G. *Crash*. New York: The Noonday Press, 1973.

Ballard, J. G. *Empire of the Sun: A Novel*. New York: Simon and Schuster, 1984.

Ballard, J. G. *High-Rise*. New York: Liveright, 2012.

Ballard, J. G. *Miracles of Life: Shanghai to Shepperton: An Autobiography*. London: Fourth Estate, 2008.

Ballard, J. G. *Running Wild*. New York: Farrar, Straus, and Giroux, 1998.

Ballard, J. G. *A User's Guide to the Millennium: Essays and Reviews*. New York: Picador, 1996.

Barthes, Roland. *Empire of Signs*. Translated by Richard Howard. New York: Hill and Wang, 1982.

Barthes, Roland. *The Fashion System*. Translated by Matthew Ward and Richard Howard. New York: Hill and Wang, 1983.

Barthes, Roland. *Image-Music-Text*. Translated by Stephen Heath. New York: Hill and Wang, 1977.

Barthes, Roland. *The Language of Fashion*. Edited by Andy Stafford and Michael Carter and Translated by Andy Stafford. New York: Berg, 2006.

Barthes, Roland. *Mythologies*. Translated by Annette Lavers. New York: Hill and Wang, 1972.

Battcock, Gregory, and Robert Nickas, eds. *The Art of Performance: A Critical Anthology*. New York: Dutton, 1984.

Baudrillard, Jean. *America*. Translated by Chris Turner. New York: Verso, 1988.

Beckman, Karen. *Crash: Cinema and the Politics of Speed and Stasis*. Durham: Duke University Press, 2010.

Bennett, Chad. "Flaming the Fans: Shame and the Aesthetics of Queer Fandom in Todd Haynes's *Velvet Goldmine*." *Cinema Journal* 49, no. 2 (Winter 2012): 17–39.

Bingham, Adam. "Merry Christmas, Mr. Lawrence." *Cineaste* 36, no. 2 (Spring 2011): 62–63.

Biro, Matthew. *The Dada Cyborg: Visions of the New Human in Weimar Berlin.* Minneapolis: University of Minnesota Press, 2009.

Booth, Mark. *Camp.* New York: Quartet Books, 1983.

Björnberg, Alf. "Structural Relationship of Music and Images in Music Video." In *Reading Pop: Approaches to Textual Analysis in Popular Music,* edited by Richard Middleton, 347–82. New York: Oxford University Press, 2000.

Bloom, Allan. *The Closing of the American Mind: How Higher Education Has Failed Democracy and Impoverished the Souls of Today's Students.* New York: Simon and Schuster, 1987.

Bowie, David. "Basquiat's Wave." *Modern Painters* 9 (Spring 1996): 46–47.

Bowie, David. "The Buddha of Suburbia—Liner Notes." Teenage Wildlife March 18, 1999 to July 14, 2014. http://www.teenagewildlife.com/Notes/Albums/TBOS/linernotes.html.

Bowie, David. Foreword. *I Am Iman.* By Iman, New York: Universe, 2001. N. pag.

Bowie, David. "Journal for Friday, January 7th 2000." January 8, 2000. http://.davidbowie. com/premium/bowie/journal/journal01-07-00.html.

Bowie, David. "Journal for 20th February 99." March 8, 1999. http://www.davidbowie. com/premium/bowie/juornal/journ2-20-99.html.

Bowie, David. "(S)now: David Bowie Interviews Damien Hirst." *Modern Painters* 9 (Summer 1996): 36–39.

Branch, Andrew. "All the Young Dudes: Educational Capital, Masculinity and the Uses of Popular Music." *Popular Music* 31, no. 1 (2012): 25–44.

Buckley, David. *Strange Fascination: David Bowie, The Definitive Story.* Rev. ed. London: Virgin, 2001.

Bukatman, Scott. *Terminal Identity: The Virtual Subject in Postmodern Science Fiction.* Durham: Duke University Press, 1993.

Burgess, Anthony. *A Clockwork Orange.* New York: Norton, 1986.

Burroughs, William S. *Cities of the Red Night.* New York: Holt, Rinehart, and Winston, 1981.

Burroughs, William S. "Introduction." In *Queer,* v–xxiii. New York: Penguin, 1987.

Burroughs, William S. *Junky.* Edited by and Introduction by Oliver Harris. New York: Penguin, 2003.

Burroughs, William S. *Naked Lunch.* New York: Grove Press, 1959.

Burroughs, William S. *Nova Express.* New York: Grove Press, 1964.

Burroughs, William S. *The Place of Dead Roads.* New York: Holt, Rinehart, and Winston, 1983.

Burroughs, William S. *Port of Saints.* Berkeley: Blue Wind Press, 1980.

Burroughs, William S. *Queer.* New York: Penguin, 1987.

Burroughs, William S. *The Soft Machine; Nova Express; The Wild Boys: Three Novels.* New York: Grove Press, 1980.

Burroughs, William S. *The Western Lands.* New York: Viking, 1987.

Butler, Judith. *Bodies that Matter: On the Discursive Limits of "Sex."* New York: Routledge, 1993.

Butler, Judith. *Gender Trouble: Feminism and the Subversion of Identity.* New York: Routledge, 1990.

Carlson, Marvin. *Performance: A Critical Introduction.* New York: Routledge, 1996.

Carpenter, Alexander. "'Give a Man a Mask and He'll Tell the Truth': Arnold Schoenberg, David Bowie, and the Mask of Pierrot." *Intersections: Canadian Journal of Music/Intersections: revue canadienne de musique* 30, no. 2 (2010): 5–24.

Carr, Roy, and Charles Shaar Murray. *David Bowie: The Illustrated Record.* New York: Avon, 1981.

Clarke, John, Stuart Hall, Tony Jefferson, and Brian Roberts. "Subcultures, Cultures and Class." In *The Subcultures Reader*, edited by Ken Gelder and Sarah Thornton, 100–11. New York: Routledge, 1997.

Copetas, Craig. "Beat Godfather Meets Glitter Mainman." In *The Bowie Companion*, edited by Elizabeth Thomson and David Gutman, 105–17. New York: Da Capo, 1996.

Cott, Jonathan. *Susan Sontag: The Complete Rolling Stone Interview*. New Haven: Yale University Press, 2013.

Čufer, Eda. "Don't." *A Bigger Splash: Painting after Performance*. Edited by Catherine Wood, 22–28. London: Tate Publishing, 2012.

Culler, Jonathan. *Literary Theory: A Very Short Introduction*. Oxford: Oxford University Press, 2011.

Davy, Kate. "Fe/Male Impersonation: The Discourse of Camp." In *Critical Theory and Performance*, edited by Janelle G. Reinelt and Joseph R. Roach, 231–47. Ann Arbor: University of Michigan Press, 1992.

Deleuze, Gilles, and Claire Parnet. Dialogues II. Translated by Hugh Tomlinson and Barbara Habberjam. Rev. ed. New York: Columbia University Press, 2007.

Deleuze, Gilles, and Félix Guattari. *Anti-Oedipus*. Minneapolis: University of Minnesota Press, 1983.

Deleuze, Gilles, and Félix Guattari. *A Thousand Plateaus*. Minneapolis: University of Minnesota Press, 1987.

Dickens, Charles. *The Adventures of Oliver Twist*. New York: Heritage Press, 1939.

Doggett, Peter. *The Man Who Sold the World: David Bowie in the 1970s*. New York: Harper Collins, 2012.

Du Plessis, Michael. "'Goth Damage' and Melancholia: Reflections on Posthuman Gothic Identities." In *Goth: Undead Subculture*, edited by Lauren M. E. Goodlad and Michael Bibby, 155–65. Durham: Duke University Press, 2007.

Duckworth, William. *Virtual Music: How the Web Got Wired for Sound*. New York: Routledge, 2005.

Duncan, Pansy. "Taking the Smooth with the Rough: Texture, Emotion, and the Other Postmodernism." *PMLA* 129, no. 4 (2014): 204–22.

Eco, Umberto. *The Role of the Reader: Explorations in the Semiotics of Texts*. Bloomington: Indiana University Press, 1979.

Edelman, Lee. *No Future: Queer Theory and the Death Drive*. Durham: Duke University Press, 2004.

Ellis, Bret Easton. *American Psycho: A Novel*. New York: Vintage Books, 1991.

Fantina, Richard, ed. *Straight Writ Queer: Non-Normative Expressions of Heterosexuality in Literature*. Jefferson, NC: McFarland, 2006.

Flugel, J. C. *The Psychology of Clothes*. London: The Hogarth Press, 1950.

Foucault, Michel. *The Use of Pleasure: Volume 2 of The History of Sexuality*. Translated by Robert Hurley. New York: Pantheon Books, 1985.

Franklin, Jamie. "Star Man—Exclusive Interview with Bowie Wingman, Gerry Leonard." May 30, 2014 to November 5, 2014. http://www.roland.co.uk/blog/gerry-leonard-interview.

Frith, Simon. "Only Dancing," *Mother Jones* 8, no. 7 (August 1983): 16–22.

Frith, Simon. *Performing Rites: On the Value of Popular Music*. Cambridge. MA: Harvard University Press, 1996.

Frith, Simon. *Sound Effects: Youth, Leisure, and the Politics of Rock 'n' Roll*. New York: Pantheon, 1981.

Frith, Simon, and Howard Horne. *Art into Pop*. New York: Methuen, 1987.

Fry, Paul H. *Theory of Literature*. New Haven: Yale University Press, 2012.

Gendron, Bernard. "Theodor Adorno Meets the Cadillacs." In *Studies in Entertainment: Critical Approaches to Mass Culture*, edited by Tania Modleski, 18–36. Bloomington: Indiana University Press, 1986.

Gibbs, Ed. "Dancing to Bowie's Tune Still Resonates 30 Years On." *Brisbane Times* May 6, 2013 to May 13, 2013. http://www.brisbanetimes.com.au/action/printArticle?id=4247082.

Gillman, Peter. *Alias David Bowie: A Biography*. New York: H. Holt, 1986.

Gilmore, Mikal. "How Ziggy Stardust Fell to Earth." *Rolling Stone* (February 2, 2012): 36–43, 68.

Goffman, Erving. *The Presentation of Self in Everyday Life*. New York: Doubleday, 1959.

Goldberg, RoseLee. *Performance Art*. Rev. ed. New York: Harry N. Abrams, 1988.

Golding, William. *Lord of the Flies*. New York: Penguin, 1982.

Grode, Eric. "A Twist of Art: Handsome as Disfigured." *New York Times* July 19, 2012 to July 19, 2012. http://www.nytimes.com/2012/07/22/theater/bradley-cooper-takes-on-the-eletphant-man.html?partner=rss&emc=rss.

Gracyk, Theodore. *Rhythm and Noise: An Aesthetics of Rock*. Durham: Duke University Press, 1996.

Hainley, Bruce. "Steven Shearer." *Artforum International* September 2003 to July 18, 2009. http://www.thefreelibrary.com/Steven+Shearer-a0108691825.

Halberstam, Judith. *The Queer Art of Failure*. Durham: Duke University Press, 2011.

Hall, Stuart, and Tony Jefferson, eds. *Resistance Through Rituals: Youth Subcultures in Post-War Britain*. London: Routledge, 1976.

Harris, Thomas A. *I'm OK, You're OK*. New York: Avon, 1973.

Hawkins, Stan. *The British Pop Dandy: Masculinity, Popular Music and Culture*. Farnham, Surrey, England and Burlington, VT: Ashgate, 2009.

Hebdige, Dick. *Subculture: The Meaning of Style*. New York: Methuen, 1987.

Hewitt, Paolo. *Bowie: Album by Album*. London: Carlton, 2012.

Hisama, Ellie M. "Postcolonialism on the Make: The Music of John Mellencamp, David Bowie, and John Zorn." In *Reading Pop: Approaches to Textual Analysis in Popular Music*, edited by Richard Middleton, 229–346. New York: Oxford University Press, 2000.

Hoberman, J. *Vulgar Modernism: Writing on Movies and Other Media*. Philadelphia: Temple University Press, 1991.

Hocquenghem, Guy. *Homosexual Desire*. Durham: Duke University Press, 1993.

Hollander, Anne. *Sex and Suits: The Evolution of Modern Dress*. New York: Kodansha International, 1995.

Horkheimer, Max, and Theodor W. Adorno. "The Culture Industry: Enlightenment as Mass Deception." In *Dialectic of Enlightenment*. Translated by John Cumming, 120–67. New York: Continuum, 1972 (1944).

Huysmans, J. K. *Against the Grain*. Introduction by Havelock Ellis. New York: Three Sirens Press, 1931.

Ipiña, Rocío Gracia, Sergio Rubira, and Marta de la Torriente, eds. *Sur le dandysme aujourd'hui: Del maniquí en el escaparate a la estrella mediática*. Santiago de Compostela, Spain: Centro Galego de Arte Contemporánea, 2013.

Jackson, Kimberley. "Gothic Music and the Decadent Individual." In *The Resisting Muse: Popular Music and Social Protest*, edited by Ian Peddie, 177–88. Farnham, Surrey, England and Burlington, VT: Ashgate, 2006.

Jacobs, Simon. *Saturn*. Tucson: Spork Press, 2014.

Jameson, Fredric. *The Antinomies of Realism*. New York: Verso, 2013.

Jameson, Fredric. *Postmodernism, or, The Cultural Logic of Late Capitalism*. Durham: Duke University Press, 1991.

Jentzen, Aaron. "The Renegade Who Had It Made: How Long Can Girl Talk Run?." *Pittsburgh City Paper* September 4, 2008. http://www.pghcitypaper.com/pittsburgh/the-renegade-who-had-it-made/Content?oid=1340712.

Johnson, Dana. *Elsewhere, California*. Berkeley: Counterpoint, 2012.

Johnson, Paddy. "Meredyth Sparks, We Were Strangers for Too Long at Elizabeth Dee Gallery." *Art Fag City* September 9, 2008 to August 19, 2009. http://www.artfagcity.com/2008/09/09/meredyth-sparks-we-were-strangers-for-too-long-at-elizabeth-dee-gallery/.

Jones, Amelia. *Body Art/Performing the Subject*. Minneapolis: University of Minnesota Press, 1998.

Kerouac, Jack. *On the Road*. New York: Viking, 1957.

Kolosko, Nathan. Personal interview. July 11, 2013.

Leigh, Wendy. *Bowie: The Biography*. New York: Gallery Books, 2014.

Loder, Kurt. "Straight Time." *Rolling Stone* (May 12, 1983): 22–28, 81.

Ludwig, Robert. Email interview. June 26–27, 2013.

Mapplethorpe, Robert. *Black Book*. New York: St. Martin's Press, 1986.

McRobbie, Angela. *Feminism and Youth Culture From "Jackie" to "Just Seventeen."* Boston: Unwin Hyman, 1991.

McRobbie, Angela, and Jenny Garber. "Girls and Subcultures." In *The Subcultures Reader*, edited by Ken Gelder and Sarah Thornton, 112–20. New York: Routledge, 1997

McRuer, Robert. *Crip Theory: Cultural Signs of Queerness and Disability*. New York: New York University Press, 2006.

Miles, Barry. *William Burroughs: El Hombre Invisible: A Portrait*. New York: Hyperion, 1993.

Mintz, Susannah B. "Lyric Bodies: Poets on Disability and Masculinity." *PMLA* 127, no. 2 (March 2012): 248–63.

Mitchell, Tony. "Performance and the Postmodern in Pop Music." *Theatre Journal* 41 (October 1989): 273–93.

Moon, Michael. "Flaming Closets." *October* 51 (Winter 1989): 19–54.

Moore, Allan F. *Rock, The Primary Text: Developing a Musicology of Rock*. 2nd ed. Aldershot: Ashgate, 2001.

Mowitt, John. "Performance Theory as the Work of Laurie Anderson." *Discourse: Theoretical Studies in Media and Culture* 12, no. 2 (Spring-Summer 1990): 48–65.

Newton, Esther. *Mother Camp: Female Impersonators in America*. Chicago: University of Chicago Press, 1979.

Newton, Helmut. *Autobiography*. New York: Nan A Talese, 2003.

Newton, Helmut. *Big Nudes*. New York: Xavier Moreau, 1982.

Newton, Helmut. *Helmut Newton*. New York: Pantheon Books and Paris: Centre National de la Photographie, 1987.

Newton, Helmut. *Playboy: Helmut Newton*. San Francisco: Chronicle Books, 2005.

Newton, Helmut. *Sleepless Nights*. New York: Congreve, 1978.

Newton, Helmut. *White Women*. New York: Stonehill, 1976.

Numan, Gary, and Steve Malins. *Praying to the Aliens: An Autobiography by Gary Numan with Steve Malins*. London: Andre Deutsch, 1997.

Odier, Daniel. *The Job: Interviews with William S. Burroughs*. Rev. ed. New York: Grove Press, 1974.

Okeowo, Alexis. "A Once-Unthinkable Choice for Amputees." *New York Times* May 14, 2012 to May 15, 2012. http://www.nytimes.com/2012/05/15/health/losing-more-to-gain-more-amputees-once-unthinkable-choice.html?pagewanted=all&module=Search &mabReward=relbias%3As&_r=0.

Orwell, George. *1984.* New York: Knopf, 1992.

Pattie, David. "Kraftwerk: Playing the Machines." In *Kraftwerk: Music Non-Stop*, edited by Sean Albiez and David Pattie, 119–35. New York: Continuum, 2011.

Pegg, Nicholas. *The Complete David Bowie.* 6th ed. London: Titan Books, 2011.

Pitt, Kenneth. *Bowie: The Pitt Report.* New York: Omnibus Press, 1985.

Prendergast, Mark. *The Ambient Century: From Mahler to Trance—The Evolution of Sound in the Electronic Age.* New York: Bloomsbury, 2000.

Rambuss, Richard. "After Male Sex." *South Atlantic Quarterly* 103, no. 3 (Summer 2007): 577–88.

Randall, Rebecca. "The Subcultures of 1970s Glam Rock and How They Influenced 1980s Glam Metal." Unpublished essay, 2003.

Ratcliff, Carter. "David Bowie's Survival." *Artforum* 21, no. 5 (January 1983): 39–45.

Rechy, John. *City of Night.* New York: Grove Press, 1963.

Rego, Paula. "The Artist's Progress: Hogarth's Legacy in the 21st Century." *The Guardian* January 13, 2007 to March 23, 2013. http://www.guardian.co.uk/artanddesign/2007/jan/13/art.classics1.

Robles, Jorge Garcia. *The Stray Bullet: William S. Burroughs in Mexico.* Translated by Daniel C. Schechter. Minneapolis: University of Minnesota Press, 2013.

Rodgers, Nile. *Le Freak: An Upside Down Story of Family, Disco, and Destiny.* New York, Spiegel and Grau, 2011.

Roelstraete, Dieter. "Painting (the Threshold of the Visible World)." In *A Bigger Splash: Painting after Performance*, edited by Catherine Wood, 29–34. London: Tate Publishing, 2012.

Ross, Andrew. *No Respect: Intellectuals and Popular Culture.* New York: Routledge, 1989.

Rosseth, Andrew. "John Chamberlain, Sculpture of Crushed, Shredded Automobile Parts, Dies at 84." *New York Observer* December 21, 2011 to December 22, 2011. http://www.galleristny.com/2011/12/john0chamberlain-dies-at-84-12212011/?show=print.

Said, Edward W. *Orientalism.* New York: Vintage Books, 1979.

Sayre, Henry M. *The Object of Performance: The American Avant-Garde since 1970.* Chicago: University of Chicago Press, 1989.

Schechner, Richard. "The Five Avant Gardes or . . . or None?." In *The Twentieth-Century Performance Reader*, edited by Michael Huxley and Noel Witts, 308–26. New York: Routledge, 1996.

Schehr, Lawrence R. "Defense and Illustration of Gay Liberation." *Yale French Studies: Same Sex/Different Text?* 90 (1996): 139–52.

Scott, Ken. *Abbey Road to Ziggy Stardust: Off the Record with the Beatles, Bowie, Elton, and So Much More.* Los Angeles: Alfred Music, 2012.

Seabrook, Thomas Jerome. *Bowie in Berlin: A New Career in a New Town.* London: Jawbone Press, 2008.

Sheppard, David. *On Some Faraway Beach: The Life and Times of Brian Eno.* Chicago: Chicago Review Press, 2009.

Sigler, David. "'Funky Days Are Back Again': Reading Seventies Nostalgia in Late-Nineties Rock Music." *Iowa Journal of Cultural Studies* 5 (Fall 2004). July 30, 2009. http://www.uiowa.edu/~ijcs./nostalgia/sigler.htm.

Shumway, David R. "Authenticity: Modernity, Stardom, and Rock and Roll." *Modernism/Modernity* 14, no. 2 (September 2007): 527–33.

Sontag, Susan. *Against Interpretation, and Other Essays*. New York: Farrar, Straus and Giroux, 1966.

Spitz, Marc. *Bowie: A Biography*. New York: Crown, 2009.

Stevenson, Nick. *David Bowie: Fame, Sound and Vision*. Cambridge: Polity, 2006.

Stiles, Kristine. "Performance Art." In *Theories and Documents of Contemporary Art*, edited by Kristine Stiles and Peter Selz, 679–94. Berkeley: University of California Press, 1996.

Stilling, Robert. "An Image of Europe: Yinka Shonibare's Postcolonial Decadence." *PMLA* 128, no. 2 (2013): 299–321.

Stoeber, Michael. "Woman As Will and Idea: Beautiful, Self-Confident, Strong and Independent." In *The Artificial of the Real: Anton Josef Trčka, Edward Weston, Helmut Newton*, edited by Carsten Aherns. 129–207. Zurich: Kestner Gesellshaft/Scalo, 1998.

Tambling, Jeremy. *Literature and Psychoanalysis*. New York: Manchester University Press, 2012.

Tatsumi, Takayuki. *Full Metal Apache: Transactions Between Cyberpunk Japan and Avant-Pop America*. Durham: Duke University Press, 2006.

Taylor, Mark C. *Disfiguring: Art, Architecture, Religion*. Chicago: Chicago University Press, 1992.

Thomas, Calvin, ed. *Straight with a Twist: Queer Theory and the Subject of Heterosexuality*. Urbana: University of Illinois Press, 2000.

Thompson, Dave. *Hallo Spaceboy: The Rebirth of David Bowie*. Toronto: ECW Press, 2006.

Tosenberger, Catherine. "Homosexuality at the Online Hogwarts: Harry Potter Slash Fanfiction." *Children's Literature* 36 (2008): 187–207.

Trynka, Paul. *David Bowie: Starman*. New York: Little, Brown, and Co., 2011.

Vermorel, Fred, and Judy Vermorel. *Starlust: The Secret Fantasies of Fans*. London: Comet, 1985.

Visconti, Tony. *Tony Visconti: Bowie, Bolan and the Brooklyn Boy: The Autobiography*. London: Harper Collins, 2007.

Waldrep, Shelton. *The Aesthetics of Self-Invention: Oscar Wilde to David Bowie*. Minneapolis: University of Minnesota Press, 2004.

Waldrep, Shelton. "Introduction." *The Seventies: The Age of Glitter in Popular Culture*. Edited by Shelton Waldrep, 1–15. New York: Routledge, 2000.

Walker, Alice. *The Color Purple: A Novel*. New York: Harcourt Brace Jovanovich, 1982.

Welch, Denton. "When I Was Thirteen." *The Faber Book of Gay Short Fiction*. Edited by Edmund White, 72–88. Boston: Faber and Faber, 1991.

Wells, Dominic. "Boys Keep Swinging." *Time Out* August 23–30, 1995 to October 20, 2014. http://music.hyperreal.org/artists/brian_eno/interviews/Bowieno.html.

Westcott, James. "A Culture of 'Perform Yourself.'" *New York Times* August 18, 2011 to December 1, 2014. http://www.nytimes.com/roomfordebate/2011/08/18/did-youtube-kill-performance-art/a-culture-of-perform-yourself?module=Search&mabReward=rel bias%3Aw%2C%7B%221%22%3A%22RI%3A10%22%7D.

White, ed. *How to Read Barthes' Image-Music-Text*. London: Pluto Press, 2012.

Wilcken, Hugo. *Low*. New York: Continuum, 2005.

Wilde, Oscar. *The Picture of Dorian Gray*. New York: Oxford University Press, 2006.

Wilde, Oscar. *The Importance of Being Earnest and Other Plays*. Edited by Peter Raby. New York: Oxford University Press, 1998.

Williams, Alastair. *Constructing Musicology*. Aldershot: Ashgate, 2001.

Williams, Raymond. "The Analysis of Culture." In *Cultural Theory and Popular Culture: A Reader*, edited by John Storey, 56–64. New York: Harvester Wheatsheaf, 1994.

Willis, Paul E. *Common Culture: Symbolic Work at Play in the Everyday Cultures of the Young*. Boulder: Westview, 1990.

Willis, Susan. "Hardcore: Subculture American Style." *Critical Inquiry* 19, no. 2 (Winter 1993): 365–83.

Wilson, Robert. "Interview." In *The Twentieth-Century Performance Reader*, edited by Michael Huxley and Noel Witts, 384–98. New York: Routledge, 1996.

Wittig, Monique. *Les Guérillères*. Translated by David Le Vay. New York: Avon Books, 1973.

Wittig, Monique. *The Lesbian Body*. Translated by David Le Vay. Boston: Beacon Press, 1986.

Wollen, Peter. *Readings and Writings: Semiotic Counter-Strategies*. London: Verso, 1982.

Wood, Catherine. "'Painting in the Shape of a House.'" In *A Bigger Splash: Painting after Performance*, edited by Catherine Wood, 10–21. London: Tate Publishing, 2012.

Media Bibliography

Åkerlund, Jonas, dir. "Paparazzi." Perf. Lady Gaga and Alexander Skarsgård. 2009.

Anderson, Laurie. *Big Science*. Warner Brothers, 1982.

Anderson, Laurie, dir. *Home of the Brave*. Cinecom, 1986.

Armstrong, Michael. *The Image*. Perf. David Bowie and Michael Byrne. Border Film Productions, 1967.

Bauhaus. *Bauhaus 1979-1983*. Beggars Banquet, 1985.

The Beatles. *Sgt. Pepper's Lonely Hearts Club Band*. Parlophone, 1967.

Beck. *Midnight Vultures*. DGC, 1999.

Bergman, Ingmar, dir. *Persona*. Perf. Bibi Andersson and Liv Ullmann. AB Svensk Filmindustri, 1966.

Best of Bowie [Bowie's collected music videos]. Virgin/EMI, 2002.

Bowie, David. *Aladdin Sane*. RCA, 1973.

Bowie, David. *Black Tie White Noise*. Savage, 1993.

Bowie, David. *Buddha of Suburbia*. BMG International Virgin/EMI Records, 1993.

Bowie, David. *David Bowie*. Mercury, 1967.

Bowie, David. *David Bowie [Space Oddity]*. Mercury, 1969.

Bowie, David. *David Live*. RCA, 1973.

Bowie, David. *Diamond Dogs*. RCA, 1974.

Bowie, David. *Earthling*. BMG, 1997.

Bowie, David. *Heathen*. ISO Records, Columbia, 2002.

Bowie, David. *"Heroes."* RCA, 1978.

Bowie, David. *Hours*. Virgin, 1999.

Bowie, David. *Hunky Dory*. RCA, 1971.

Bowie, David. *Let's Dance*. EMI, 1983.

Bowie, David. *Lodger*. RCA, 1979.

Bowie, David. *Low*. RCA, 1977.

Bowie, David. *The Man Who Sold the World*. Mercury, 1970.

Bowie, David. *Never Let Me Down*. EMI America, 1987.

Bowie, David. *The Next Day*. Virgin/ISO, 2013.

Bowie, David. *Outside*. Arista/BMG, 1995.

Bowie, David. *Pin Ups*. RCA, 1974.

Bowie, David. *Reality*. ISO Records, Columbia, 2003.

Bowie, David. *The Rise and Fall of Ziggy Stardust and the Spiders from Mars*. RCA Records, 1972.

Bowie, David. *Scary Monsters (and Super Creeps)*. RCA Records, 1980.

Bowie, David. *Station to Station*. RCA, 1976.

Bowie, David. *Tonight*. EMI America, 1984.

Bowie, David. *Young Americans*. EMI, 1975.

Buñuel, Luis. *Un Chien Andalou*. Perf. Pierre Batcheff, Simone Mareuil, Luis Buñuel, Salvador Dalí, and Jaime Miravilles. Les Grandes Films Classiques, 1929.

Buñuel, Luis. *Viridiana*. Perf. Silvia Pinal, Francisco Rabal, Fernando Rey, and Margarita Lozano. Films Sans Frontières, 1961.

Byrne, David, and Brian Eno. *My Life in the Bush of Ghosts*. Sire/Warner Brothers, 1981.

Byrne, David. *The Catherine Wheel*. Sire, 1981.

Byrne, David. *Music for "The Knee Plays."* EMI, 1985.

Carlos, Walter [Wendy]. *Switched-On Bach*. Columbia, 1968.

Cronenberg, David, dir. *Crash*. Perf. James Spader, Deborah Kara Unger, Elias Koteas, Holly Hunter, and Rosanna Arquette. Fine Line Features, 1996.

Curtiz, Michael, dir. *Mildred Pierce*. Perf. Joan Crawford, Jack Carson, Zachary Scott, Eve Arden, and Ann Blyth. Warner Brothers, 1945.

Eno, Brian. *Another Green World*. Island, 1975.

Eno, Brian. *Discreet Music*. EG, 1975.

Eno, Brian. *Here Come the Warm Jets*. Island, 1973.

Eno, Brian. *Ambient 1: Music for Airports*. EG, Polydor, Virgin, GRT, 1978.

Eno, Brian. *Taking Tiger Mountain (By Strategy)*. Island, 1974.

Eno, Brian, and Jon Hassell. *Fourth World, Volume 1: Possible Musics*. EG, Polydor, 1980.

Eno, Brian, and Jon Hassell. *Dream Theory in Malaya: Fourth World Volume Two*. EG, Caroline, 1981.

Gehr, Ernie, dir. *Serene Velocity*. Independent film, 1970.

Glass, Philip. *Einstein on the Beach*. CBS Masterworks, 1979.

Glass, Philip. *"Heroes" Symphony*. Point Music, 1997.

Glass, Philip. *North Star*, 1977.

Glass, Philip. *"Low" Symphony*. Point Music, 1993.

Godard, Jean-Luc. *Alphaville*. Perf. Eddie Constantine, Anna Karina, Akim Tamiroff, and Howard Vernon. Athos Films, 1965.

Haynes, Todd, dir. *Velvet Goldmine*. Perf. Ewan McGregor, Christian Bale, and Jonathan Rhys Meyers. Miramax Films, 1999.

Henson, Jim, dir. *Labyrinth*. Perf. David Bowie and Jennifer Connelly. Tri-Star Pictures, 1986.

Hitchcock, Alfred, dir. *Psycho*. Perf. Anthony Perkins, Vera Miles, John Gavin, and Janet Leigh. Paramount Pictures, Universal Pictures, 1960.

Hitchcock, Alfred, dir. *Rear Window*. Perf. James Steward, Grace Kelly, Wendell Corey, Thelma Ritter, and Raymond Burr. Paramount Pictures, Universal Pictures, 1954.

Hitchcock, Alfred, dir. *Vertigo*. Perf. James Stewart, Kim Novak, Barbara Bel Geddes. Paramount Pictures, Universal Pictures, 1958.

Hobbs, Christopher, John Adams, and Gavin Bryars. *Ensemble Pieces*. Island, 1975.

Horn, Andrew. *The Nomi Song*. Perf. Klaus Nomi. Media Luna Entertainment, Palm Pictures, National Film Network, 2004.

Kubrick, Stanley, dir. *A Clockwork Orange*. Warner Brothers, 1971.

Kubrick, Stanley, dir. *Eyes Wide Shut*. Warner Brothers, 1999.

Kubrick, Stanley, dir. *The Shining*. Warner Brothers, 1980.

Kubrick, Stanley, dir. *2001: A Space Odyssey*. Metro-Goldwyn-Mayer, 1968.

Lady Gaga. *The Fame*. Interscope Records, 2008.

Lang, Fritz, dir. *Metropolis*. UFA, Paramount Pictures, 1927.

Lean, David, dir. *The Bridge Over the River Kwai*. Perf. William Holden and Alec Guinness. Columbia Pictures, 1957.

Livingston, Jennie, dir. *Paris Is Burning*. Perf. Dorian Corey, Pepper LaBeija, Willi Ninja. Miramax Films, 1991.

Lynch, Jennifer Chambers, dir. *Boxing Helena*. Perf. Sherilyn Fenn and Julian Sands. Orion Classics, 1993.

Mahoney, Brian, dir. *Pierrot in Turquoise, or The Looking Glass Murders*. Perf. David Bowie, Jack Birkert, Michael Garrett, Annie Stainer, and Lindsay Kemp. Scottish Television Colour Production, 1970.

Mallet, David, dir. *David Bowie: Serious Moonlight*. Perf. David Bowie. Concert Productions International, 1983.

Mallet, David, dir. *Glass Spider*. Perf. David Bowie. AAVA Australia, MGMM, Tall Pony, 1988.

Marker, Chistopher, dir. *La Jetée*. Perf. Hélène Chatelain, Davos Hanich, and Jacques Kedoux. Argos Films, 1962.

Nivrana. *MTV Unplugged in New York*. DGC, 1994.

Pennabaker, D. A., dir. *Ziggy Stardust and the Spiders from Mars*. Perf. David Bowie, Mick Ronson, Trevor Bolder, and Mike Woodmansey. 20th Century Fox, 1973.

Oshima, Nagasa, dir. *Merry Christmas, Mr. Lawrence*. Perf. David Bowie, Tom Conti, Ryuichi Sakamoto, and Takeshi Kitano. Universal Pictures, 1983.

Polanski, Roman, dir. *Repulsion*. Catherine Deneuve, Yvonne Furneaux, Ian Hendry, and John Fraser. Compton Films, Royal Films International, 1965.

Polanski, Roman, dir. *Rosemary's Baby*. Perf. Mia Farrow, John Cassavetes, and Ruth Gordon. Paramount Pictures, 1968.

Polanski, Roman, dir. *The Tenant (Le locataire)*. Perf. Roman Polanski and Isabelle Adjani. Paramount Pictures, 1976.

Pop, Iggy. *The Idiot*. RCA, 1977.

Pop, Iggy. *Lust for Life*. RCA, 1977.

Pop, Iggy. *Blah Blah Blah*. A and M, 1986.

Ray, Nicholas, dir. *Rebel Without a Cause*. Perf. James Dean, Natalie Wood, and Sal Mineo. Warner Brothers, 1955.

Reiner, Rob, dir. *This Is Spinal Tap*. Perf. Christopher Guest, Michael McKean, Harry Shearer, and Rob Reiner. Embassy Pictures, Studio Canal, Metro-Goldwyn-Mayer, 1984.

Renoir, Jean, dir. *La Grande Illusion*. Perf. Jean Gabin, Dita Parlo, Pierre Fresnay, and Erich von Stroheim. World Pictures, Janus Films, 1937.

Reznor, Trent. *The Downward Spiral*. Nothing/Interscope, 1994.

Roeg, Nicholas, dir. *The Man Who Fell to Earth*. Perf. David Bowie, Rip Torn, Candy Clark, and Buck Henry. Cinema 5 Distribuing, 1976.

Romanke, Mark, dir. "Closer." Perf. Trent Reznor. 1994.

Ross, Herbert, dir. *Pennies from Heaven*. Perf. Steve Martin, Bernadette Peters, and Christopher Walken. Metro-Goldwyn-Mayer, 1981.

Schnable, Julian, dir. *Basquiat*. Perf. Jeffrey Wright, David Bowie, Benicio del Toro, and Dennis Hopper. Miramax Films, 1996.

Scott, Tony, dir. *The Hunger*. Perf. Catherine Deneuve, David Bowie, and Susan Sarandon. Metro-Goldwyn-Mayer, 1983.

Specht, Patty Ivins dir. *Hollywood Rocks the Movies: The 1970s*. Perf. David Bowie. American Movie Classics, 2002.

Talking Heads. *Fear of Music*. Sire, 1979

Talking Heads. *Remain in Light*. Sire, 1980.

Temple, Julien, dir. *Jazzin' for Blue Jean*. Perf. David Bowie and Louise Scott. Sony Video, 1984.

Thomson, Malcolm J., dir. *Love You Till Tuesday*. Perf. David Bowie. Polygram, 1969.

Waits, Tom. *The Black Rider*. Island, 1993.

Waits, Tom. *Blood Money*. Anti, 2002.

Warhol, Andy, dir. *Empire*. Independent film, 1964.

Wiene, Robert, dir. *The Cabinet of Dr. Calagari*. Perf. Werner Krauss and Conrad Veidt. Goldwyn Distributing Company, 1920.

Welles, Orson, dir. *The Trial*. Perf. Anthony Perkins, Orson Welles, and Jeanne Moreau. Astor Pictures Corporation, 1962.

Yentob, Alan, dir. *Changes: Bowie at Fifty*. Perf. David Bowie. BBC2, 1997.

Yentob, Alan, dir. *Cracked Actor*. Perf. David Bowie. BBC, 1974.

Young, Terence, dir. *From Russia with Love*. Perf. Sean Connery, Pedro Armendáriz, Lotte Lenya, and Robert Shaw. United Artists, 1963.

Zinnemann, Fred, dir. *From Here to Eternity*. Perf. Burt Lancaster, Montgomery Clift, Deborah Kerr, Donna Reed, and Frank Sinatra. Columbia Pictures, 1953.

Index

David Bowie's albums are listed without parenthesis, and songs are filed as subheads under their respective album title.